THE LAST CANNIBALS

The Last Cannibals

A South American Oral History

ELLEN B. BASSO

UNIVERSITY OF
TEXAS PRESS
AUSTIN

This book has been supported by a grant from the National Endowment for the Humanities, an independent federal agency.

∞ The paper used in this publication meets the minimum requirements of American National Standard for Information Sciences—Permanence of Paper for Printed Library Materials, ANSI Z39.48-1984.

Library of Congress Cataloging-in-Publication Data

Basso, Ellen B., date
    The last cannibals : a South American oral history / Ellen B. Basso. — 1st ed.
      p.   cm.
    Includes bibliographical references and index.
    ISBN 0-292-70818-1 (cloth : alk. paper). — ISBN 0-292-70819-X (pbk. : alk. paper)
    1. Apalakiri Indians—Folklore. 2. Apalakiri Indians—History. 3. Oral tradition—Brazil—Xingu River Valley. 4. Ethnohistory—Brazil—Xingu River Valley. 5. Discourse analysis, Narrative—Brazil—Xingu River Valley. I. Title.
F2520.1.A63B366   1995
398.2'0981—dc20   94-25376

Some material in this book has been previously published in different form. Grateful acknowledgment is made to the following for permission to reprint: *L'Homme* for excerpts from "A Kalapalo Testimonial," XXXIII (2–4), April–December 1993, pp. 379–407; University of Pennsylvania Press for "Saganafa," from *A Musical View of the Universe* (1985); "Kalapalo Biography: Psychology and Language in a South American Oral History," reprinted by permission of the American Anthropological Association from *American Anthropologist* 91:3, September 1989 (not for further reproduction); Cambridge University Press for excerpts from "Contextualization in Kalapalo Narratives" in *Rethinking Context*, ed. A. Duranti and C. Goodwin (1992); Folklore Institute, Indiana University, for material from "The Last Cannibal" in *Native Latin American Cultures Through Their Discourse* (1990).

For David

CONTENTS

PART

PREFACE

In this book, the third in a series on Kalapalo narrative discourse, my observations and interpretations of Kalapalo history unfold around nine stories that were told to me by Kalapalo storytellers at various times between 1967 and 1982. I am especially concerned with what these sometimes grotesque yet deeply moving stories can tell us of a particular Native South American history, about how individuals are remembered, and about meanings given to decisions and choices made in the past, together with what the narratives might offer to the comparative study of ideology, biography, and history.

The series itself is the result of a long-standing collaboration I have been privileged to enjoy with Kalapalo storytellers, translators, and commentators, men and women who, as long as I have known them, have wanted to make known to outsiders so much that is crucial to understanding their lives. As an occasional participant in those Kalapalo lives, for many years I have been fascinated with what can be learned from their stories, for it is through narrative communication, above all, that Kalapalo represent themselves both collectively and as individuals.

The continuing discoveries of patterning in stories recorded in a wide range of Native American languages are part of an exciting process in which a focus upon talk is beginning to serve as a bridge between various orientations within anthropology. More and more, we are coming to recognize that everything anthropologists have historically (and with increasingly greater complexity) thought of as "language" and "culture" can be properly located in "discourse"—the concrete and unfolding instances of communication and expression that make so much of social life "speech-centered" (Sherzer 1987; Urban 1991). Discourse, as Hayden White has written in connection with literate communication, is "our most direct manifestation of consciousness seeking understanding, occupying that middle ground between the awakening of a general interest in a domain of experience and the attainment of some comprehension of it" (1978: 22). These signs of human intelligence at work are of special interest when so much that a people remember, dispute, fantasize, and speculate about are conveyed through oral narrative. In these discourse forms, elaborate visual imagery and a particularly condensed kind of speech (closely related to that of daily life but carefully modified and polished in keeping with ideas about how things should be said) play especially important roles by contributing to certain dominant tropes that govern how things are to be understood by the listeners. Discourse in the Foucauldian sense is therefore also our subject, for we often consider the choices narrators make about, and the limits placed on, their saying things in specific ways—"the permitted versus the false" (Foucault 1973, 1976, 1980).

Of all forms of discourse through which a meaningful past is remembered, those forms of narrative we call myth (and especially myths of origin) have been singled out for the greatest study, in part due to the ease with which myths—in the form of written texts—could be ordered, classified, and compared with written genres of literate people. "Myth" became emblematic of a kind of consciousness in which events, because they are given to be original, are constituted as "sacred," just as history, with which myth was inevitably contrasted and found lacking, stood for that other kind of "objective" consciousness associated with literacy. With the critical scrutiny and resultant breakdown of this distinction (in anthropology at least) which has occurred during the last twenty years, we have begun to think of myths not just as collections of ideas but as narrative activity, to listen more carefully to what individual storytellers are saying, and to concentrate as well upon their audiences. By complementing our concern with "what a myth is about" with an interest in "why it was told," we have been able to remove rather quickly the boundaries drawn earlier between myths and other kinds of stories.

Suggestive of this climate, the study of personal narratives has become more and more popular, as the analytic focus of anthropologists has changed from structure to discourse, and as those attending to psychological matters have recognized the need to understand how ideas of subjectivity, emotion, and identity are realized in and through discourse. Unlike their predecessors, these anthropologists are not content to justify studying life histories by the long-standing claim that individuals are somehow representative of their cultures, that cultures alone shape people's fate. We hear an insistent call for consideration of what people have to tell about themselves so as to learn about what is significant to them about their experiences of life, to understand the various tactics they use to speak about those experiences, and to capture the processes whereby people define themselves and others, how they come to change their senses of who they are and of what the future has in store for them—how they shape their own fates. The study of personal narratives that is oriented to discourse rather than to text challenges anthropologists, as the editors of a recent volume on Native American discourse have written, to recast the relations between our received ideas about language, culture, society, and the individual.

Some writers have already made plain how crucial to an understanding of people's histories are biographical and autobiographical narratives. Yet most still treat biographical narratives as if they were "microhistories," exemplifying more generalized and subjectively decontextualized trends and processes. Lévi-Strauss posited a connection between the two in terms of a scale of explanatory power, writing:

> Biographical and anecdotal history, right at the bottom of the scale is low-powered history, which is not intelligible in itself and only becomes so when it is transferred *en bloc* to a form of history of a higher power than itself. . . . but it is the richest in point of information, for it considers individuals in their particularity and details for each of them the shades of character, the twists and turns of their motives, the phases of their deliberations. This information is schematized, put in the background and finally done away with as one passes to histories of progressively greater "power." (1966: 261)

Searching these stories about individual experiences for clues about social processes in time, authors hope to find in these narratives evidence for the origins of particular values, or for changing notions of "role," of "self," and of "(moral) identity" that serve as models for contemporary people to follow. Less consideration is given to subjective processes and personal development that may actually be central to how the past is remembered. These are the very processes that make history concrete, a way in which people—by remembering the past in particular ways— give meaning to their own most deeply felt concerns and interests.

As long as history is treated as a precast environment that surrounds the progress of individuals, a kind of tunneled space down which people march on their way to self-discovery, biographical narratives and other forms of talk in which there is considerable attention paid to private interests will have a secondary status for understanding historical con sciousness, still regarded (particularly in the case of people without writing) as primarily a collective consciousness, a "social memory." On the other hand, a closer look at these ideas of subjective process can help us recognize biography and the ideas about personal development, emotional events, subjective speech, and individual agency that are developed through narrative, some important testimony about what past experiences were like. And formal analyses that are centered on the dis course itself show us how different ingredients of these stories make sense in terms of how people use their ideas about the past to comment on the present.

In this book, I do not intend to tell a story of the Kalapalo past, no more will I try to reconstruct from the many partial memories a coherent whole. Rather, I present what I understand to be the conventions from which a particular South American historical understanding emerges. I am especially interested in the role of individuals—both storytellers and the people they tell about—in this understanding. The stories in this book are telling examples of the art of Kalapalo narrative, fleeting acknowledgments of that art crystallized during the course of individual lives. Kalapalo do not memorize their narratives word for word, so there is no mechanical reproduction of stories between generations of tellers. Nevertheless, any teller's stories have a secure place in the history of Kalapalo narrative, because they are always retold by at least some of those listeners to younger people. And some were first told because ancestors specifically instructed people to make their lives known to "those who come after us." For these reasons I regard the biographies presented here much as heirlooms (and in some cases verbal monuments) that people examine from time to time in order to make their own lives continuous with those lived at various times in the past.

I am particularly interested in matters pertaining to psychology and language, interests that have suggested the questions I have asked. How (in a story about the past) do the Kalapalo narrators render apparent to their listeners descriptions of the more subjective actions of an individual? How are these personal actions linked so as to constitute the story of a life, a biography? In what contexts do these stories get told, and in what ways do the tellings themselves create contexts? What are the particular features of telling that distinguish a narrator's own personal qualities?

How are these Kalapalo stories presented to an audience? Is the life a model to imitate, an example to follow, or is it something to ponder in connection with other experiences, other stories, "beacons by which to gain an orientation" (as Karl Jaspers wrote about the men he called "paradigmatic individuals")? What are the critical dimensions of such biographies? In what ways are individual lives portrayed as exemplifications of problems faced by people living in a certain place and time, and in what ways are they presented as unique attempts at resolution of those problems? By addressing myself to questions about how biographies were understood by the Kalapalo men and women who told them to one another, I began to understand biography as an important way that the past is remembered and historical processes made meaningful. The meaning of a Kalapalo story is not just in the events we are being told about or in the matching of those events with real or plausible worlds in the Kalapalo universe. The meaning is also in the ways that complex and specific forms of knowledge are evoked and partly questioned through the subtle use of language.

The more I explore the narrative art of the Kalapalo, the more the feeling of humility and wonder at their achievements increases. Anyone who has tangled seriously with the task of understanding the deep complexities in Native South American storytelling will readily be able to appreciate my deep gratitude to those who took time to discuss, provoke, encourage my various attempts over the years. Although I name the storytellers and their listeners who participated in the narrative events described in this book, I will not single out Kalapalo men and women by name for acknowledgment. To do so would be contrary to the Kalapalo way of representing as a community endeavor their own willingness to share with me the good things of their lives and their efforts to teach me about themselves. What I must acknowledge, as always, is their continuing to allow me to learn from them in so many different and lasting ways.

Back home, I was fortunate to have been able to offer some tentative versions of Kalapalo warrior biographies at various meetings and colloquia held between 1983 and 1991, when the departments of anthropology of the universities of Arizona, Pennsylvania, Chicago, Texas, and Virginia invited me to present this work. I am also especially grateful for the helpful comments made by Raymond Fogelson, Emiko Ohnuki-Tierney, and Douglas Price-Williams at a session entitled "The Self in Discourse" held during the annual meetings of the American Anthropological Association, Chicago, 1987. It is my pleasure to acknowledge as well Donald Bahr, Richard Bauman, Dan Ben-Amos, Ray DeMallie, Alessandro Duranti, Bruna Francetto, David Guss, Steven Feld, William Hanks, Jane Hill, Judith Irvine, Arnold Krupat, Susan Phillips, David Shaul, Peter Stromberg, Terrence Turner, and especially Jonathan Hill, Joel Sherzer, and Greg Urban, who made many useful observations and suggestions. I also wish to express my deep appreciation to Professor Roque de Barros Laraia of the Universidade de Brasilia and to thank the officials of the Conselho Nacional de Desenvolvimento Científico e Tecnológico and the Fundaçao Nacional do Indio for their considerable assistance in furthering my research in Brazil. My work among the Kalapalo during 1966–1968, 1978–1980, and 1982 was supported by the National Science Foundation, the Wenner-Gren Foundation for Anthropological Research, Inc., and the University of Arizona. In 1987 a research professorship in the Social and Behavioral Sciences Research Institute of the University of Arizona allowed me time off from teaching to further explore the significance of Kalapalo biographies. Preparation of this book continued under a grant from the National Endowment for the Humanities during 1990.

Some of the material appearing here was previously published in different form in the *Journal of the History of Religions* (August 1989), the *American Anthropologist* (September 1989), the *Journal of Folklore Research* (1990), *Rethinking Context*, edited by Alessandro Duranti and

Charles Goodwin (Cambridge University Press, 1992), and *L'Homme* (1993). My translation and analysis of Muluku's story of Saganafa (first published in *A Musical View of the Universe*, University of Pennsylvania Press, 1985), has been revised in keeping with further insights into the Kalapalo language.

A GUIDE TO PRONOUNCING
KALAPALO WORDS

The following phonetic symbols have been used to write Kalapalo words:

a, as in opera (low front open)
e, as in best (middle open)
ë, as in "oe" in French *coeur* (middle closed)
i, as in seem (high front open)
ï, as in should (middle open)
o, as in old (middle rounded)
u, as in moon (high back rounded)
Vowel nasalization is indicated by a *tilde* (as in ĩ)
Nasalization usually occurs in a stressed syllable

CONSONANTS

d, as in English (voiced alveolar stop)
dy, somewhat as in the name Nadia, but with more breath (voiced alveopalatal fricative)
f, pronounced while blowing air through loosely opened, untouching
   lips (voiceless bilabial fricative)
g, as in English, but slightly farther back in the mouth (voiced glottal
   fricative)
h, as in English (voiceless glottal fricative)
k, as in coffee (voiceless velar stop)
l, as in English, but tongue is held slightly longer and farther back in the
   mouth (voiced alveolar lateral)
m, as in English (voiced bilabial nasal)
n, as in English (voiced alveolar nasal)
ñ, as in Spanish *mañana* or Portuguese *linho*
ng, similar to sing, but pronounced farther back in the mouth (voiced
   palatal nasal). This sound is often followed by a syllable beginning
   with g, hence there will be some instances of ngg (as in *fangguinga*,
   "river"); normally, there is a syllabic break between ng and g.

p, as in English (voiced bilabial stop)

s, as in English (voiceless alveopalatal fricative)

ts, as in cats (voiceless dental affricate)

t, somewhat softer than tooth (voiceless alveolar stop)

w, as in went (voiced bilabial semivowel)

zh, as if pronouncing sh farther back in the mouth (voiced alveopalatal fricative)

Where only two syllables occur in a word, stress is usually on the first syllable. In noncompound words of more than two syllables, the second syllable of the word is normally stressed. Nasalized vowels also indicate stressed syllables.

PART

1

1

Introduction

One of the more remarkable stories of Native South American ethnic survival is that of the people who live in a region of the country Brazilians call the Alto Xingu (Upper Xingu), centered around the headwaters of the Rio Xingu, a major northward-flowing tributary of the Amazon. Although most likely visited by eighteenth-century *bandeirantes* (adventurers in search of slaves and precious minerals), the scientific exploration of this region was first undertaken in the last two decades of the nineteenth century by the German explorer-scholars Karl von den Steinen and Hermann Meyer (Meyer 1897, 1898, 1900; Steinen 1886, 1894). In 1884, Steinen, traveling north with mules from the frontier town of Cuiaba, came down from the dry, *cerrado*-covered plateau onto the Rio Culiseu, entering a region of complex aquatic environments, an ancient river basin whose main tributaries led to numerous deep embayments drained by narrow channels (*igarapes*), swamps, inundated woodlands (*igapos*), and large, shallow lakes.[1]

Both Steinen and Meyer considered language an especially useful instrument for the reconstruction of cultural-historical processes, the principal orientation of their theoretical interest in Native South Americans. Using at first Bakairi interpreters from the Rio Teles Pires, south of the Xingu Basin, whose Carib language turned out to be related to some of those spoken in the area, and then working with Alto Xingu people who could speak other local languages, Steinen collected detailed word-lists for the purpose of identification and classification. He quickly recognized that at least five mutually unintelligible languages were spoken, that most people were monolingual, but that there were individuals who could speak more than one language. This work of classifying languages was continued by Steinen's colleague, Hermann Meyer, who described two different Carib linguistic groups, the "Yanamakapï" and the "Akuku," who resided in more than eighteen communities. The settlements these German explorers actually visited, or those they heard about from the local people, were placed into one or another linguistic grouping. This method led to estimates of population

Rio Culuene with *mata* forest on the far bank.

An *igarapé* (embayment) near the Rio Culuene.

View of Aifa settlement and the lake.

as high as three thousand, far higher than exists at present. In the case of the Carib speakers, Steinen and Meyer included in their lists of village names words for places that were either summer settlements or abandoned sites and perhaps also regional names that referred to places within which settlements were shifted over time.

Despite the inability of most of the local people to understand languages other than the particular one they spoke, Steinen and Meyer observed many shared practices, which they attributed to the extensive trade network. This idea of the existence of a single culture was used in later years by Brazilian anthropologists to define an Alto Xingu "culture area" (perhaps the only one ever labeled with reference to a pubic ornament, *o área do ulurí*, "the *uluri* area," after the Tupi word for the bark triangle once worn by women).

The people had developed elaborate fishing techniques that enabled them to work the many different aquatic environments, from deep, narrow lakes formed from the embayments of the larger rivers (across which dams were built, set with large basketry traps) to shallow creeks that could be poisoned with plant stupefactants and in which small children set traps of their own for minnows. The image of the naked male standing on the prow of his canoe while aiming a drawn bow into the calm waters of a river below became an Alto Xingu stereotype, just as were to be the photographs of the women working at processing their bitter manioc (*Manihot utilissima*), the staple crop. Twenty to thirty varieties of manioc are grown, typically interplanted with the seeds of *piqui* (*Caryocar brasiliense*), a fruit-bearing tree reaching about thirty feet tall at its maturity which forms extensive orchards around the older settlements. Large fields cut from the high forests (in places barricaded with fences to keep herds of peccary from devouring the manioc plantings) surround settlements of several hundred people and can also be found at more distant sites to which smaller groups of people move during the dry season. People plant these more distant fields with manioc, as well as cotton, *urucu* (*Bixa orellana*, whose seeds yield a brilliant red dye), beans, squash, gourds, corn, tobacco, and a variety of medicinal plants. In addition to their shared techniques of environmental orientation, Alto Xingu people practice identical body techniques, accept local specializations in the production of certain highly valued items of exchange (ceramic vessels, hardwood bows, salt, shell ornaments), and share ritual activities associated with hereditary leaders (in some of which several settlements participate jointly). Most important, I believe, they share an extensive oral tradition that identifies certain places with events in the past when humans and powerful beings could approach one another more easily than now.

After the Germans, we know of a number of other (mostly exploratory) expeditions that entered the region. We know too about the tragic effects of these expeditions upon the local population.[2] With the establishment of various outposts along the upper Rio Paranatinga to the southwest, people from the area also began to travel upstream to trade for European goods. The immediate consequences of these visits were often disastrous to the residents of the Alto Xingu, who succumbed to repeated epidemics of infectious diseases. Meyer's third expedition in particular seems to have had awful consequences, as did the Spanish influenza epidemic of 1920–1921. But in the memory of living people, the most terrible invasion of disease was measles, brought back to the region in 1954 by some local people who had been taken for a visit to a Brazilian outpost to the south of the Upper Xingu Basin. After that epidemic, the population of the Alto Xingu was most likely at its lowest since Steinen first descended the Rio Culiseu.

Despite these disasters, the Alto Xingu people seem to have preserved much of their ways of living described by the nineteenth-century explorers after several centuries of direct experience of Europeans. By the time of this writing, they still maintained their hold over a large piece of territory which in the 1980s had become nearly surrounded by Brazilian ranches. Today, there are ten local communities in the Upper Xingu Basin of central Brazil, with a population of approximately thirteen hundred. The area is still unique in that country (if not South America more generally) in being relatively free of harassment by outsiders, though this is a fearfully tenuous situation that might change at any moment. We must attribute this unusual situation to the designation of much of the Upper Xingu Basin as a reserve in 1961 and to the fact that this reserve was far more than a paper concept, coming as it did under the protection of the federal government rather than the local authorities responsible to the state of Mato Grosso.

The making of the reserve is part of the modern history of Brazilian penetration into the central regions of the country. During the 1950s, the new capital, Brasília, was being built in the then-isolated hinterlands of Goiás State, an area that was culturally and socially marginal because of its geographic separation from the majority population living along the coast. President Juscelino Kubitschek hoped that the building and occupation of Brasília would shift attention toward the immense, undeveloped resources of the Amazonian forests, whose exploitation would change the future of his country. As part of this grandiose project (named a "March toward the West"), the government planned a variety of heroic gestures to inspire Brazilians in a new pioneering spirit. One important goal was national integration, in which the most distant regional population centers would be united through national development emanating from the new capital. An expedition to burn an airstrip at the exact geographic center of the country (where, at least in theory, the president himself could land) was one such scheme. The leaders of the Xingu-Roncador Expedition were Orlando and Claudio Villas-Boas, employees of the Central Brazilian Foundation, a government body organized around 1943 to explore from the air the vast central regions of the country. Explorations of this area entailed building a line of airstrips, a project that eventually took over fifteen years to complete.

In the course of their work, the Villas-Boas brothers had become officials of the Serviço Proteção aos Indios (Indian Protective Service), another government agency formed at the turn of the century to administer Indians in a progressive manner. In this capacity, they had encountered many native peoples, some peaceful toward outsiders, others clearly unfriendly. They had observed firsthand the destructive consequences of contact with members of the national society. One of the airstrips they helped build, named Capitão Vasconcelos, was located in the very region Steinen and Meyer had visited less than seventy years earlier. This was a "friendly" region near the confluence of the Ronuro and Xingu rivers. To the north were people who were hostile to the Indians who lived near the airstrip. An important goal set by the Villas-Boas brothers was to contact these "fierce" Indians in order to have them settle peacefully among their neighbors, free from harassment by Brazilian prospectors and rubber gatherers, who had, it was assumed, caused these people to become suspicious of all outsiders. Their violent responses to the presence of outsiders were seen as a protective reaction. Posto Capitão Vasconcelos (later called Posto Leonardo Villas-Boas, in memory of a third brother) became the center of the Villas-Boas brothers' activities. Over the years, they and others who had visited the region on scientific expeditions from the National Museum were to conceive of "a National Park that might serve as a reserve and a showpiece of a sector of Brazil in the throes of transformation and extinction" (Agostinho da Silva 1972: 252). Access to the region would be restricted in order to protect the local inhabitants from incursions by Brazilian society, which in the Villas-Boas brothers' experience offered nothing of benefit to Indians.

In 1952, discussion sponsored by the Vice-Presidency of Brazil resulted in a legal draft of a plan to be submitted to the Congress from the Executive Authority. The state of Mato Grosso had begun to sponsor putative colonization projects that were actually speculative ventures with the idea of profiting from land sales. These projects resulted in the paper transfer of almost 75 percent of the area proposed for the park. Yet, with the very important support of air force officers and important officials who had been invited to Capitão Vasconcelos (where they were encouraged to give presents to the Indians and in return were taken on hunting and fishing trips with Indian guides), the government reserve (formally called the Parque Nacional do Xingu, or Xingu National Park) was finally established in 1961. Some 22,000 square kilometers had been set aside, to be enlarged to approximately 30,000 square kilometers in 1968.

The Villas-Boas brothers tended to separate the Indians they encountered into either a "friendly" or "fierce" category, the former being characteristic of the Alto Xingu people, who, they wrote, formed an authentic "society of nations" (Villas-Boas 1970:16). They described this Xinguano society in the following manner: "at the present, in the Xinguano society, there is no preponderance of the stronger, no controlling superalliances, no subjection of the weaker. Since the human potential and productive capacity of each group are not taken into account, a perfect balance and respect prevail among its co-participants. They all live under a regime of mutual and beneficial dependency" (1970: 17).

In contrast to this state of affairs were the more independent and hostile tribes whose cultures were distinct from each other and from the área do uluri. Earlier accounts by Steinen and Meyer suggested that this was an oversimplification. While the people who lived in the more southerly region of the Alto Xingu certainly did seem to live peacefully with one another, some groups (especially the Ge-speaking Suya) in this early period were not clearly "hostile" to each other nor were they clearly compatible. It was also apparent that the Alto Xingu people were capable of fierce attacks upon these other tribes.

After the establishment of the park, the Villas-Boas brothers managed to make contact with several groups of Indians, eventually bringing them into the boundaries of the protected area, which they had come to think of as a refuge for native peoples fleeing Brazilian incursions onto their lands. Over the years, the work of the Villas-Boas brothers in contacting groups who had formerly attacked local communities or who were known to have killed European outsiders tended to reinforce the distinction between "fierce" and "friendly" Indians. Undoubtedly, to a certain extent the Villas-Boas brothers' practice of labeling tribes in this way reinforced a similar contrast that was made among the Alto Xingu people. Furthermore, the brothers' practice was to settle most of these culturally distinct peoples in the northerly regions of the park. There, the geographical juxtaposition of groups formerly isolated from each other resulted in much illness, causing a heightened tension between people who more and more frequently came to accuse one another of witchcraft. The death rate soared as men were killed to avenge death by sickness. In later years these northerly groups confronted Brazilians clearing land they considered their own, exacerbating the practice of distinguishing between the peaceful people in the south and the violent people in the north. By the time of my first visit in 1966, this distinction was already quite important to the Alto Xingu people.

At present most of the Alto Xingu settlements cluster in an area about a day's travel from Posto Leonardo, although the Kalapalo settlement of Tangugu (close to the confluence of the Rio Tanguro and the Rio Culuene) is a three-day canoe trip upstream on the Rio Culuene from their older settlement called Aifa. The Kalapalo who decided to settle at Tangugu were in fact returning to the region they had occupied before the establishment of the park, after which they were persuaded by Orlando Villas-Boas to move to Aifa, a site he selected for them. (The name means "finished" or "ready," which was simply what the leader, Ahpĩũ, said when the houses were completed.)

The other Carib-speaking groups in this area (the Wagifïtï, Dyagamï,[3] and Kuikuro), as well as the Arawakan-speaking Mehinaku and Yawalipiti, began to move northward in the years after 1950 in response to attacks by the so-called Txição (also Carib speakers, but their language is markedly different from other Alto Xingu communities). They joined the Tupian-speaking Kamaiura and Aueti, the Arawakan Waura, and the Trumai, who lived farther to the north, toward the confluence of the Culuene with the Rio Ronuro. The presence of the Xingu-Roncador posts was undoubtedly an attraction, both for their European goods and the protection they offered against attack.

The airstrips built for the Central Brazil Foundation eventually were used by air force planes as refueling bases, and some became the sites of small outposts that serviced the military. (In the Alto Xingu, a base called Jacare was established for refueling and, later, military training.) Over time the more southerly outposts were joined by roads (including the monumental highway project BR-80 Norte, which nearly bisected the original park), eventually leading in the late 1970s to the intensive occupation of the region by large cattle-ranching operations. In 1973, the boundaries were changed and the name was changed to Parque Indígena do Xingu, or Xingu Native Park.

There have been repeated and continuing attempts by outsiders to occupy this area (especially in the northern sections of the park, but most recently on its southwestern margin as well), to turn the *cerrado* environment into cattle ranches, and lately to dam the Rio Xingu in one of the worst-conceived development schemes in Brazil. Nonetheless, the reserve has as of this writing successfully resisted settlement by outsiders, enabling many local communities to continue to pursue their traditionally defined goals. They do so while gradually learning about the outside world and through carefully planned contacts with Brazilians at the local air force base and ranches outside the reserve, devising strategies of their own to engage Brazilian society.

Orlando and Claudio Villas-Boas did not envision the Xingu National Park as a place where Indians would systematically be taught about Brazilian life. Their policy was to isolate them, to strictly control, as best they could, access to the local people by outsiders. Very occasionally, men who were important leaders (and, rarely, their wives or sons) were allowed to fly out on a Brazilian Air Force plane to visit São Paulo or Rio de Janeiro for medical reasons, carefully chaperoned by one of the brothers or a trusted associate. In turn, the visits of Brazilian dignitaries were carefully supervised; such visitors were often treated to a well-orchestrated performance of local ceremonial dances under the "sponsorship" of the Villas-Boas brothers. After the performance ended, they would formally distribute the gifts that had arrived with the visitors as the performers lined up outside their small house at the post. The two brothers strongly objected to schools, which were consequently founded only after their retirement in 1978. For a few years after their departure, a program of schooling was begun under the park directorship of Olympio Serra, but this effort became more a matter of the whim of the occasional teacher than according to the many ambitious plans conceived in the distant cities. Although with greater frequency young men have left the area to be schooled in Brazilian cities and, most recently, to participate in various conferences focused on environmental and political concerns of importance to Indians, the continued absence of functioning, widespread literacy has meant that essentially oral means of preserving knowledge and sharing information with neighbors in other communities have continued in vital relationship with Kalapalo realities. The artificial isolation of the area constantly intruded upon the attempts people made to understand their place in the greater world. I often heard people say, when making plans to travel to Posto Leonardo, that they were going to the *pahki*. They had heard of the park, but identified it completely with the immediate area of the administrative post and airstrip that was now controlled by Brazilian officialdom.

As early as 1967, before there was much thought being given by the local people to the dangerously close Brazilian settlements, fears of being attacked by the *kagayfa* (people of European culture, or "Christians") would surface at unpredictable times. On one occasion in 1967, I was traveling with several Kalapalo men along the Culuene when we came across a group of canoes from the community of Mïgiyape crossing the river. It seemed as if the entire community were traveling to Posto Leonardo. "We are going to the *pahki*," they told us, "because Orlando is calling everyone there." "Why?" the Kalapalo leaders asked them. "The Christians are at war, and they might bomb us," was the answer. "All right," was the peculiarly diffident response from the Kalapalo. As we drew away, the men began to laugh, saying that the Mïgiyape couldn't speak Portuguese well enough to really understand *ka-gayfa*, so that they had probably misunderstood something that had been said. Or maybe, it was suggested, someone had played a trick on them. I began to think of the political situation in Brazil, at the time a military dictatorship. "Had there been a coup?" I wondered. Only several months later, when I happened to travel to Posto Leonardo myself, did I learn of the Six-Day War.

Fragmented Communities, Fragmented Memory

Alto Xingu settlements are formed when several communal family households decide to occupy permanently a place that is being used only during the dry season, the agricultural time of year. Often, two families related to each other through kinship or marriage or both form the core of these households, but there are always several different kinds of arrangements in a settlement. There are no units based on descent, ceremonial societies, ritual moieties, age grades, or other formal ways of complicating a person's relationships to others in the community, such as is (or was) the case among such central Brazilian groups as the Bororo, Mundurucu, Tapirape, and various Ge-speaking peoples. In the Alto Xingu, the persistence of both household and settlement groups depends on the particular ties between relatives by blood and marriage for their perpetuation. Additionally, for various reasons, the communities are relatively permeable and all settlements include at least some people who were born elsewhere (and thus identified with other places). Some of these people have left their natal settlements to marry (which is a relatively unusual practice). More commonly, others have been forced to flee because of witchcraft accusations, joining relatives in more distant places when that is possible. Yet others, now exclusively very elderly people, are the last survivors of communities which had been decimated by disease prior to the 1950s. Since people have been moving around in these ways for generations, most Xinguanos participate in multiple and cross-cutting relationships, both within their own community and elsewhere; these ties form a network extending into every Alto Xingu settlement. The communities together thus constitute a composite society, apparently formed from a number of groups of very different origins.

Presently, each settlement (or cluster of closely related settlements formed from factions originally living in a single place) is named and politically as well as territorially autonomous. The earliest published accounts of people living in this area used these settlement names to refer to "tribes," which resulted in outsiders coming to use the names long after the people in the settlements had moved elsewhere, died off, or merged with other communities (some recent ethnographers also persist in writing of these communities as "tribes"). Thus the name "Kalapalo" is actually that of a very old settlement, paired with a place called Kwapïgï, that was eventually abandoned perhaps eighty years ago. Kalapalo is mentioned in several of the stories I include in this book, but the people only use the word in self-reference when they are speaking to foreigners. After they had abandoned Kalapalo, people lived in a place called Kanugidyafïtï. Contemporary Kalapalo occupy the settlements called Aifa and Tangugu and call themselves *Aifa otomo* ("Aifa community") and *Tangugu otomo* ("Tanguro community"), as do other Carib speakers. Yet the word "Kalapalo" has become a shared means for both local people and outsiders to refer to the descendants of that earlier community, though these people actually live together with men and women whose parents and grandparents came from other Alto Xingu communities.

Some of the people in present-day settlements are said to be descended (although sometimes vaguely and imprecisely) from male and female hereditary leader-ancestors (*anetau*) who are considered the ultimate sources of particular stories, rituals, and songs as well as owning the rights to the resources of particular territories associated with the earlier settlements; consequently there are local specializations in manufactured objects (shell ornaments, pottery, hardwood bows, water hyacinth salt, and body paints) produced for trade. Present-day hereditary leaders are supposed to be descendants of these founding personages, though in practice many are only very collaterally related. Furthermore, the hereditary leadership itself had to be reconstituted, Kalapalo tell me, after the early invasions of *kagayfa* slavers (described in the story of Saganafa), who decimated the population on yearly forays into the region. New forms of leader's talk, too, had to be reinvented, since memory of the earlier formal genres was lost with the leaders who had been killed or taken by the *kagayfa*. In the "new" oratorical address, leaders call upon their community as "children," and they are considered sponsoring owners (*oto*) of the settlement.

The leaders are primarily ritual officers and persons who mediate between communities, but they are locally important as repositories of traditional knowledge. Those who are able to demonstrate direct genealogical continuity with past leaders are particularly important because they are among the few who embody memory of the distant past. Their physical presence, their names, their behavior, their own children are all evidence of inherited practice that is truly "traditional," *Kalapalo ekugu*, "really Kalapalo," as they say. Their legitimacy is extremely important to them, not for any political consequence it might have but because it is an important way for them to save remembrances. They live the past in a way other leaders cannot. But even for these leaders, the series of disasters endured in the Alto Xingu shapes their existence through the kinds of stories they tell. Neither the idea of an *área do uluri* nor that of an "Upper Xingu society"—ideas that emphasize shared "traits" and social relationships—makes this extreme fragmentation of memory apparent. To understand the stories in this book, we need to keep the reasons for that fragmentation in mind.

Ifutisu and *Angikogo*

This notion of the moral whole, an ethical community, centers on the idea that all Alto Xingu people (called *kuge* by the Kalapalo community I focus on in this book) were born from a single mythic mother who lived in the Upper Xingu Basin and whose trickster sons' activities made the place what it is today. The ethical community, whose very origins are embodied in the landscape (in the rivers that the trickster Taugi made, the lakes created by an ancestor who let loose a monstrous fish, causing a flood), was made to stand in marked contrast with the unpredictably hostile groups (called *angikogo*)[4] who lived at some distance from the Rio Culuene and its larger tributaries and who, it seemed (before many were displaced by Brazilian ranchers and prospectors), surrounded the Alto Xingu people. To the Kalapalo, what remained for many years the inexplicable rage of the club-carrying Suya and Kayapo (Ge speakers) and the seemingly random killings of the Txicão (a Carib-speaking group) contrasted with what they felt was their own disciplined dignity and restraint when angered. "We only fight with words," as Enumï put it. The stories about killings suggested that people executed men only when there was substantial consensus about a witchcraft accusation, but even these executions seemed rare given the large number of people who were accused. Lots of men were able to flee to settlements where they had relatives who were willing to shelter them; they were able to do so because local people let them know they were about to be killed, so they had a chance to get away before the attack occurred. While the Alto Xingu peoples were not entirely defensive in their response to outside aggressions, the idea of attacking and exterminating an entire neighboring community, seemingly because they were simply there, was something only the violent *angikogo* did.[5]

When I first visited the Kalapalo in 1966, people often described the Alto Xingu communities as valuing a "distanced" personal composure called *ifutisu*, involving a modest, respectful calm in their relations with one another. A theme that invariably ran through our discussion of *ifutisu* was the importance of generosity; a person who was willing not only to share things with others but to cheerfully give away possessions was particularly admired. Leaders in particular were expected to live in relative poverty; newly married men and women, at the moment they were given gifts, respectfully passed them on to their older in-laws. Children learned quite early, through a "trading game" called *uluki*, to give away their own possessions. (Usually they were supervised by someone older, but once in a while children got carried away and traded their parents' valuables, which meant that embarrassed older people found themselves in the position of having to ask for their things back.)

Ifutisu can also mean that a person is willing to publicly agree to share goals and is known for a willingness to validate the opinions of others. Here again, leaders were expected to speak this way. It was also important to greet a person encountered on a path, even if the sight of that person evoked anger at some past slight. A young leader failed to respond to the greeting of another man who passed him on his way to bathe. "He's not yet a leader," a cousin of the young man told me. "He's not like our older leaders, who know how to behave. You see that old man over there, my uncle? His wives were always causing trouble for him, lots of men came to them both, but he never, never got angry. He always smiled at people. He was a very good leader."

The exchange of food was also particularly important; during the best times for fishing, men and women walked continually between the houses distributing portions of the catch their relatives had brought home. Shamans also moved from house to house, diagnosing and treating the sick. Older women came to help during childbirth; burial and mourning were collective endeavors, highly ritualized community responsibilities. People repeatedly told me that what distinguished them (and others in the Alto Xingu) from all the other native people with whom they were familiar (especially the club-carrying Ge and the marauding Txição), was simply that they were not "fierce" (*angiko*) or "violent" (*itsotunda*) but "controlled" and "respectful" (*ifutisunda*).

The Kalapalo also distinguished themselves from others by their unusual dietary customs, especially by the fact (apparently unique in South America) that they refrained from eating game animals (*ngene*).[6] The practice of hunting game must have been discarded fairly recently, though, since quite a few Kalapalo stories contain vivid descriptions of people hunting, butchering, and smoking meat, just as the habits of the tapir, peccary, and deer are meticulously described in some of those same stories. Why this emphasis on diet? The Kalapalo took considerable notice of what people ate, since eating only the "right" things was a significant public demonstration of individual responsibility for engendering qualities of restraint and respect. This ideology was projected into the frequent discussions about witchcraft accusations. A young woman died suddenly leaving three young children and her grieving husband. Her relatives attributed her death to a powerful being (*itseke*) they said she had passed on the trail as she returned one afternoon alone from the manioc fields. But an older woman who had been visiting her Kamaiura relatives at the time reported that one of the Kalapalo men was being accused of the first woman's death through witchcraft. As soon as they heard about this the man's closest relatives immediately gathered around the accused man, who sat weeping with frustration and anger. A brother of his blurted out, "Those worthless Kamaiura, eaters of animals, eaters of people!" A second brother picked up this theme: "When I was there, on my way to the Waura festival, I saw those men cooking and eating agouti. They were outside, behind their house. That's where I saw them eating that."

I thought at first that these ideas about *ifutisu* were simply ways the Kalapalo expressed their fear and scorn of the native people who lived on the margins of the Alto Xingu Basin, particularly at a time when the Brazilian *chefe do posto* administrators and some foreign visitors showed greater admiration for the rugged character of the more flamboyantly aggressive Ge-speaking Shavante and Kayapo communities. At the time, the Kayapo appealed to a certain Brazilian male ethos, which took pleasure in their swaggering displays of physical strength and beauty, their intimidation of others through barely suppressed violence. The local Brazilian officials described the Kalapalo leaders to me as "weak," in contrast to the "great chiefs" of the neighboring Kayapo, who "had no fear of anyone, not the diamond hunters, not the generals, not even us." But I now also think that in these practices and attitudes about themselves a different kind of contrast is being made by the Kalapalo. This is a contrast between their present life and their past. In the stories they tell about how their ancestors lived, they reveal that in important ways the distant past is somewhat abhorrent to them; just as they have gladly (they say) given up eating most meat, so have they freed themselves from activities of the kind they see continued by their violent neighbors. No longer do they engage in violent battles with enemies, suffering the grotesque mutilations associated with trophy taking after death in battle, the lack of an appropriate burial, and cannibalism; families are no longer afflicted with the anxiety and grief such a violent life created. Yet the past is fascinating, too, for the newness of contacts with strangers, the exploratory quality of life at the time, and the rigor with which young men were trained to be warriors. For some, it is perhaps most fascinating for the violent life ancient heroes led.

These particular stories are about distant ancestors, people who can only be linked in a general way to contemporary communities. This kind of ancestral connection is actually founded in the narrative tradition itself: the idea that certain stories were originally learned from members of particular communities ("Wapagepundaka" from Kamaiura people, for example). The ancestors are distant from contemporary Alto Xingu people because they seem to have lived precariously, frequently being attacked by fierce people. In contrast to the large, long-settled communities of today, in the past people lived in small groups and moved about with some frequency, suspicious and often hostile toward one another. Some tried to create ties with *angikogo*, but the consequences were often grim. The stories Kalapalo tell about such encounters portray a violent life of cannibalistic blood feuding, of survivors of brutal attacks encountered during journeys or suddenly appearing at settlements, of children and young women abducted, of cannibal feasts and the grotesque mutilation of the victims of war. There is a special encrusting of imagery around the behavior of *angikogo*, whose grotesque practices may in fact be a mingling of observations and hearsay about enemies and strangers accumulated over many centuries. This imagery of cannibalistic and sadistic warfare builds upon both ancient and recent practice.[7]

While in many narratives (as the name for his status suggests) the warrior or "bow master" figures as a person who is particularly adroit at using bows and arrows in battle, clubs seem to be the weapon of choice for the ultimate blows of extermination. Some narrators use a word that is translated "bladed instruments" to speak of these weapons; they are a sort of sharpened weapon made of wood that acts with both a clubbing and a cutting action (perhaps similar to the so-called *takape* of the Tupinamba). In yet other stories, simple clubs of wood are clearly being used in battle. The club was an instrument as much of mass extermination and the formal execution of captives as of fighting battles. Scenes of people being clubbed to death have considerable emotional force for the Kalapalo because today witches are executed in similar fashion, typically being taken by surprise by a group of outraged mourners and bludgeoned to death. Since contemporary use of war clubs is especially associated with the Ge-speaking Kayapo groups who live to the north of the Alto Xingu Basin, people who disagree with decisions to execute others sometimes liken the executioners to *angikogo*.

The club is not a weapon associated with training and preparation, for even essentially untrained women, it seems, could use it. It is, however, a weapon of assassination, suggesting a violent personality, an essentially generalized hatred. It is thus far more horrible than the bow and arrow, which takes great skill and strength to use successfully. In story after story, arrows are specially prepared, associated with individualized power, restricted in use to people who have been "chosen" through their parents' dreaming. Arrows, however, are weapons of controlled, even objective violence, associated with fishing and hunting, the procurement of food. The bow (by the same token) can be used successfully only when a man is unflinchingly in control, "distanced" from the act of killing by his need to concentrate more on the instruments and less on his hatred for the victim. Such implications may have contributed to justifying rejecting animals killed with clubs as food and ultimately all "land animals" (ngene) except monkeys and birds, which are shot with bow and arrows (as are fish, the main source of protein in today's diet). The bow is thus an appropriate symbol for a person whose wish to kill is "distanced" or "objectified," impersonal and oriented toward a large social good: feeding those at home, even to the extent of not eating what he himself kills. The club, on the other hand, even when used during hunting, remains the weapon of execution, which is a personal act of revenge during which a witch is confronted with his crime and executed by the relatives of his victim.

While some of the practices appear to be those of the neighboring Ge-speaking Kayapo and Suya, more likely the Ge images (use of "stinking" palm oil; clubs the weapons of choice) have been combined with Tupian and Cariban cannibalism, Tupian palisaded villages, trophy taking, and the torture of captives. In some complicated sense the angikogo in these stories are all the different kinds of enemies experienced over the past centuries.

Life as described in these narratives of the past stands in marked contrast with the present life of Alto Xingu peoples. This is not to deny the presence of violence in their communities but rather to emphasize that among them the values of peaceful interaction between and within communities and spontaneously generous, modest demeanor are paramount. It is as if a dramatic and drastic ideological shift at once social and deeply personal in meaning has taken place. From perceiving neighbors as strangers at best but more frequently dangerous adversaries, to whom one could respond only with a corresponding ethic of ferocious aggression, these people gradually came to create a moral sphere of action extending beyond the immediate settlement, recognizing that there were others sharing a sense of common purpose. They knew this because those others seemed to also value highly what the Kalapalo called ifutisu. This moral ideal does not delimit a universal domain of ethical judgment, for there are people who fall outside this sphere of action, yet the possibility of incorporating them into a community of shared interests against outsiders' incursions into the region arises with greater frequency. That possibility is also often the subject of stories describing more recent ancestors living very much in the way present-day Alto

Xingu people do, though far more precariously insofar as they are very much aware of the presence of strangers always in danger of penetrating the boundaries of their known territory.

A passage from one of the stories Kalapalo tell about these times makes clear that some people entering the Upper Xingu Basin were refugees fleeing from other native people, sometimes after their own relatives had been decimated by enemies. One story concerns people who lived before the ancestors of the Kuikuro, Carib-speaking neighbors of the contemporary Kalapalo. These people, appearing in the Alto Xingu after having wandered through the forest with little to drink, eventually join another small group of people, who have already made a settlement. These wanderers are described by the narrator as "people like us," although they are also *angikogo*, which in the context of their sharing values with present-day Xinguanos should be translated "strangers."

Refugees were not always "people like us." Sometimes, people who became known for their violence and their different customs also appeared. In a story about the ancestors of the Trumai people (see chapter 10),[8] Ausuki the narrator talks about how these wanderers searched along the Rio Culuene for a place to live. In this story, "strangers" are clearly not like the narrator's own people (*kuge*) but "enemies," what in another story Kudyu called "our killers." The Trumai ancestors were not suffering from obvious hunger as they traveled through the open country, even though they killed hummingbirds for food. But Kalapalo ancestors occasionally came across other starving and thirsty wanderers, as we learn from the poignant account which opens Tsangaku's story of the Carib-speaking Dyaguma people. Yet other stories refer most specifically to non-Indian strangers, *kagayfa* or "Christians," as I translate the word (for its essential use to emphasize cultural rather than racial differences; some *kagayfa* [in the story of the Saganafa, for example] were most probably native people who had adopted European ways).[9] Trying to sort out the identities of persons and groups in some of these stories can be difficult, since individual and group identity are often deliberately obscured and because of the various ways Kalapalo use the word *angikogo* to label both "strangers" (people who are considered ethnically distinct) and "fierce people" (who are enemies).

In warrior biographies, a contrast is first developed between the hero's local community and some nearby hostile group, variously called *angikogo* (translated, in these contexts, as "fierce people"), *i oto* ("club masters"), or the worst insult, *tifitsengekiñe* ("stinking people"), this last, according to Kalapalo, from the palm oil with which they anointed themselves. But later, as we learn that these people are often known by name to the hero, may even be relatives of his, and are sometimes remembered for what happened to them after the events in the story took place, we become unsure of who those ferocious, stinking, treacherous, club-carrying cannibals really are. Are they a separate and distinct enemy community? Or are they the hero's own people, whose hurt pride and whose notions of personal honor we are initially supposed to accept? The answers to these questions are never as clear as we would like, and the fact is that these crucial moral issues are left unresolved, even in the social biographies, which describe the conditions under which new communities were formed. Our own concern with closure demands we seek some resolution of these ambiguities, but this is never the case in Kalapalo history. What we learn from Kalapalo stories about the past is that some of the persons most involved in warfare attempted to alter the patterns of raiding, kidnapping, and cannibalistic blood feuding by expanding the locus of ethical judgment so as to redefine themselves and their enemies as members of a single moral community. In particular, warriors (the people who are remembered most in biographies) seem to have become memorable because they were concerned about refashioning critical ideological forms. They ended up formulating personal versions of reality that were different from those around them.

Although these newer ways of modeling experience did not achieve fully regularized shape as ideological forms until much later (long after these individuals ceased to live), the words of warriors registered subtly new understandings of self and identity (particularly regarding personal responsibility) and engaged new themes in social life. In stories about the origins of communities, these newer ideological themes (closely associated with contemporary Kalapalo thinking about social life and social persons) are developed more fully, lending substance to the strategies more recent ancestors of Kalapalo and others used to form new communities. Storytellers speak of people coming from different places who attempt (successfully or not) to marry, trade, and make musical ritual together much as contemporary Alto Xingu people do. From the point of view of stories about the past, the end of warfare had less to do with the physical extinction of enemies than with an ideological shifting of the boundaries of the moral community to include people in different communities (even strangers). What was being destroyed was the idea of the enemy defined a priori by the acts of others, for which one's own group could take no direct responsibility. And yet, despite this shift from an ethic of aggression toward other communities to one of peaceful interaction, the ancestors of the Kalapalo were hardly able to create for themselves a nonviolent paradise. Once the "enemy" was omitted from discourse about relations between social groups, acts of revenge were redirected into much more specific local contexts, toward groups of brothers who lived in the same community and who came to be known as "witches" who had attacked specific, local victims. Thus suspicion and revenge turned inward, into the group, rather than being directed outward. Once the warrior recognized the essential sameness of people in groups, his own and others', then responsibility became very localized indeed. Only then did *angikogo* become an idea that needed radical rethinking.

At the same time, people who belonged to different communities got along with one another in more personalized ways. Since they were no longer so constrained by their local community affiliations as before, the possibilities for a community of many local groups speaking different languages but sharing a common set of values arose. Local groups whose customs were deviant in one way or another adopted what was more commonly accepted. The Kalapalo themselves, for example, continued to eat meat well into this century but were, they said, discouraged from doing so by the Kuikuro. Hereditary leaders sat together in hammocks and shared ritual and mythological knowledge, often across language groups. This sharing was not only done because they were leaders but because they chose to emphasize their solidarity with men who had fled their natal settlements after witchcraft accusations. Individual ties were developed and evaluated in keeping with a set of values about "good" behavior and "correct" action in daily practice (particularly focused on the treatment of the body in a great variety of contexts) and in ritual, marriage, and trade, whose powerful emotional meanings—often most clearly expressed in the songs that are collectively sung in the central village plaza[10]—also came to be shared. This sharing may explain why Kalapalo tell stories said to be about neighboring people's ancestors, such as the story of Wapagepundaka (said to be an ancestor of the Tupi-speaking Kamaiura); the story of the Trumai migration down the Tanguro into the floodplain of the Rio Culuene; the histories of Tapoge and Tamakafi, belonging to the Lake Community people, themselves ancestors of Carib-speaking people known today as Kuikuro. It might also help explain the encrusting of imagery around *angikogo*.

Accompanying this increasing "personalization" was the development of personal networks of social ties developed through marriage and kinship relations. Witchcraft accusations, involving complex political alliances that cross-cut settlements and always focusing upon individuals, apparently replaced blood feuding between communities. (Of course, people do challenge one another's adherence to such a common purpose, and difficult and delicate maneuvers have to be made when relatives in different communities are forced to take sides as conflicts arise; see Basso [1973].) In any event, there is no mention of witchcraft until the community biographies. And warriors—men who were earlier trained to protect their fellows against enemies—came to be regarded more and more as "great hunters" (still especially well trained in the art of the bow) until, with the appearance of firearms, male puberty seclusion came to be focused less on skills associated with feuding and with hunting and more upon agriculture, fishing, and wrestling. The stories about very recent times, where individuals can be directly related to the actual tellers (or who lived in communities abandoned within the last few generations), show very different processes of contact and a different role for warriors, one that is generalized and in which they cease to be individualized (though they usually are named) as they were in the far distant past.

With these changes came new variations in the use of words that formerly referred to "enemy," "fierce people," and "warriors." With increasing consciousness of the common problems of indigenous Brazilians and a much sharper understanding of the motivations behind the violence of the Ge people, in particular, who are almost always actively defending their lands against Brazilian invaders, the category label *angikogo* itself has begun to lose its more pejorative meanings and to stand for native persons whose customs differ from those of Kalapalo particularly and people of the Alto Xingu more generally.

I used the word *ideology* in this chapter when considering matters concerned with choices among values that people make, their judgments of relative political and ethical value. This emphasis on judgments and choices complements an approach that is oriented to the "subjectivities" or "voices" of Kalapalo identity. Such judgments and choices allow people to shape their own fates. From the narratives, one learns about personal versions of reality manifested through dialogue that became integrated into the social etiquette of contemporary people; these voices have particular meaning when it comes time to make judgments about values and to make decisions and choices about action in connection with those values. Understanding the particular anxieties that motivated those ancient heroes can further assist our comprehension of how an ideology of reconciliation is verbally constituted, the reasons why personal attitudes take the form they do in public contexts, with understanding the manner in which the discourse of history reminds contemporary Kalapalo of the moral and political consequences for future generations of their own decisions and choices.

CHAPTER
2
The Language in Storytelling

Kalapalo told me stories from the very first week in Aifa, their settlement. As a novice, my first research goal was to try to learn how to speak to the residents in their own language, and for this purpose I began my work by asking for lists of words for things, using as a translator the single Portuguese-speaking man present in the settlement at that time and the only person who used a Portuguese name. In 1952, Antonio had been taken as a teenager to live in Rio de Janeiro along with his sister Dyaqui, who was being married to a Brazilian worker who had come to the Alto Xingu during the time of the Central Brazil Foundation expedition.[1] After having been inducted into the army, he was eventually returned to the Alto Xingu, where it was expected that he resume the life he had left years before. He was filled with bitterness about the forced change, was the only man who consistently wore clothes in my presence, and gladly spoke Portuguese (particularly to reminisce about his experiences in the city). One day, as I sat with him in the plaza center writing down my simple words and sentences ("house"; "man"; "woman"; "dog"; "fish"; "He is old"; "She is young"; "This one is good"; "This one is red"), a tall robust man whom I hadn't seen before came to stand very close before me, intently watching my writing. He spoke to me in Portuguese. "I will tell you a story," he began, "and you will write it down. Then I will tell it to you in the *kagayfa* language. Will you like that?" Of course. We began that afternoon, in the house he shared with his sister and brother-in-law. From that day, continuing for almost a year, Waiyepe sat with me face to face, narrating stories, patiently repeating sentences I was unable to capture at first on paper. While his stories were nothing like the elaborate performances I later heard from people who were talking to their relatives and visitors, or the ones people asked me to tape for them, Waiyepe's narratives eventually led me deeper into Kalapalo life as I transcribed and attempted my first translations with his help. And this early experience of being taught Kalapalo through narratives was a significant, continuing lesson, one that never ended throughout my time among them.

All Kalapalo stories, including historical narratives, personal accounts, and myths of the dawn people and powerful beings, involve organized bodies of knowledge, not just empirically focused talk but discourse emerging from fantasy, dreaming, speculation, alternative states of consciousness characteristic of shamanistic practice, and defensive projections that make use of shared symbols in special, privately focused ways. The study of these discourses is a very useful way of learning something about how people organize what they know, remember, and fantasize about their pasts so as to explain to one another what they think happened. From the present kind of study, which is discourse-centered rather than simply concerned with topics or themes extracted from stories, we can also learn about how people think about their present lives and what concerns them about the future. Narratives are not only "about" the past but reminders, warnings, encouragements—in other words, models for people to use as they project forward. These stories are, in an important sense, "kept for use," mulled over for very different reasons by different people and in many different contexts. Like all narratives they comment on the present as much as the past.

The telling of a Kalapalo story is an elaborate kind of commentary, developed over the many different tellings and refined by the particular storyteller to suit the conditions of the particular audience, be they children (who know nothing and are said to be easily bored), a foreign anthropologist (who also knows nothing but who is willing to listen for hours to stories she barely understands), local women (who are very much interested in learning the names of ancestors and determining who was married to whom so they can construct genealogical connections for their younger kin and suggest appropriate names for children), youths in puberty seclusion (whose dreams should be influenced by vivid narratives of powerful beings), or (what is most usual) a mixed audience with many concerns and interests and, it should be said, quite varied degrees of interest. It is hard, in fact, to generalize about the nature of storytelling contexts, for they are the substance of Kalapalo day-to-day life itself.

Although they may not be the targets of specific stories, people begin hearing stories when they are very small. They continue to listen, and to narrate themselves, throughout their adult lives. But only the oldest leaders (anetaü) are recognized as the true akiña otoi, the people who "possess" the most detailed versions of stories about both mythological times (ingila) and the distant past when the first Xinguano communities were being formed. To these storytellers come younger relatives and friends who wish to learn. Some people who claim distinguished story-teller ancestors seem to make use of their birthright in ways that are admired by their contemporaries. Others, particularly younger men and women who are related by marriage to older, powerful leaders, refrain from this kind of public display in order not to appear immodest before their relatives. It is particularly important for hereditary leaders, especially men, to learn narratives, because they are expected to be able to share them with both local residents and outsiders. Stories are considered "gifts" to their listeners and are characteristically "given" to visiting dignitaries as an important element in the hospitality of local leaders. But other men (and women) also learn narratives and are expected to be adept in storytelling as well. However, such people typically do not tell the more fundamental stories of the dawn people that are told to young people in puberty seclusion and to visitors. Though they usually know such a story, they reserve the telling for the community elders. But they usually know some of the more esoteric stories, as I discovered was the case with Kudyu (not *anetu*) and Tsangaku (a female *anetu*), both of whom had learned much from her *anetu* father, Tadyui, the leader of Kanugidyafiti. This knowledge was given to each of them when they were quite young, especially during their time of puberty seclusion. Like many narrators, Tsangaku and Kudyu would sometimes tell me whom they had learned their stories from, including this information right in the narrative. Tsangaku, while telling me about the Dyaguma, said:

I remember Tadyui telling me this.

["I see," I replied.]

Father.

["Um."]

While I was secluded he was telling me this.

["I see."]

Yes.
The arrival of the Dyaguma, right to Kalapalo.

["I see."]

Children of theirs to Kwapïgï.

["I see."]

Mm.
And far away at your own settlement you'll play this.

["Yes."]

Far away, at your settlement you'll do that with this.

["Yes."]

This tape, will that happen to it?

["That's what I plan to do."]

And Kudyu, during a story about Christians who came to the very early settlement at Wagifitï, told me:

I remember him telling me that's what they sang, Tadyui did that.
He really taught me a lot.
He was my teacher.

Storytelling cannot always be specifically correlated with immediate concerns motivating both storyteller and listeners, since stories are often told to people like Kudyu and Tsangaku, who ask for them as part of an ongoing process of learning to narrate. There are special stories that seem to be told by women (focused upon a female character or oriented toward female sexuality), others, such as the complex, lengthy myths of the original dawn people and other powerful beings, that are more appropriately told by older men, and yet other stories parents and grandparents tell that seem oriented toward small children: short tales about animals, often with songs that the listeners are encouraged to learn. Stories are frequently told at night, after the evening meal, as people relax in their hammocks gossiping. Narratives begin when people wish to evoke a particular setting (the grand and mysterious lake called Tafununu, for example) or to teach about the (always deeply moving) role that women played in maintaining peace between people, to emphasize the value of fundamental ethical principles and ideals of personal conduct, or when concerns with current strategies for dealing with threatening outsiders surface. Older people may take several weeks telling complicated histories of long-extinct communities with which they were associated as children, considering these narratives to be part of their younger relatives' heritage. Stories are recalled during trips to special places or may be narrated after someone returns from such a place.

Narratives often seem to be contrasted implicitly with "everyday talk" by theorists perhaps because of the connection that is often made between practical necessity, common sense, and "ordinary" conversation, on the one hand, and narrative and "artful" performance, on the other. With performance connected to highly creative speech, narrative talk is associated in this view with specialists. Among Kalapalo, however, narrative is part of everyday talk but distinguished from conversational speech by how responses are managed. Conversations may evolve into stories, as someone begins a narrative in order to elaborate on some general theme. The opposite frequently happens when a listener begins to ask questions of the storyteller. It can take as long as several months for a storyteller to get through a very long story, and episodes from stories may be told in connection with ongoing relationships between storytellers and listeners. I heard a story because it was being told to some children by an old leader, at first because the old man wanted to be remembered as a master storyteller and then because he was happy to hear himself talk on tape. (The possibilities of tape-recording stories as well as music for sharing with people in other settlements were beginning to be understood then, in 1966.) Twenty years later, the old man and his grandson, who had by then inherited his grandfather's old name (the one he had used when I made the recording), listened to the narrative and helped me transcribe and translate it. In 1982, the old leader (by then using the name Ulutsi) was able to tell me more about bow masters, cannibals, the ritual music described in his story, and other matters I wanted to ask about, now that I heard some of the other bow-master biographies and knew how to ask more intelligent questions. These kinds of discussion occur when outsiders, visitors from other settlements as well as foreigners, are told all kinds of stories as gifts from the distinguished members of the local group. The visitors, in turn, may exchange stories of their own. There is a lively interest in storytelling and, more and more, in stories about foreigners told by foreigners, as the Kalapalo become more and more aware of their and other native peoples' place in national Brazilian society. Talking with me one afternoon about *akiña*, Kudyu said to me:

> You are right to think our own offspring are taught these things. We want them to understand and accept what we say. While they listen to us. Someone tells someone else something. And someone tells another person something. But not all our people have such things. Only the ones who know them have them. Yes, only the ones who know them have them. In that house over there, there's someone who is a storyteller, and someone over there in that place is a storyteller, that's how they are. That's how they are.

"*Eh he*. I see," I replied, letting him know in proper form that I understood and accepted what he was telling me.

There are, then, so many reasons Kalapalo tell stories. Most generally, stories are a way of preserving, and passing on, knowledge. Even the most casual conversations can easily change into situations of storytelling, drawing a small group of listeners. Storytelling includes the narration of what might be called sacred myths, which concern the origins of people and the world as known to the Kalapalo, but the word *akiña* refers to any kind of narrative speech. So in addition to traditional stories, we should also consider the relatively short narratives that people relate to one another privately every day, stories about fishing trips, honey gathering in the forests, trips to Posto Leonardo or to visit relatives in other settlements, and, even more brief, gossipy narratives about encounters at the lake or along a path, what one person said to another about a third party whose behavior is cause for concern, and what someone else heard as she passed outside a house unseen. These *akiña* are an important means of sharing rather ordinary information and transmit the substance of community gossip. Most of them contain such sensitive information that I would not have wished to record them under any circumstances. I must therefore speak very generally about them.

These little narratives have an important explanatory component to them insofar as people present their understandings of events this way, framing conversations within a narrative structure. Like the longer stories told more publicly, they make extensive use of quoted speech; indeed, one reason for narrating is to tell others what people said about certain things, or to describe how people who are related in one way or another are getting along with each other, itself the subject of extended scrutiny. Surely some of these autobiographical stories become over time historical narratives; in the past some must have been joined together by more socially distant observers to form the kinds of traditional stories I present in the chapters that follow.

Narration is informally practiced by the young and carefully cultivated as an art by certain older men and women. By thinking of Kalapalo stories as "narrative art" I am writing of a certain kind of verbal performance that involves a storyteller or narrator (the *akiñoto*) and a listener-responder (*tiitsofo*) who receives the story in an active, dialogical manner. One way to describe the *akiñatunda* (the practice of simultaneously telling and receiving a narrative) is to say that it is like an extended and rather one-sided conversation, during which one party does most of the talking while expecting the listener to reveal how the events of the story are being heard: with interest, excitement, awe, or apparent boredom. Questions, too, are encouraged, sometimes asked for. What makes the *akiñatunda* different from a conversation is not only the regularity of the dialogical interaction but the extended, narrative quality of the emergent text: a story is being told and received. I believe that Waiyepe was able to sustain his interest in telling me stories because, while writing them down, I repeated each utterance of his during his pauses before actually recording it on paper. In an extreme way, I replicated the behavior of the listener-responder, working with the storyteller and thus enabling his narratives to emerge. But, not knowing in the early months of my work that there even was such a thing as a what-sayer, I was unable to get many other people to agree to tell me stories. I simply didn't know how to receive them properly. Even as time went on, like a distracted child I would occasionally have to be prompted to say *"eh he"* by a narrator. My problems understanding Kalapalo certainly contributed to my distractedness at times, as I tried to translate what was being said, but I often found my thoughts set loose by the remarkable images in many of the stories. Clearly, the role of the responder involved dutiful concentration upon what was being said.

Performance of Kalapalo stories is a matter of degree, with careful, elaborate versions, marked by changes in the speaker's voice to suggest different characters, being at one extreme, and rather repetitive, halting attempts at another. Many stories emerge from, and later are submerged by, conversations (in the Kalapalo sense of short, nondiscursive, often overlapping remarks; these are usually associated with "gossip"). Always, a story is framed as such by the introductory remark "Do listen" ("Ahtsakefa") and a conclusion such as "That's all there is to that" ("Aifa, apïgï aketsigey"). This frame creates and then releases a certain tension between teller and listener which involves an increasingly shared imaginative intimacy, as the narrator tries to make the listener "see" the events of the story. As with English speakers, the metaphor involves understanding and appreciation; the good Kalapalo listener is alert to the need for reinforcing the images in the teller's own mind by the responses necessary for having the story move forward.

My translations of these stories are arranged to show the line structure that storytellers created together with their listener-responders (tiïtsofo). The most common response is "Eh" ("Yes"), which to make the texts easier for my publishers to accept I have omitted in these presentations. The position of lines (determined by the responses made by listeners) is arranged according to the narrator's voice quality. Those lines which appear near the left margin were spoken with relative force, while those arranged near the right margin were spoken rather softly. Typical of Kalapalo oral performance is the beginning of a rhetorical segment with a relatively loud voice, which during ensuing lines becomes softer and lower-pitched. Subsidiary units within the larger segment usually add more information to the proposition given initially in the segment; these are also spoken rather loudly and with a higher pitch than the opening line of the verse.

To use as an example the story about Dyaguma told by Tsangaku, this narrator regularly used five typical cadences and tones. Although she was often interrupted during her story, I consider her one of the most consistent in her prosody. Arranged according to how I eventually decided to place the lines marked by her listener-responders, these can be summarized as follows:

(a) louder, lower-pitched voice
    (b_1) higher-pitched voice (qualification) and/or (not necessarily in order indicated by numbers),
    (b_2) quickened pace (description of action)
      (c) increasingly softer and low-pitched voice
      (d) low-pitch, softest voice

An example from the story itself follows:

lepene, ohsifa. (a)
   asinïngolefa. fugombonga. [um.] (b₂)
   teh ekugumbenipa ukuge (b₁)
   tamitsinafa tafite agage tuipïgï, (b₁)
   añatula ataguetue atufuguko. (koh.) (b₂)
   kufitseke apuguko, (b₁)
   aguetugele, aguetugele, aguetugele, aguetugele, aguetugele. (b₂)
aifa. (a)
   Kalapalo otomo. [um] (b₁)
      ukuge. [um.] (c)

(translation):

Then, "Let's go."
   They came into the plaza.

                                                           ["Um."]

So many beautiful people must have been there.
They must have just erected a grave enclosure, because they
were all lined up behind the grave.

                                                           ["Wow."]

They were very serious, they had all run up to line themselves
up, one by one by one by one by one.
Readied.
   The Kalapalo people.

                                                           ["Um."]

      Our people.

                                                           ["Um."]

Compare this style of presentation (which of course can best be accomplished with a narrative that has been put on tape) with the following notebook reconstruction in English of an untaped story told to me
around the same time. When I wrote this down, I was trying to remember as much of the story line as I could, in order to be able to ask about
it later on:

A young man (*angifolo*) was beaten by his father for having lovers
and so left his village for the forest. At night he crept into a large
rotten log to sleep. This was the home of a very large snake (*eke-
fuegï*). The snake entered the log, removed a small arrow from behind his ear, and left. *Angifolo* grabbed this and fled. He came to a
bathing place where a secluded maiden was bathing. "Who are
you?" she said. "You are the one whose father beat him?" "Yes, I
am that same person. I want to marry you," the man said. This was

the daughter of the jaguar. She told him to wait and went to tell her mother . . . (and so forth, without any paragraphs).

The reader might be puzzled by the fact that the stories are neither introduced nor followed by commentary made by narrators or listeners. Kalapalo stories are in fact commented upon through/by their telling, rather than being framed by interpretive remarks. We are much accustomed to people chatting about a story after the fact, we don't like storytellers to be interrupted, and acknowledgments of what they're saying sometimes make them think we've heard them all before. Nothing could be more different for storytellers like Tsangaku, Ulutsi, Ausuki, and Kambe.

A Kalapalo story, then, is something to ponder, to remember, "good to think," but only "good to discuss" during pauses left open by the narrator specifically for questioning by listeners, to which the storyteller responds. Sometimes, the discussion does turn back into conversational speech, with the what-sayer ending up asking so many questions the speaker in effect stops the narrative to provide extensive explanations and details. Discussion might also occur through the telling of other stories. Conversations themselves in Kalapalo tend to be focused around rather short narratives (like the brief accounts of their experiences during the measles epidemic I was told), only more moderately responded to (according to our standards) by listeners than do listeners to stories. *Akiñatunda*, storytelling or "narrative speech," is more formal and extended narrative, though not necessarily always traditional or mythological, and often in fact concerned with current events.

Imagery of Traveling, of Time and Space

Traveling by air over the Alto Xingu, one sees land that is relentlessly flat, densely covered in places with forest, but often as much grassland with scattered, lower-growing trees. During the period of low waters, it is easy to see how often the serpentine rivers have changed their courses, leaving a myriad of small embayments and oxbows, the newer ones fresh with dark water, the older turning to swamp, covered with a green blanket of water hyacinth and weed. As the waters dry up, extensive sandbanks are exposed, upon which turtles lay their eggs.

Traveling by canoe along the larger rivers and streams, the land seems far more varied. On one bank might be some open *campo cerrado* habitats of mixed spiny palms and dry-looking scrubby trees extending beyond the steep sandy bank, while on the other side, behind a curtain of vines, is the tall *mata* forest. These are so heavily flooded during the rainy season that canoes are able to pass through in the wetter months of the year. In the *cerrado*, too, are areas that are extensively flooded.

Although from the air much of the Alto Xingu seems empty beyond the obvious settlements and fields, as one walks through this country the evidence of human occupation is startlingly pervasive. In many places there are clearings still visible where old settlements existed. Even in the deepest forests there are trails, log bridges laid across creeks and through swampy places where flooding occurs in the rainy season. Here and there people have left stumps from their cutting of the tallest trees and drying racks across which the materials for a canoe, a new house, or ritual objects like musical instruments or memorial posts were laid prior to being brought back to the settlement. Trees are scarred from having been repeatedly tapped by men for their resins, used to fasten arrow heads or as special medicines or body paints. In certain densely overgrown places, where manioc once grew in large, open fields, women have stripped other, more graceful species of their bark for making pubic ornaments with which they decorate themselves when they dance in ceremonies. The groves of *piqui* trees, visited each year for their remarkable fruit, surround the older settlements. And always trails—trails between settlements, trails to fishing places and canoe landings, trails to *piqui* groves and manioc, corn, and cotton fields, trails to trees bearing edible wild fruit and yielding special resins. The land is well used and well known, marked by incidents of experience and memory among the living and by ancient stories that describe how lakes, rivers, and rapids came into being.

It is not surprising that a subtle matter of concern in people's memories of their past is the Alto Xingu environment and most particularly the water and its multiple associations. Almost all the stories summon, over and over again, the names of special watery places near where people settled. the lake Tafununu, a broad expanse of shallow water nearly surrounded by burity palms, on whose muddy bottom the canoeing traveler sees endless numbers of stingrays; the stream called Tangugu, which cuts through low semideciduous *mata* forests, along which fishermen travel from one small embayment to another, each more abundant with fish than the next; the Iña creek, salvation of refugees in the deep high *galeria* forest, dying of thirst and hungry for the game that could best be caught near water; the Rio Culuene, called Fangguinga, "Fluidity." This is the largest river in the region, eventually joining the Rio Xingu itself, a major northward tributary of the Amazon. We must pay some attention, then, to what is said about these waters, to the kinds of animals, monsters, and powerful beings (*itseke*) people encountered as they canoed or walked near these places. A story told by Kudyu preserves the memory of how one young man, searching for a new place to live, discovers high ground from his canoe by following the sound of a particular kind of cicada which only lives in open, sunlit places located at some distance from flooded forests. Ausuki talks repeatedly about the giant catfish killed by Trumai bow masters as they travel into a new land. Remarkable, too, are the seemingly casual references to species of plants, but these too are significant for enabling the Kalapalo listener (any one of whom, adults and children alike, might easily name plants for hours on end if they didn't have more interesting things to do) to picture the events of the story as occurring in very specific kinds of places and seasons. Ausuki, in his story of the Trumai ancestors, tells of the *akaga* tree, common on the open *cerrado*, swarming with hummingbirds who are feeding from the flowers that (the listener should know and thus need not be told) bloom just before the rains begin, when the "hands of Duck"—Procyon and Canopus—appear on the southwestern horizon. The turtles should be laying their eggs on the sandbanks; this is confirmed later in the story. Tsangaku also mentions people gathering turtle eggs, which prompts her daughter to ask, somewhat rhetorically as a good listener should, if the time of year is *isoa*, the dry season. Toward the end of his story, Ausuki describes a certain kind of tree that leans over a stream where the water has begun to erode the bank. This tree creates just the right kind of cover for a man aiming his bow at the fish below. Ausuki doesn't have to tell a Kalapalo listener that the fish are there because they are waiting for the fruit of the tree to drop into the water. At the same time, the branches of the tree conceal the fisherman's enemy waiting farther up the bank, so that the fisherman is easily ambushed. Given the complexity of the watery environment of the Upper Xingu Basin, a land of numerous swamps, pluvial and oxbow lakes (or embayments), and creeks, streams, and rivers, each with their special configuration of sandbars, outlets, and distinctive plant communities, these stories are poetic field guides for the native traveler concerned with the substance of the environments, with the local dangers, and most particularly with the psychological journeys of people who passed through in earlier times.

On a long trip up the Rio Culuene, from the newer area of Kalapalo settlement (Aifa) to the older region called Kanugidyafitï, I listened to Kambe name each meander we approached, reminding his youngest son of stories about things that had happened in each place to the dawn people and to their more recent ancestors. The river for Kambe was far more than a convenient way to travel and a place to fish, though he was readily able to tell the grandsons exactly where fish of specific species were to be found, whether in the shallows along the sandbanks, in deeper water, or near certain bushes whose fruit would drop into the water below.

The old settlement of Kanugidyafïtï was abandoned around 1961, when the Kalapalo were persuaded to move north to Aifa during the establishment of the reserve. This was a place that had been settled for many years, as attested to by the extensive groves of *piqui* that were still bearing fruit in the late 1960s. Once at Kangidyafïtï, those of us who were visiting for the first time were told whose house was located in which part of the house circle, from which other settlements the formal entrance path led, where the paths were to bathing places and canoe landings. And each day, as we gathered *piqui*, the older people pointed out the manioc fields, the secondary growth, the *piqui* groves; concerning the latter, their names, what the names meant, who had planted them, and who had inherited them.

Near the landing place at Kafindzu Meander from which people walked to Kanugidyafïtï was a site very important to the older Kalapalo, for it was there that some of the people who had died in a terrible measles epidemic in 1954 were buried by *kagayfa*, workers for the Brazilian Air Force who were camped along the river. On our trip to Kanugidyafïtï, while Kambe's family prepared camp nearby, prior to our next day's walk to the old settlement, Kwanakwana gently took my wrist and led me to the unmarked grave, where she solemnly listed the names of the people who were buried there. I had first heard about the measles epidemic when I asked people about their relatives, shortly after my arrival at the beginning of the rainy season in 1966. At the time I was attempting to learn how people in Aifa were connected to each other by collecting genealogies. There were then many young people living with relatives who were not their parents. They, and the older women who were most knowledgeable about recent ancestors, always took care to mention how individuals had died; often, witchcraft was blamed, or else powerful beings. Death was a subject they were constantly occupied with in their discussions of the past. Almost casually, people began telling me of the *sagampu*, the measles: of parents dying in their hammocks while children slept below, of the sick burying the dead, of the continuous weeping from all the many houses of the settlement, so densely populated until then. Weeks before, while talking to other older women about their grandparents, Tsangaku and Kanaigu kept returning to the subject of the measles, because so many people they were telling me about had died. Finally, they listed over fifty people from the Kalapalo settlements who had been lost in this epidemic. I was told that it had begun very suddenly after a pair of Kalapalo returned from the Brazilian outpost at Shavantina, where they had been taken for medical treatment. Those two were the first to show signs of the disease.

The even tone with which Kalapalo told me these stories concealed a terrible fear they still carried with them. In 1968, while we were visiting the Yawalipiti settlement for a trading ceremony (*uluki*), some visitors from the neighboring Kamaiura told the Kalapalo that several people in that settlement had measles. Almost immediately, the Kalapalo leaders decided to leave the Yawalipiti before the ceremony had even begun. It was almost nightfall at the time, and we had settled inside the house where our hammocks had been slung by our hosts. Urged on by the leaders, we hurriedly packed up our things and walked out through the rain to the canoe landing several hours away. Chilled by the heavy rain, we paddled in the dark until we arrived at the Kalapalo landing place on the east bank of the Rio Culuene from where we walked another half hour until we reached Aifa.

Experiences like these, in which critical events and spatial sensibilities are formed through traveling and other experiences of time, are the basis of more abstract ideas about time and space that in turn are revealed in narrative imagery. All Kalapalo narratives share images of space and time that serve to break up the narrative flow into thematically discrete units, to define events as occurring at different "times." While these conventional segmenting devices create something like the spoken equivalents of written paragraphs, they are important as segmenting devices precisely because they distinguish among different kinds of "time." Quite often, characters are said to "sleep" a certain number of days. This reference introduces new action possibilities for them. What follow are different events, often new orientations. While events in a narrative are separated from each other in this way, they are also connected logically through the persistent imagery of the cyclical succession of time conveyed by the words used to refer to movements of the sun, seasonal changes, and day turning to night turning to day (suggested by the speaker mentioning that a character has "slept" a certain number of times). The specific expressions used by Kalapalo all express concrete ways in which temporal changes or natural processes of time are experienced rather than an objectification of them. These references also serve to emphasize the way time is experienced differently by different types of characters (men walking through a *cerrado*, watching the sun move across the sky; a woman in her pregnancy), which contributes to a sense of different experiential worlds existing side by side in the same story. Using these references to a character's experiences of time helps to segment the narrative. However, it would be wrong to consider these segments as corresponding to analytic "stages." What I suggest are segments that the narrator organizes into a story with developmental progression; the segments can be isolated because they emerge as the narrator uses the very features in question to orient the listener to changes in how different characters are experiencing events.

Finally, the experiencing of time through traveling is another important segmenting device. What is particularly important to a Kalapalo listener is how a character travels through space. The frantic movement back and forth between places, traveling on foot, in a canoe, in the form of an animal, or in magical flight between home and a dangerous, mysterious realm of powerful beings, enemies, or Christians are all symbols for different kinds of consciousness, that is, ways of perceiving and understanding. Associated with persistence, determination, and the goal of creating an "alternative self" (different from a man or woman's humdrum life), traveling is characterized by experiences of creative, transformative power.

The changes in how people experience events and how they participate actively in making decisions and choices are made to seem inseparable from and, to put it somewhat differently, are both foregrounded and cross-referenced by descriptions of the passage of time, the repetition of activities, interaction with others as indicated by the differences in the sounds made by participants (speech, calls, expletives, songs), and traveling.

A reviewer of an earlier book in this series complained of the large amount of space I devoted to the narratives, relative to "analysis." This is, I will always maintain, as it should be. It is probably true of this book as well. The sheer number of pages given over to text translations is a consequence of my use of writing conventions (arrangements of texts into lines rather than prose paragraphs; indenting lines in different places; using capitals to indicate differences in emphasis) that help a reader to see the narrative structure of each story and to imagine in a sensory way something of what the storytellers did with their voices during their performances. If the stories were to be presented as if they had been written prose, the analytic sections would have been more balanced in terms of quantity of pages, but what was said in those sections about the importance of prosody and discourse form and their relationship to expressive and rhetorical functions would have been utterly contradicted by how the reader sees them on the page.

One might try to read the stories only, skipping the commentary and contextualization. A person who does this probably won't like the stories, won't find them very interesting. For reading Kalapalo stories can be hard on those accustomed only to reading Western literature. In Kalapalo narratives, every detail is splayed before us for our minute examination and reflection. A story seems to drag on without much happening besides talk. ("Where's the story?" a writer asked me about one Kalapalo narrative I asked him to read.) Also, there is frequent repetition, because a repeated line is a response to the listener's verbal cue that the teller is being heard and understood. The listener's responses are therefore very important because they help develop the story rhythm, one reason why I have not removed repetitions. Another is the fact that certain numbers of repetitions have significance: four means completion; five, that a goal is reached.

Another problem for the Western reader is that sentences are often short and uncomplicated. People, objects, events are described as conglomerations of minutiae. Descriptive adjectives emerge in single file: "He was this, he was that, he was thus and so." Words like "because," "and," "also" don't appear in Kalapalo; their functions are signaled by grammatical particles attached to verbs. This can make a close English translation hard to follow because the logic of a relationship between events may not be transparent. Perhaps most perplexing of all are the conversations, whose presence is the basic reason why readers "can't find the action."

In all Kalapalo narratives, reported or, as I prefer to say, quoted speech is the most important means of developing individual characters and their interpersonal relations. I estimate that at least 50 percent and in some instances as much as 80 percent of a story consists of quoted speech. Another way to think of this is that events in stories tend to be centered on speech and therefore instances of interpersonal contact. Even when acting alone, a person will be described as speaking.

Quoted Speech and Evidentiality

In many of these narratives, people tend to validate each other, as they agree with one another's goals and plans, verify evidence, and sympathize with one another's feelings. We shall see how important these processes are in the community biographies discussed in part 2 of this book.[2] Such ideologically centered processes are also markedly characteristic of day-to-day conversations between Kalapalo, who seem quite concerned to seek and receive validation and verification of ordinary plans and interpretations from one another.

Validation results from the use of conventional "agreement" responses (especially the simple "eh he," "all right," "very well"; and the verbal suffix apa, "as you wish," "if you want to") that imply shared imaginative intimacy: shared feelings, shared goals, indeed for the Kalapalo a social creation that is shared. A typical "suggestion-agreement" example is found in the story of Saganafa (chapter 3); the younger speaker's use of the hypothetical mood suggests that he is being especially polite to the much older man:

apiti nïgifeke.
ekitsoto ukwembugopeta, kanga ukwembeta.
kigeapa, nïgifeke.

"Grandfather," he said.
"Could we go meet the fish migration, go meet the fish?"
"Let's go if you wish," he answered.

But the expression of a different point of view involves considerably more specification of reasoning processes, the nature of contradictory evidence, and how conclusive is the result of that reasoning. Different opinions forthrightly spoken do occur but are considered rude and in certain contexts (witchcraft accusations) seriously divisive. In the Kalapalo language, different points of view are more usually indicated by more subtle differences in the certainty and directness with which speakers respond to each other. The more forthrightly expressed the differing opinion, it seems, the less socially satisfying the interpersonal relation. It is clear that material truth is secondary to the social truth of relations that are contextualized by Kalapalo linguistic processes.

These processes of constituting "social truth" revolve around the use of "evidentials," ways of indicating the speaker's attitude toward the validity of what is being said, marking both varieties of evidence and of certitude that occur in statements; the latter include the shifting valences of opinions (as, for example, when someone wishes to say the equivalent of the English "I don't know but perhaps . . ." and "Now I'm more than ever convinced that . . .").

By "evidentials" I refer to several kinds of linguistic phenomena. The first type includes a large and complex set of suffixlike forms that constitute an important morphological category in the Kalapalo language; in sentences, these forms are found after nouns, verbs, and demonstratives, thereby qualifying descriptions of existential phenomena (such as size, number, location) as well as depictions of events which are under the control of agents. So far, I have discovered twenty-five basic forms belonging to a single form class, as well as eight forms clearly compounded from these basic ones. Also having evidential functions are certain expletives (such as "koh," an expression of ignorance, and "um," expressing introspection); words like *engikomungapa*, "I'm not sure but maybe"; and a set of conventional responses that indicate either validation ("eh he"; "eh he kingi") or denial ("afïtï," "afïtï kingi") of the validity of a proposition. The grammatically based evidentials interact in important ways with words (such as *afïtï*, "that's wrong") and the conventional responses used in agreement and disagreement.

As one might expect, the most elaborate use of evidentials occurs at moments of heightened tension between persons: in situations of doubt, of potential discord, and of actual disputes, and especially in situations of dialogue where persuasion and resistance to persuasion take place. As we shall see in the many examples discussed in connection with particular stories, they occur when a shared meaning is sought (on the one hand), or where it is being thwarted (on the other): during initial contact between persons hesitant or even overwhelmed by doubt about the propriety of such contact, and moments of poor insight (when someone can't seem to understand what is happening), of negotiation, of resistance to an interpretation, or of outright denial of shared experience.

In these stories, we can see Kalapalo evidentials being used to "contextualize" (Gumperz 1984) relationships, to qualify the sentiments that are emerging from interpersonal contact, and which, for the Kalapalo, serve as motivations for continuing action. Another way to describe this is to say that evidentials help to create an intersubjective experience falling somewhere along an axis between fully shared imaginative intimacy and self-isolating resistance. By explicitly corroborating, deducing, or speculating in terms of degrees of certainty and uncertainty about any of the marked forms of evidence, Kalapalo speakers in fact convey impressions in a kind of conventionalized verbal shorthand not only about how the making of inferences leads to particular conclusions about experience but about how reasoning contributes to different points of view or to shared interpretations. Evidentials are used when speakers perceive the need to isolate themselves from others, to create new boundaries around groups (to which they choose, or do not choose, to belong), or to join themselves to people in newly significant ways.[3]

3

An Early Experience of Europeans Told by Muluku

An anthropological understanding of the history of a people without writing, which will necessarily be communicated orally, must be effected both with respect to their particular ways of remembering and understanding events and to how they communicate this understanding and memory within one or another speech genre. Thus, for example, if we are to know how people construct an awareness of historical processes, we must learn why certain events have become memorable, how they are given explanatory meaning, and how they are integrated into earlier life experiences. History has an explanatory or clarifying function which is inherent in its constant creative involvement with changing worlds of experience. Insofar as it involves narrative (this is certainly not always the case), history might be seen as a theory of the relations between events—an explanation or clarification of what occurred—that exists within a selective description of those events. What I mean by this is that the very structure of the narrative, as it emerges through the speech of the teller, has rhetorical significance. This structure, or form, contains clues any knowledgeable listener can follow. (A "knowledgeable listener" would be a person speaking the narrator's language and thereby knowing something about what life is like for the narrator's contemporaries.)

The first story I introduce is one that to many readers might seem mythological. I have deliberately chosen it for this reason, because it is a story about the past which seems to be very carefully organized through conventional, even perhaps stereotypical, narrative expression. The narrator, Muluku, was a youngish man when he told me the story of Saganafa, in his early thirties, and thus not known as one of the more skilled speakers. As a hereditary leader, though, he was a person who was supposed to convey such knowledge to others as a formal duty. Although he had enjoyed making a few tape recordings of stories before, this was the first "serious" story he told me, and thus, I feel, his speech was particularly careful during the telling.

I call the reader's attention to the many regularities in form in this story. I have arranged Muluku's narrative into lines, according to pauses he made in order to hear the what-sayer's response. In addition, I use four degrees of indentation to suggest the modulations in Muluku's voice, which like that of all Kalapalo storytellers is extremely regular. These different degrees of pitch are important, I believe, in helping speakers remember the details of what are often quite complicated stories that are infrequently told. In Muluku's story, the introduction of voice modulation and line structuring that was produced by the interaction between teller and what-sayer created extreme regularities—rhythms—in the way he quoted speech. Orders given from one person to another are normally single lines. Declarations and descriptions (found within conversational segments) are usually given three lines, but conclusive, even fateful, utterances are given five lines. Conversational segments are always in pairs of utterance-response. Another type of regularity concerns lists of things. Metal tools given in payment for Saganafa; the types of people stolen; the types of payment given for a revenge murder are all grouped into sets of four, a complete set.

I have divided the story of Saganafa into six major, distinct thematic parts or "verses," corresponding to important rhetorical divisions the narrator made in his narration. These divisions are signaled by the use of the expression "lepene aifa" ("then, it was over" or "then, ready") followed by a long pause and some stretching (indicating that this was the appropriate time for Muluku's listeners to ask questions; I have inserted my comments as often as possible in these places).

The first "verse" concerns Saganafa and his relationship to his father; the second focuses upon his separation from Kalapalo society; the third describes his capture by Europeans; and the fourth continues with his life among them. The fifth division, the most lengthy and complex, proposes a certain judgment about Indian-European relations. Finally, the sixth involves the culmination of all those preceding, what can be called the consequential effect. Each thematic division is located in a distinct setting, all six places or sites being linked together by the characters' experience of traveling, that common Kalapalo narrative device that serves to contrast by means of spatial symbolism qualitatively distinct forms of experience. Traveling, in other words, is a way of establishing boundaries, which seem to be treated less as visual entities than as spatial relations experienced through the sensitivity of human beings to time. These spatial relations are conceived as psychological ones as well, insofar as they are associated with very different kinds of subjectivity. And the nature of the traveling—reasoned, directed to a single place, or compulsive and arbitrary—signals how the travelers themselves are thought of as moral actors.

Some Christians stole Saganafa.
  At that time he was secluded.
    He was secluded.
  That was happening at Kwapïgï.
    Kwapïgï.
  Saganafa was there,
    secluded.

1

Then on one occasion someone slandered him to his father.
  "It certainly looks as if your son did something.
    Your son has begun to touch women," that person addressed
  him.
  "Something has got to be done about that," his father answered.
    Now his father was altogether disappointed with him.
    In that mood, he came to him.
  "Can this be true about you, that you've finally spoken with
  your sister?" he asked.
    "Someone just warned me about you."
  His son was silent.
  The father was angry with his son,
    he was truly angry.
      He was enraged.
        More than he ever had been before.
  "I'm really going to give it to you now!"
  He removed the chord from his bow,
    the father did.
    Next he whipped him.
    Because he was not allowed to have sex with women,
      Saganafa was whipped by him.
  When he was done his father scraped him all over.
  After that was over his mother said,
  "That's enough, stop doing that to your son.
    Beat him only a little," his mother declared.
  "If you are so disappointed with your son use your speech."
  That was all that happened then.
Saganafa was left alone.

The formula of a sexually rebellious youth who enrages his father
constitutes a conventional beginning for a story about a youthful hero,
who heads for the forest, where he plunges into a world of mysterious
and powerful beings. (Another example is the excerpt from the story
about a man who married a jaguar's daughter, given in prose form in
chapter 2.) The youth is made out to be contemptuous of convention,

unwilling to remain in celibate seclusion, but, more positively, is a person whose moral judgment and social curiosity are beginning to extend beyond his own family. At this time, a man is the most vulnerable to the social difficulties that so often prove tests of his composure and resilience.

2

Afterward he remained silent, then he fled.
   "I'll go to Grandfather," he said,
     "Grandfather and his companion."
  At that time they had come,
     his grandparents had come to pull out salt plants at Kafindsu
      where they had a house.
Then when night fell,
     finally he gathered up his arrows.
      By then it had become dark.
  "All right now." He was ready.
     His father thought he was still there inside his seclusion
     chamber.
     It must have been very windy by then.
VERY late in the day he arrived.
  "Here is our grandchild," the grandfather said as he arrived.
  "All right," his grandmother answered.
  "As you see, I've come here now to you both, Grandfather," he said,
     "to see you two."
  "All right."
     That was all.
Then he stayed there and they all slept.
     And the next day.
After they had slept two days,
  "Grandfather," he said,
     "could we go meet the fish migration,
      go meet the fish?"
  "Let's go if that's what you want to do," he answered.
  "Go ahead," she told him,
     "with our grandchild," his wife said,
      so they left,
        they left *pupupupu*
         paddling toward Kafindsu Meander.
Bah! a flood of migrating fish were approaching.
     They went shooting at them all the while,
      shooting all the while at *wagiti*.

Saganafa went,
    shooting all the while at the migrating fish.
That was all that happened then.

Saganafa's grandfather takes him to fish along the Rio Culuene at a meander still known as a good place for shooting *wagiti* on their way downstream during the spawning migration. This event suggests that the time of year is late April or early May, the onset of the dry season, when the forests are beginning to be drained of floodwaters. The events of the story do not take place in an abstraction of a forest nor in the typically hyperanimate setting of powerful beings. The places are named, known. And the events are, for the time being, fairly commonplace.

3

It was still very early, before dawn.
    While they continued to do that other people were beginning to
    come toward them,
        some Christians were coming toward them.
    They saw something white on the sandbar, a lot of them,
        some distance from where they were at that time.
    "Look at all the *jabiru* storks," he said to him,
        to his grandson.
    "Grandfather," Saganafa answered,
        "at night I've not been well because of that very thing,
           not well at all.
                That's how I've been at night."
    "All right."

Mention of dreaming tells us that what is to take place has been fated to occur; the Kalapalo understand dreaming to metaphorically present possibilities for future life experiences to the dreamer. Then, it is up to the dreamer to make explicit decisions to act, to allow those possibilities to become reality (Basso 1987). Muluku describes Saganafa's dreaming as "unfortunate dreaming" (*sïngufesu*), advising the listener that something terrible will happen to him if he encounters a crowd of people in white clothing. Despite this warning, Saganafa (who has intended to abandon his father's settlement) persists in drawing nearer to the "*jabiru* storks."

He continued to go on, shooting *wagiti*.
    Toward Tefupe.
While he was doing that the Christians had already come there.
"Grandfather. I think some Christians are here!"
    They held on to their canoe, the Christians did.

Traveling along the Rio Culuene at the end of the dry season. *Cerrado* vegetation can be seen on the far bank.

"Say, where are you two going?"

"We've come here for fish."

"I think you should come along with me."

"I will!" Saganafa answered.

"Come with me, come be my daughter's husband."

"I will! Grandfather, I really am going now, I'm going away."

"Very well."

"Believe me, I came here before because of the pain of my father's speech, Grandfather," he said.

"I came here because that's how he was with me.

That's why I'm leaving.

Tell the others, you'll tell those who come after us the story of my departure," Saganafa said.

"That's why I'm leaving."

How sad he was when he said that!

"All right," *bok* he got into the canoe.

Bok, the Christian gave him payment.

Bok, a knife to his grandfather.

"Here, take this."

Again, *bok* an axe.

"Here, take this."

Again, *bok* a cane cutter.

"Here, take this."

Again, a pair of scissors.

He gave him many things in payment,

the Christian gave payment for Saganafa.

"Take this, because now I'm taking this boy of yours with me for good.

I'm taking your grandson away.

I'm leaving right now."

That was all.

"Grandfather, go away!

I must leave now for good with our grandfathers.

Believe me, I didn't come to you for nothing."

"All right," his grandfather answered,

"go then if that's what you want to do."

"Grandfather, my necklace must be where I left it a long time ago. At Ogi.

I put it inside a tree there.

I hid my necklace there.

You must take it," that was the last thing he told him.

Then finally they all left,

they all left that place,

they all went away.

When the sun was at its height his grandfather paddled
downstream.
   He arrived home.
"Our grandchild is no longer alive.
   A Christian has just taken him away."
How sad were the two old people!
They walked away from there *ti ti ti ti*.
Very late in the day they arrived at Kwapïgï.
   "*Kaah! Kaah!*" shouting out in grief the elderly man walked on.
   "Your son is really no longer alive.
   Our grandchild is really no longer alive.
   A Christian carried him off."
      How sad he was!
Because the father had been so angry with his son,
   with his son he had been angry.
"You were never calm with your son, were you?
   You never spoke very nicely to him.
So here's your son's payment, here."
      The axe.
   "Here are your things, here,"
      and the old man went away.

All that has taken place so far is the consequence of a specific psychological complex connected to family life rather than an abstract and
arbitrary fate, as underscored when the grandfather presents the tools to
Saganafa's father, implicating him directly in his son's departure.

After that the others were all paddling home on Kafitsekugu, the
Rio Culiseu.
   This was how the Christians used to go to their canoe
   landing.
"Let's go now, far away from here."
   I guess they all went on the road after that.
And they slept, they slept, they slept.
For a LONG time they went on,
   toward the horizon.
      To where Kagifugukuegï the Monstrous Toad stayed.
"Quickly, hurry everyone!"
   They all scraped some vines.
      "Quickly, hurry everyone!"
Next they threw the balls of vine scraping in front of the
creature
   and it pounced on them.
      That's how they did it.

The edge of the sky rose up,
   and while the creature was occupied with the balls,
      they hurried past.
"Quickly, hurry now, let's go,"
   and they went on.

The sky is held down like a sprung curtain by the body of this monster, who must be fed balls of vine scrapings before the travelers can pass. The presence of such a monster (in another version, it is an equally loathsome Giant Tick) as well as the fact that they have traveled beyond the horizon suggest Saganafa's entrance into an unknown and dangerous region occupied by powerful beings, a place where human experience is shaped by very different kinds of dispositions than what are known in the normal world. Muluku's description of Saganafa's journey to the Christians' settlement emphasizes the extraordinary endurance necessary to arrive successfully, and this conforms to other Kalapalo accounts of trips to the realms of powerful beings. The developing image of Christians as humans whose attributes are those of powerful beings (dangerous, transformative) actually begins with Saganafa's dream and continues when he exhorts his elderly relative: "Grandfather, go away! I must leave now for good with our grandfathers." Here, reference to human beings as "grandfathers" is an allusion to the extraordinary hyperanimate power of *itseke*, in this context the power of mysterious enticing spells that are, in the end, deadly.

After a VERY long time
   they arrived at their settlement.
   And he was with them,
      Saganafa was with the Christians,
         he was.
It was over.
   They had arrived.
"Well, it's over. Now you can be my daughter's husband."
   He became so,
      Saganafa became so.
"Go ahead," he urged him to become his daughter's husband
just as he had promised him earlier on.
   The Christian promised him.
"Go ahead," so they were married.
Then it was over.

Although Saganafa has married the Christian's daughter, this does not necessarily mean a European woman; most likely she, like the *kagayfa* themselves, is not racially European but native or *mestiço*. What is significant is that they are culturally very different, which is why I translate *kagayfa* "Christians."

4

She became pregnant,
    his wife became pregnant.
When she was ready a boy was born.
Again she was pregnant with a boy.
Again she was pregnant with a boy.
Again she was pregnant with a boy.
    There were four children of Saganafa.

Mention of the woman's pregnancy not only conveys information (that children are about to be born to the pair) but is one of those time experiences that is used by a storyteller as a segment division marker. All that Muluku has told me so far concerns Saganafa's relations with his father and grandparents; what follows concerns Saganafa, his sons, and the Christians.

Kagayfuku (that's his name),
    and Kagasafegï,
    and Paymïgasa,
        and then Paypegï.
    Four of them.
Teh! That last one [pointing to his little finger] was the beautiful one!
    Beautiful.
        Paypegï, no one else.
            He became the most beautiful of all his sons.
                That's all.

Paypegï the last-born son is highlighted in this section and given the special status association with his birth order position; he is the most beautiful of all the sons and thus the one destined to become their leader. (Kudyu described to me how Paypegï as a young man never walked but rather was carried from place to place in a hammock.) By contrast, the first-born Kagayfuku is devalued. As an adult, he shows himself to be the worst of the Christian raiders. The relative birth order of these two sons and their respective moral and physical attributes are indications (metaphors, perhaps) of how others will perceive and act toward them and how they in turn will respond.

"You should do it now," he went to kill some deer.
    Saganafa went to do that,
        he always went to do that.

Those who talked with one another were Saganafa and Paymigu,
   and I don't remember the name of the other one now. . . .
There were three of them,
   people like us who were also Kalapalo,
      who always worked together when they went to their tasks.
That's all.
Kagayfuku was this high at that time.
   Another one was still this way, smaller.
      Another one was still this way, even smaller,
         like that.
Then, he went to kill fish at an oxbow lake,
   Saganafa went there.
      He went fishing.
Doing that same thing, he now acted like a Christian.
   That was all that happened then.

Over a long period of time those serving the Christians come to act like them. We might think of this as the first strategy proposed for Kalapalo-Christian relations: to adopt the ways of enemies. This strategy of assimilation is shown to be fruitless and dangerous, as the vicious power over human life that is characteristic of the Christians is developed throughout this section.

5

He went to work,
   Saganafa went.
One of our people was feeling lazy.
"Do your work," the Christian said.
"All right," he answered,
   "but I'm going to wait for a while."
Next, "You should go."
"I'm going to wait for a while," he answered.

The negative moral implications of the English word do not apply to the Kalapalo verb -ege-, which has more of the sense of a mood, a temporary feeling rather than a habitual disposition. So, when the Christian curses his slave, "So you will remain then" ("lafa eytsani"), he means, "As you lived lazily, so you will die a lazy person." This indicates to a Kalapalo listener the imminent death of the man to whom it is addressed. For not wanting to work on a certain day, he suffers a terrible execution at the hands of the extraordinary figure of the cannibal "Christians' grandfather." Such ferocity is a distinctive attribute of both fierce people and powerful beings and provides another context for associating them with Christians.

Then it was over.
   "Go now!" the Christian told him.
    "You're really feeling lazy this time, aren't you?"
   "Yes," he answered, "I'm feeling very lazy."
    "Then you will remain as you are now," the Christian said.
   "Come along with me.
    Come along to be eaten by the Christians' grandfather."
Next he tied him up,
   the Christian tied him up.
He was one of us.
   Saganafa had gone to hunt deer,
    he was fishing.
Then they went away.
   "You'll remain just as you are since you don't seem to want to
   live any longer," as he took him away.
He took him far away,
   far away from there,
    he took him,
      the Christian did.
They came to the edge of some water,
   the edge of a lake.
Out in the middle of the lake was a house.
   The house of the Christians' ancestor.
"*Kaah!*" he called out to him.
   "*Kaah! Kaah!* Come get your food over here!"
Then he came,
   the Christians' ancestor came.
    He arrived.
"Here," the other man said,
   "here's your food."
"Very well," he answered,
   "very well."
Then the Christian took hold of the Kalapalo man.
   "Look," the Christian said,
    "look.
   Because of your laziness this Christian here will kill you.
   This is what this Christian will do because of your laziness.
    You're going to be killed.
      He's an evil Christian."
   "Very well."
Then he brought him to the other man,
    and that person took hold of him.
   On the back of one knee the Christians' ancestor *tsïk* cut him.
   His blood flowed out.

On the other side *tsïk* his blood flowed out.
On the inside of one elbow, here on the inside of the other *tsïk*.
   One wrist *tsïk*. The other *tsïk*.
      Here, on his neck *tsïk*.
And when he died the Christians' ancestor took his body
away.
He carried him away with his daughter.
   With his daughter.
He was the Christians' grandfather.
   He was a very old man.
   Believe me, long ago Saganafa spoke about him.
   Believe me, long ago Saganafa used to tell us about him.
As he carried him away,
   his axe coagulated,
   his knife coagulated. [That is, the blood of the dead
   Indian turned into the metal tools of the Christians.]
"I think we should go now," the Christian said to another
person who was with him.
   Then he arrived home.
Saganafa was fishing and hunting deer.
   He had gone to hunt wild animals.

According to Muluku, the statement concerning coagulation of an axe and knife was Saganafa's original explanation of the origin of the miraculous metal tools. He himself was skeptical, and he later asked me for a detailed description of how metal is made. Concrete manifestations of European power are often linked with the physical substance of Indians: their body fat (as in the Andean countries) or blood (as in the present story). As with other objects whose creation is mysterious (such as paper and radios), the association of metal tools with Christians lends credence even today to their ability to use and control the hyperanimate, hyperillusory power of *itseke*, the power of creative transformation (*itseketu*).

The dreadful manner in which Saganafa described the creation of metal tools is a forceful allusion to the most significant attributes of Christians, their *angiko* and their *itseketu*. The gradual unfolding throughout this and later sections of ever more terrible images of the psychological attributes of Christians is accompanied by a description of the feelings of local people and the reasons for killings they might initiate. The decision to execute a person is not made frivolously, we learn, and the act itself is surrounded by great solemnity.

Then his friend told him what had happened.
   "I've been wondering where you've been," his friend asked.
   "I was traveling around far from here."

"We must escape,
     let's escape from here."
"Why should we do that?" Saganafa asked.
"You'll see our brother is no longer alive.
     He's dead," his friend told him.
          "The Christian killed him."
"Where was he?"
     "Far from here."
"All right then," Saganafa answered.
     "But consider our children. If I were to do this you would see
     that I'd really miss our dear children," he said.
          "Only one of our children,
               our son.
     I'd really miss him if I were to do this."
"That's too bad," the other man answered.
     "Let's flee now, our children must be left behind here."
     "Very well," he answered.
"Let's run away, certainly we'll run away if that's what you want
to do! That's settled.
     But I must take one of our sons with me.
          Our son."
"All right."
"We'll have to wait a while longer.
     We'll come and go carefully from time to time for a while."
"All right."
So then they left for the oxbow lake,
     Saganafa and his companion left.
"Let's go to the oxbow lake," he said.
     "All right."
Then, another time,
     "Let's go to the oxbow lake."
     "All right."
          They went away.
"How many days will you sleep there?"
     "Two."
"All right," his wife replied.
Then they returned.
Once again, "We've got to go to the oxbow lake again."
     "All right, let's go again," he answered.
"Now let's go, let's run away!
     Because the Christians are sure to kill us if we wait here any
     longer.
Let's get away from here right now,
     let's get far from here right now!"

"All right!" the other answered.
They left.
    "We have to go to the oxbow lake," Saganafa told his wife.
    "All right," she answered.
    "I've got to take this son of yours with me."
        Paypegï.
    "Come along, come along with me, my son."
        "Where to?"
    "To the oxbow lake."
    "You must not go there with him.
        I'm sure your father is running away this time," his wife told
        her son.
    "Very well."
    "Father, let me go there with you," Kagayfuku said.
    "You continue to stay here,
        I'll take you another time,
            another time.
    Right now I want to take this boy here,
        your youngest brother."
    "All right."
    "No, none of you must go," his wife said,
        their mother said.
    "Because your father is running away this time.
        Your father is going far away from here."
So then they began to come back and while they were still far away,
        they slept.
    The next day they were still far away and they slept,
        and on the following day
            the Christians went to search for them,
                to search for Saganafa and his companion.
    They came on the backs of horses,
        the Christians came.
    Lots of them were searching for the two men.
Then the others watched as they continued to come closer.
    "It looks as if they're right here!
        They're right herc!
        It looks as if we're about to die this time!"
    "We'll wait for them to come here to us," Saganafa answered.
    "Look, we really should exterminate them now. I'm sure that's
    what they're about to do to us."
    "They'll have to defend themselves against the *angikogo*, so
    they won't do that. I'm sure of it."
They waited there for the others to come.
        But they didn't.

They were afraid of the *angikogo,*
  the Christians were afraid of them.
Following that the two men kept coming back.
After a very long time had passed they arrived.
  They arrived here, at Kwapïgï,
    Saganafa arrived.
  He had become VERY old by the time he arrived,
    when he arrived he was very old.
The truth is, now he went looking for their father.
  Kagayfuku left as soon as he and the others had grown up.
    Traveling all over to each of the settlements.
    Going about in this place.
  Kagayfuku kept killing all the people as he went.
  And the Christians were stealing as many people as they could.
  Everyone.
    Leaders,
    men,
    women,
    children,
    everyone.
  During one dry season of theirs they came, during the next dry
  season of theirs they came.
  The Christians continued over and over again to come here to
  us, wherever there were people.
    To this place.
  Kagayfuku was the worst.
When he had become an adult person,
  Kagayfuku was the leader of them all.
  Kagayfuku, Kagasafegï, Paymugasï, and Paypegï, look.
    He was their beautiful one,
      teh, their beautiful one.
Then he too became a leader. Yes.
  When Paypegï became so,
    he became a leader,
    they all left for a place far from here called Angafuku. [This is
    a stretch of the Rio Tamitatalo on which the old Dyagamï
    village was located.]
  "All right, now is the time.
    Let's go get Kagasa."
    That's the word Kagayfuku used to speak about us, Kagasa.
      His name for us was Kagasa.
  "All always, we should go get Kagasa."
    That was how Kagayfuku spoke about us.

Concerning someone who we know did something else earlier on.
   This other thing that he did was to shoot at them, he shot at
   Kagayfuku and his companions.
   He did that at Angambutï.
      That was the name of his settlement.
   They killed this Angambutï person, he was killed.
   When he came to fish, the Angambutï person came,
      the Christians killed him while he was doing that.
         They cut him with a knife,
            Kagayfuku did, all of them.
   Teh, he was one of their beautiful people.
After he died,
   his father left, weeping for him.
   "Your younger brother is no longer alive, children.
      No.
   The Christians killed him."
      "Very well," the others answered.
Right after the boy died, his father arranged for someone else to
avenge his son.
   The Angambutï person [his name was Asuti] went to a
   Kwapïgï man,
      to Kwigalu.
         That's his name, Kwigalu.
   He was an enemy of the Christians.
   He was a person who clubbed Christians.
      He was one of their killers.
         He was a person who clubbed them.
            That man.
            Teh, that boy had been pale and beautiful [that is, he had
            just exited from a particularly long puberty seclusion].
So then the father gave this man a shell belt,
   a shell collar,
   a toucan feather ornament,
   eagle tail feathers,
      as payment.
   "Very well," he agreed,
      "because you cherish your son."
   "Look," the other told him,
      "I've come to you in order that you do just as you have been
      doing, because they wanted to murder our son."
   "Unfortunately so," Kwigalu answered.
      "Very well."
   "Very well."

So he remained there. That was all.
Over and over again the others kept coming.
"All right, let's go."
They arrived.
Then for the very last time, it was just before the end of our rainy
season, they came,
that's when the Christians came,
Kagayfuku and his companions came.
"All right everyone," he told them.
They arrived.
They went to a place far from here,
they came close to Angafuku.
Right after that they went to Kwapïgï,
and to Kalapalo,
to the real Kalapalo,
that's its name.
(Kwapïgï and Kalapalo were two settlements, Kwapïgï was here,
and Kalapalo here.
There was always just one watering place, only one.)
The others arrived.
They slept there, they slept, they slept, they slept,
the Christians slept five days.
Then they went looking for their father,
looking for Saganafa.
He had fled to a distant place,
he was far away.
Kagayfuku and the others,
the Christians went looking for their father.
He wasn't there,
because he had fled from them.
That was all that happened then.

                                        6

Kwigalu waited for them.
"You must kill their older brother, their Kagayfuku."
"All right," he answered,
"if I must kill only one of them,
let it be Paypegï.
Their beautiful one," he decided.
"Very well."
So then he came to bathe,
Paypegï came.
That was all.

Right there while he did that the hidden one waited.
  He shot him right here in the chest with an arrow,
    Kwigalu did.
      He shot Paypegï.
"*Akahm!*" after which he fell down.
  He didn't move.
"Go ahead," others said.
  Others went to let the Christians know about it.
Some children went,
  those who were blood of the Kalapalo.
"Your younger brother is no longer alive."
So then he came, Kagayfuku came.
  He was furious, furious.
Then he fired his gun, over and over,
  until the other man ran away from where he was.
    The one who had killed Paypegï ran away.
But he wasn't shot.
  He ran and ran.
    He wasn't caught.
Enraged,
  so enraged was the Christian there at Kalapalo.
"Yes, this is the last time we're going to do this,
  the last time.
'Now that it's our dry season, now is the time for us to
take away Kagasa,'
  you won't say that anymore."
Then he beat his followers,
  Kagayfuku beat them.
    They carried Paypegï away,
      they carried him away.
And so they left,
  the Christians left after that.
They slept for a while,
  and the next day they slept,
    and the next day they slept.
      Three.
He had died,
  Paypegï had died.
    They were so sad!
  And so they buried his things after he died.
It was all over.
  No longer did the Christians come.
    No longer.

Because he died they gave it up.
   They gave it up because of him.
This was to be the last time.
   No longer did the Christians come, did Kagayfuku come.
      No longer.
Those people were his children,
   Saganafa's children.
That's all.

Segmentation, Meaning, and Kalapalo History

In his story, Muluku constructs a lineal sequence of events by means of conventional narrative formulas that break up the flow of time into distinct and structurally significant elements. All these elements seem especially concerned with people's psychological qualities and with how they affect concretely motivated action. The links between one element or segment of the narrative and another is the motivational system; the backbone of this story seems to be constructed, in other words, of motives that are developed through quoted speech. These serve as causal explanations of events. If this story is in any way characteristic, the reasons underlying events, reasons that are a matter of people's attitudes toward one another, are what the Kalapalo are especially concerned with. Such reasons, we might say, are a crucial ingredient of their "sense of history."

In Muluku's story, people's attitudes toward one another are implicated by the physical distinctiveness of the characters (old or young) and by the underlying tendency to reinforce the contrasts among them, to assert the differences between Kalapalo and Kagayfa. By their violent transformative power, Christians are associated with powerful beings. Saganafa is an image of the good relations between Kalapalo Christians, both from the perspective of the Kalapalo themselves (for whom he is a Kalapalo with knowledge of the ways of Christians) and of the Christians (for whom he is a nice young man who works hard and can be trusted to marry one of their women).

Although a character's feelings are usually portrayed as inherent and immutable, relationships between people are the contexts in which strong motivations arise. A character's action is thus the result of relationships with others, not a spontaneous outburst devoid of an underlying cause. Feelings are therefore portrayed as causing motivation and motivation as causing actions and events, which as a consequence of their own logical relations (subsequent-prior) are thereby linked together into a narrative sequence.

In this story, Muluku's "sense of history" is constructed much more from ideas about actors, their moods, motivations, and goals, than upon abstractly conceived events. His ideas about actors, moreover, are expressed in terms of their relationships to one another, the feelings they provoke within each other, and the motives arising from these feelings. This focus gives Kalapalo historical narrative a distinctively different character from a more familiar historical sensibility, in which personal motive is subservient to generalized processes, forces, ideas, or interests that are held to exist in the abstract, independently of individuals.

In anthropology, the distinction between myth and history emerged from an assessment of how accurately a narrative form reflected or described reality (see Hill 1988). Myth, considered an essentially metaphorical form of narrative, was seen less as a representation of reality than as a moral commentary upon it. History, on the other hand, was conceived as a form that focused upon the succession of events, resulting in a more or less accurate representation of those events. The less literally interpretable the content, the less historical narrative was taken to be and the more distorted and inaccurate the representation of events that are the narrative content. The distinction between myth and history thus seems to parallel attempts to distinguish the communicative and formulative functions of language, trying to sort out imputedly rational elements from those that seemed not to obey the laws of logic and that were considered peculiar and fantastic.

From a Kalapalo perspective, no easy contrast can be drawn between "history" and "myth" because all narratives are constructed by means of discourse elements and verbal images that are symbolic and that imply others within a general worldview. The story of Saganafa is clearly concerned with describing the succession of certain events held to have occurred in particular times and places, but the selective nature of the description of these events (how they were remembered), the treatment of places and times when they occurred, and the properties of persons who participated in them suggest that they are themselves symbolic. They are symbols that stand for the abstractly conceived contrast between Europeans and Kalapalo, as represented by how these peoples' respective ways of feeling result in motivated action.

The most "mythological" images (metal tools coagulated from human blood; a monstrous toad whose repulsive bloated body holds down the horizon) are far more significant as allusions to certain ideas about Europeans and about the known world than they are statements of literal belief. Rather than consider them mere fanciful esoterica, to treat these ideas as allusions makes them both plausible and comprehensible, even concretely meaningful in a way abstractions might not be. In these allusive descriptions, figurative images assist in comprehending what may be inherently difficult or complex notions.

CHAPTER
4
Kambe's Testimony

In 1927, searching for the remnants of the lost civilization of Mu, the English explorer Sir Percival Fawcett, his son Jack, and their friend Raleigh Rimell disappeared somewhere in the central Brazilian Upper Xingu Basin. Colonel Fawcett was no ordinary eccentric. An engineer and distinguished member of the Royal Geographic Society with connections to the Court of St. James, his trip was sponsored by none other than the famous writer H. Rider Haggard, author of *The Ring of the Queen of Sheba* and *King Solomon's Mines*. Fawcett's first attempt to obtain the permission of the Brazilian authorities was thwarted by Gen. Candido Rondon (soon to organize the first Brazilian Indian Service, the Serviço Protecção aos Indios), who advised them of the foolhardy nature of the Englishman's quest. Letters from the court written in Fawcett's favor eventually made them relent.

Consequently, when the Fawcett party did not reappear in good time, a relief expedition led by the American captain George Miller Dyott was sent, only to discover that they had been last seen by the Kalapalo, who claimed the Englishmen had insisted on traveling east, in the direction of fearful *angikogo*, or "fierce people." Perhaps, the Kalapalo told the American, the foreigners had died of thirst in the forest. Or, even more likely, they had been treacherously clubbed to death by the Suya. By the time he heard this story, Dyott was beginning to fear for his own life, thinking his party was about to be killed for the trade goods they carried with them. He began to believe that the Anafukwa [*sic*], whose leader was someone Dyott called "Aloique," had actually killed them. These people agreed to escort Dyott to the place where the killing had taken place. On the very eve of this trip, Dyott broke camp and fled. "I began to realize," he wrote, "the difficulty of depending on anything told me by this pack of savages. Of course I could not understand everything that was said, and no doubt I misinterpreted many of their stories; yet, on the whole, the main facts of the case were gradually taking definite shape in my mind's eye and the finger of guilt seemed to point to Aloique" (1930: 175–176).

Dyott's version of the end of the Fawcett party was accepted by later visitors to the Alto Xingu. Orlando Villas-Boas, assuming the murderers had buried their victims, made many attempts to learn the location of the grave. Finally, he was led to a certain place where, indeed, bones were discovered. The Kalapalo were liberally rewarded with trade beads and metal tools, but upon being sent for study to São Paulo, the remains were determined to be those of Indians, not Europeans. Someone who had died long ago away from his settlement (someone with only a few living relatives) had been dug up and reburied in the forest.

While living with the Kalapalo in 1982, I was told that the old heredi-tary leader Kambe had actually seen the three Englishmen as a child. Kambe's father had even been one of the men accompanying them to the end of the trail, from which they disappeared into the forest. When I asked Kambe if he remembered the Englishmen, he said, yes, he had been a small boy at the time, and then proceeded with a long narrative of the encounter.

Testimonial Features of the Narrative

What is particularly noteworthy is the "testimonial" character of Kambe's narrative account. By this I mean two things. First is the fact that it is an elicited memory of a dramatic event in which the teller speaks as a witness rather than as an active participant in events. In other words, the story is not really about the teller's own life—as in an autobiography, also a collaborative account—but focuses upon someone or something else. In this story, it is clear that any autobiographical "I" that is actually present is subdued, with the Englishmen and the Kala-palo leaders—their conversations and the activities that are of special interest to Kambe—taking center stage. When he speaks about himself, Kambe tends to use the "exclusive we" pronoun forms rather than the singular "I." Although a firsthand account, it is not clear that this is an autobiographical one. Such ambiguity is characteristic of the testimo-nial. On the other hand, it is clear that, as with all Kalapalo narratives, the device of quoted speech (which results in stories within stories) blends accounts from various eyewitness sources, especially older people who were present at the time. Kambe includes the conversations held between his father and the other local people, as well as observa-tions his father and the other men made when they followed the En-glishmen's trail.

We should not expect the Kalapalo, any more than (most of) our own authors, to consistently follow a single, narrow autobiographical per-spective on events, for without what to each of us is important contextual information, the narrative would simply not be sufficient in detail. But for the Kalapalo, something more seems to be going on. That is, the use of other people's experiences, opinions, and judgments when telling a firsthand account are crucial pieces of evidence, lending credence to what the speaker is saying about his own memories of events. Kambe spreads responsibility for what he is saying with the rest of the community, sharing that responsibility with others whose own firsthand (quoted) opinions are included in the narrative.

Testimony is noted for a significant depth of time between the telling and the events that are remembered. Testimonials are often made by people who were much younger—even small children—when the event or person that is the subject of the elicited memory was experienced. This is certainly the case with Kambe's narrative. As is often the case with childhood memories, Kambe's descriptions of events are often extremely vivid, emphasizing visual details that an adult might find trivial but which recall the child's perspective: people appear exceptionally tall; objects, very large and heavy.

But the experiences described in testimonials are strikingly rare, even unique, and thus charged with powerful feelings. Testimonials convey this paradoxical character of personal distance (or lessened subjectivity) within a context of heightened emotional significance (Young 1988). This complex mix of deliberate objectifying and highly subjective dimensions is somewhat special to the testimonial. Young writes, "Implicit in the testimonial act seems to be the possibility for making more witnesses by informing others of events." We see this possibility developed in several ways in Kambe's narrative, which is not just "about" the distant past but about the present relationship between local people and the Indian Service, and, also, a statement about his relationship to me, the foreign listener.

Kambe's narrative is "witnessing" in character because it is testimonial in another sense, being replete with what Roman Jakobson called "shifters of listening." Jakobson used the term "testimonial" to refer to this category, in which "all mention of sources, all testimony, all reference" is to a listening of the historian (Barthes 1987: 128). Roland Barthes suggests that this explicit listening of the historian is a choice, "for it is possible not to refer to it; it relates the historian to the ethnologist who mentions his informant" (1987: 128). The shifter of listening in Kambe's narrative that so strongly contributes to this testimonial quality is the Kalapalo evidential *wãke*.[1]

In ordinary conversational or narrative speech, a speaker uses the evidential *wãke* to assert eyewitness certainty in the distant past ("Believe me, I remember"). A somewhat different use of *wãke* is heard when a hereditary leader (*anetu*) engages in formal oratory (memorized speeches called *anetu itagiñu*). The speaker is an inheritor of this special tradition, and what is being said concerns traditional knowledge and the formal behavior (usually during ceremonial gatherings) of hereditary leaders. Presence of *wāke* in *anetu itagiñu* thus marks a culturally valid conclusion based upon inherited (perhaps not exactly firsthand) knowledge. But this strong assertion of truth is also found in the way people sometimes use *wāke* in their historical narratives, when a speaker (whose contextual knowledge is firsthand) is making strong claims or, better, judgments about events that have not been personally experienced. (Such assertions can be made by combining the probability or suppositional evidential *ngapa*, which emphasizes that the event described has not been personally experienced, with *wāke*, as in example 3 below.) The tone is something like, "I bear witness," which is especially the case when speakers include it in each phrase in a sentence rather than simply a single phrase, as is more usual with other Kalapalo evidentials. In all three uses (whose differences must be understood through their discourse contexts), *wāke* marks a conclusion of utter certainty. The implication is that there is no other possible interpretation; the speaker stands as an individual voice against any possible different others.

Some examples from Kambe's narrative follow. In example 1, *wāke* indicates the speaker is relating a firsthand experience in the distant past.

(1) *ina wāke sinïgï, amañu etutongoka wāke tetiñui.*
    "I remember that time long ago when he came up this way, near where Mother's settlement was located long ago, I remember, so that we people might guide him."

In example 2, the evidential emphasizes common knowledge, judgments based on cultural expectations that are shared by the speaker and his people. As *anetu*, Kambe represents his people in telling me this story, but since the story is a firsthand account it also contributes to his special authority, lending further credence to his claims to valid *anetu* status.

(2) *uletofo tuilïlefa wāke idyufeke wāke tuilïlefa wāke.*
    "We know from experience that's how they kill people, that's how the fierce people kill people, believe me."

In example 3, Kambe's use of *wāke* indicates that an inference he is drawing from events he witnessed is valid because it is based upon cultural expectations.

(3) *ule atani ngapa wāke, eh he tago atani, idyufeke wāke apifolï ifïgïtsïgïï.*
    "Believe me, if he had agreed, it would have been that man's fault alone if the fierce people had clubbed him to death."

In example 4, the evidential *nafa* is used specifically to indicate a conclusion based upon cultural expectations (regarding the fact that another leader's people lived in a different place and consequently couldn't have known anything about the Englishmen). Not incidentally, the descendants of this leader are Kambe's current political rivals. Kambe's remark reinforces his particularly strong sense of being a "real" Kalapalo leader with the traditional knowledge to prove it. And he appeals to my own knowledge of Kalapalo life to drive this point home. In the example, *nafa* is joined to the "experience confirmation" evidential *aka* ("as you see"). Without in any way directly criticizing the others, Kambe is drawing my attention to what he knows I know very well: that this group often lives apart from his, particularly during the summer months when new manioc fields are prepared and old ones harvested. (In fact, most of this group eventually relocated to the settlement they call Tangugu.)

(4) *ago otomo wāke inde, Mugika akanafa anïngo etuko.*
    "I remember there were other people, Mugika and his relatives, who were living at their own settlement. As you know that's how they live."

Another example of Kambe's use of *nafa* comes late in the story when the Kalapalo try to persuade the Englishmen they will be killed if they travel in the wrong direction:

(5) *eunguluingo nafa igey, embukinenïmingo ifekeni. apadyu kita wāke.*
    "'While you're asleep there, being what they are, they will betray you.' I remember Father saying that."

Kambe's repeated use of *wāke* is perhaps the most important formal linguistic basis of his testimonial character. *Wāke* also constitutes his voice as an authoritative one, which functions at least three different ways. First, it lends credence to Kambe's status as an authoritative leader, a person who may be relied upon by me to tell an accurate account of incidents involving Kalapalo. Second, Kambe is made out to be an authoritative rememberer, someone whose account is firsthand, not based upon hearsay. Third, the authoritative voice lends credence to the idea that Kambe is a legitimate leader, particularly in contrast to the "leaders" chosen by the Indian Service who are supposed to serve the local Indians. Together with other evidentials used in this story, *wāke* helps substantially to constitute Kambe's autobiographical voice. The speaker's relationships to me, to his own people, and to Brazilian administrators are all underscored as of particular importance, even as Kambe tells his story of the events of fifty years ago.

It is useful to compare what I have said about Kambe's narrative voice with that of Muluku. Returning to his narrative of Saganafa, there are several places where that younger leader used the evidential *wāke*. Several appear in lines spoken by Saganafa, as for example in segment 3b:

(6) *talokila kugu wāke eiña wenïgï.*
    "I didn't come to you for nothing."

This off-hand remark is actually an important declaration, because Saganafa is referring to how badly he was treated by his father. He needs to give his grandfather a good reason for leaving with the Christians. We know the grandfather accepts this reason because he validates it with his response: "Eh he," "All right."

Three other instances of *wāke* are each found within a section describing the gruesome behavior of the Christians. These are all sentences in which Muluku is commenting upon the events of his story. The first occurs in section 5, where, after telling me about the Christians' grandfather, Muluku says,

(7) *tsufïgï elei Saganafa kita wāke. Saganafa wāke ifatatiga.*
    "Believe me, a long time ago Saganafa spoke about him.
    Believe me, it was Saganafa who began teaching us."

A second instance occurs later in this same section, which introduces Muluku's description of Kagaifuku's murderous travels among the people of the Alto Xingu:

(8) *tuwïko ufisale wāke, Kagaifuku tetalefa.*
    "The truth is, now Kagaifuku went looking for their father."

Muluku's final use of *wāke* appears at the end of section 5, which describes the killing of the Angambutï boy:

(9) *ulekoguwafale wāke.*
    "Concerning someone who we know did something else earlier on."

In examples 7, 8, and 9, *wāke* appears in the rare comments Muluku made about his own story, where it was apparently very important to him to bear witness to the character of the Christians. Perhaps he thought their behavior was so horrible as to be unbelievable. (At the time he told me the story, the Kalapalo knew very little about the lives of native people who lived beyond the Alto Xingu.) When he speaks to me as someone telling this story, his voice is clearly authoritative—much like Kambe's. In contrast, during the telling itself, Muluku speaks with the voice of someone by and large reporting hearsay, the voice of a person narrating stories of the mythological past. But while certain parts of the story may seem mythological, the activities of the Christians are decidedly to be believed, because of the way Muluku repeatedly frames his account of their doings in an authoritative fashion.

The Englishmen

In my translation of Kambe's narrative, sentences with *wãke* evidentials are highlighted by being given in Kalapalo, along with the English version. Notice that both the opening lines and the three final conclusive lines include repeated appearances of *wãke*, which thereby serves as a kind of framing device to present the entire narrative as an authoritative explanation. Within the story, Kambe describes seemingly trivial matters using *wãke*. These are, though, some of the very things we would expect a child to wonder about: the huge size of the visitors, the large packs they carried, the fact that they refused to eat the heads of fish, and so forth. His descriptions of how the Kalapalo lived fifty years earlier, the location of their settlements, the ignorance with which they dealt with outsiders because of their lack of Portuguese, and their interest in the new tools that were being offered them are all marked with *wãke*. More important, Kambe repeatedly describes the fear he felt about his father's going with the *kagayfa*, that he would certainly have been killed by *angikogo*, that his father might have been persuaded by the *kagayfa* despite his better judgment. Together, then, these *wãke*-marked descriptions bear witness to a kind of person, the *kagayfa*, who is clearly very different from the child's own people. The childhood memories are used by the adult *anetu* to make a significant statement about differences between *kagayfa* and *kuge*, and these differences have strong moral significance: the *kagayfa* are wasteful, they are stubborn, they act despite their ignorance, having little regard for the lives of people who have helped them. While indirect, these *wãke*-marked criticisms seem to legitimate the complaints Kambe made to me about the FUNAI officials who were present in the Alto Xingu during the preceding months.

The story begins in a typical fashion, with the narrator summarizing the entire narrative and placing the events in a particular setting, all the while presenting what he is about to tell me as authoritative. In the opening lines, the evidential *wãke* has a "witnessing" function:

ina wãke sinïgï, amañu etutongoka wãke tetiñui.
I remember that time long ago when they came up this way, near where Mother's settlement was located long ago, I remember, so that we people might guide him.

egea wāke taifeke.
This is what I remember he told him that time long ago.
   Told my father.
"Come with me way over that way, just so you can be our guides
to that place.
   You go with me way over that way so you can guide me."
      Standing next to him he said that to him, "With me as our
      guide."
   inde wāke igelisi itsa wāke.
   The Englishman was here, I remember.
tseta wāke titsetu atani,
I remember seeing them when they were there at our settlement,
   at the oxbow lake.
   That's where our houses were.

The narrative then proceeds to describe the arrival at this dry-season
settlement of a messenger from the main settlement, informing the
people at Tefupe that *kagayfa* are at Kanugidyafitï.

   As for that one, think if you will, the sun was like this.
   It was during the dry season, the way it is now.
"*Kaa, kaa,*" a messenger sent to us
   there at that place I spoke of.
   On his way to Tefupe.
      On his way to Tefupe.
"*Kaa,*" the messenger called to us as he walked on.
That was, think of it, the one who came to us to tell us something.
   Wagitsu.
      Yes, it was none other than Wagitsu.
   He was the one who came to us to tell us something.
"*Kaa,* Christians, Christians."
   But his correct name was Nauke.
He was the one who came to tell us something.
He hurried toward Tefupe to tell us something.
When he approached our people went out to meet him.
   My father and the others went to him.
   My relatives, there were a lot of relatives of mine.
Then, when we were all together,
   "Who is it?"
   "Christians are here," he answered.
      "Some Englishmen."
   "Where are they?" "At the other settlement."
   Near where Oso lived, he meant.
      By Oso.
      They were by the one who had stayed behind all alone.

There were houses there. [I asked, "What was the settlement
called?"]

　It was called Kanugidyafïtï. [This was the main settlement at
　the time.]

　　People also made Akutsa there.

And, what was it? Think carefully about it,

　Think carefully.

Think carefully of what happened next. The sun was over there.
"Let's go," myself, my father, my grandfather, another father of
mine. Leaders, my fathers were leaders of our group.

　　Their daughter is Angasagu, the leaders' daughter. [This
　　woman was one of the important female leaders at the time of
　　my visit.]

　　Agifiga's daughter.

　　　His daughter.

　　　She.

　　Think, if you will, Agifiga's only remaining child.

　　　Agifiga had even more children.

　　Another person was one of Father's brothers. [I said, "That one
　　you spoke of."]

　　　Yes.

Kambe then mentions the main leader of the community, a man named
Isagagi (probably the last male leader in the direct line of the original
founders of the community), and this leads him to begin comparing the
Kalapalo tradition of hereditary leadership with Brazilian practice; at
this point, the authoritative voice appears for a second time.

　Isagagi wãke apadyu fïsuagïi gehale.

　I remember seeing Isagagi, also Father's brother.

　There were these many of them, Father and the others.

　Many of them were there!

　Yes, my relatives.

　The leader of our group, the chief of our group.

Kalapalo leaders are never removed, no.

　But among the Christians, it's like this: "Our leaders aren't
　working out," the leaders of the Christians.

　　So they're removed.

　They never replace them with their younger brothers, no.

　The leaders are always removed, over and over.

　And more of them come.

Think, if you will. I am a Kalapalo.

Since I have a son now, he will come on top of me.

　And his descendant, his own son here will come on top of him.

　　When he dies.

After my son is removed.

He will be the person on top of him.

FUNAI doesn't . . . when someone else comes on top of another, he sleeps a day or so, and then for no reason he goes away. He's only begun and he's removed as well.

And another time, before we know it he's removed.

Kambe then resumes his narrative, but only for a moment. Telling me where the sun was when the group arrived at Kanugidyafïtï (this temporal reference is a major narrative segmenting device), he pointed out that another group (those who were connected to his rival's faction) lived in another place. The authoritative evidential is heard once more, and here Kambe makes it clear that those other people knew nothing about the visit of the foreigners because they were living so far away.

So listen.

"There are Christians here," he said.

So then we came there to see them.

To the settlement.

We came to see them at Kanugidyafitï.

Coming away from Tefupe.

We walked *titititititi*, oh, it was far!

We walked a long way.

Tititititititi.

It was late in the afternoon, just around this time of day, the sun was just over here when we arrived.

While the sun was over here.

I mean, to where the one who stayed by himself lived. There weren't any of our people there.

ago otomo wāke inde, Mugika, akanafa anïngo etuko.

I remember there were other people, Mugika and his relatives, who were living at their own settlement. As you know that's how they live.

igea wāke fisunduko wāke.

I remember there were these many of those brothers. [As he says this, he holds up several of his fingers.]

There were people living on this side and on the far side as well, across the river from us.

They never saw them.

Nor did they know they were there.

Nor did anyone come to tell them.

No one ever told them, they didn't.

It was too far for them to travel there.

It was so far, it would have been surprising had they gone there. That's how it was. Far from there.

ulemïñigeyalefale egey, Kafindzu itsa wāke.
Because that was how things always were there at that time, the others kept to Kafindzu Meander, believe me.

Continuing his narrative, Kambe describes how they arrived to see the foreigners walking around the house circle while looking at a piece of paper. This provides him with another example of how different the Kalapalo are now from that time, when not only could no one read, writing itself had no meaning.

Then, that's all.
    That's all.
  We had come into the plaza, we had come.
  "Where is he?" they asked the other man.
    Oso was the person about whom they spoke.
    Oso stood over here.
    He stood just inside his house.
  They were led to his house.
    To his house.
"Here they are," they answered.
  "Here, they've come out to the plaza."
    At his house, by the doorway.
  They were standing there, they were.
  They kept examining a piece of paper.
    They kept examining a piece of paper.
  While they kept doing that they walked around the house circle.
  None of the Kalapalo knew anything about what they were doing.
  How could they have known anything about them?
  While the Kalapalo were still ignorant, still ignorant.
But now we have learned about things like that. The Yawalapiti people have done that,
    those people have done that.
  Much later, we have such things.
  ifitseke kualehale wāke tsitsagele.
  I remember how truly different we were then from how we are now. [He is referring here to their ignorance of Portuguese.]
  ingilagele wāke.
  I remember it was still in the beginning. [That is, of their relations with non-Indians.]
  "Give me this, give me that."
    titsita wāke tahofeke,
    I remember that's what we were like around knives,
    igefungu wāke tsahogoi, ñegikini tilako.
    I remember there were only three, one for each man.

Sahasïsï itïtë wāke.
I remember his name was Sahasïsï.
  "What's your name,"
    my father said.
  Sahasïsï.
  This one here is "Sïhadyo."
  "Very well."
  "And this one here," he said, "Dyoi."
    Dyoi.
  "All right," we answered.
Next we went inside, *tiki.*
  We got up after we had slept.
  "That man is their chief," he said.
    Oso was the one who said that.
  "That's their chief," he said.
  "All right," they answered.
  That was all. [Since one source claims they traveled with Bakairi
Indians, I asked, "Were they with Bakairi people?"]
      There weren't. They were by themselves. By themselves.
Then, as we stayed there,
  "Why are you here?" someone asked.
    We people asked them that.
    Father and the others spoke.
  I was still a child then.
  This is how small I was.

Kambe points out how small a child he was; this seeming irrelevance
may be his way of reminding me that although he was present and the
conversation that he is about to describe is accurately reported, he was
still too young to have participated directly.

"I'm going over that way," he said. "I'm going over that way to my
settlement."
"That's the wrong way. You need to go THAT WAY to get to where
the Christians live." They didn't really know what was over there.
Father and the others knew nothing of Christian people.
  "That's the direction I'm going to follow."
  "You're wrong about that."
  "You're wrong," Father and the others said.
    Our people's relatives said, "You're wrong."
  "Go that other way, you should go the right way, on the
Atatsinu, that way.
    On the river."

"You're wrong. That's the way I'm going to travel.
Because my settlement is over that way."
    "You're wrong, in that direction are fierce people who will
    club you. Over there." [Like his wife, Tsangaku, he can't say
    angikogo because it is his daughter's husband's name, so he
    uses the Portuguese *indio* (*indyu*).]
"You're wrong.
    You're wrong.
No one will club me."
Look, he had one of these, *tsitsitsitsi*, a watch. He owned one of
those things.
"That won't happen because *tsitsitsi* this thing alone is going to
protect me," he said.
"The fierce people will surely club you."
"No, they won't."
*eunguluingonafa igey, embukinenimingo ifekeni. apadyu kita
wāke.*
"While you're asleep there, being what they are, they will betray
you." I remember Father saying that.
*embukinenïmingo indyufeke. eingupïgï atanilefa, apilïingo
ifekeni. uletofo tuilïlefa wāke indyufeke wāke tuilïlefa wāke.*
"Those fierce people will betray you. While you're sound asleep,
they will club you. Believe us, that's how they kill people, that's
how the fierce people kill people, believe us."

Notice the increasing use of evidentials in the conversation, as the Kalapalo double their efforts to dissuade the stubborn Englishman from
taking the direction he has chosen. And again, at the end of this segment of the conversation, the authoritative voice appears, this time in
the words of the leader from the distant past. The foreigner tries to persuade them with payment.

"Come with me." To my father.
    To Atafulu. "Come with me.
    Let's go there to get things for you. We'll get axes for you, things
    like these.
And I'll give you guns.
    You'll get your own hammocks.
        Everything.
You'll be given pets like ours, dogs."

But again, authority intervenes. Now it is Kambe's own voice which, in
commenting upon his father's refusal, lifts the encounter out of its context in a distant time and sets it firmly in the present, as if to serve as a

comment on how seriously others have misunderstood the Kalapalo. Rather than being murderous deceivers, they in fact tried repeatedly to help the Englishmen. The visitors, on the other hand, seem to have cared nothing for the lives of their hosts.

ule ataningapa wāke, eh he tago atani, indyufeke wāke apifolï ifïgïtsïgïi. la wāke apïngïmbolïlefa, apadyupe apïngïmbolïlefa, ifïgïtsïgïi.
Believe me, if he had perhaps agreed to what that other man had said, it would have been that man's fault alone if the fierce people had clubbed him to death. Believe me, if he had died over there, if Father had died over there, it would have been that other man's fault alone.
"I can't," he answered.
    "I don't want the fierce people to club me to death.
        I won't let them club me to death."
    He told him.
ila! eteke efutanipa egetomi.
"Don't you realize you have to go by canoe in that other direction?" [Here, the evidential *nipa* indicates an inference about another person's thoughts. The quotation suggests that the Englishmen are perhaps a bit crazy not to listen to them.]
    On the Tatsinu.
    "No, I'm going in that direction."
    They really argued.
    itagiñu ekugu wāke!
    I remember seeing how much they argued!

But on the following day, they decide to return home. The foreigners decide to follow but first spend three more days in the main settlement. Upon returning home, the men tell the women that the foreigners will be coming to their place, and the women agree that that is a good thing to happen.

    Someone told him:
    "Go in that direction!"
    "No, I won't."
    "You have to go that way by canoe!"
    Nothing doing. "I'm going that way to my settlement, despite what you say."
    Although they were going to travel, they didn't have any food to take with them, nothing.
The next day, "Let's go," they kept urging us there.
    While they walked away toward our settlement.

Our people left.
We went back from where we had come to see the others.
   Where we had come to. To see the others.
Very late in the day we arrived.
   "Anything?" they asked.
   Mother and the others spoke.
   "There are some Christians there," we answered.
   "They're coming right here,
      To this place.
      They're coming here."
   "That's alright with us."
      They slept three more days.
         They slept some more back there at that other place.
         That was all.

Next, Kambe describes these foreigners a bit more (using *wãke*), comparing their enormous size to one of the FUNAI officials, a man named Chico.

   mbuh! itsapohondu wãke. mbuh ha haa!
   Mbuh! I remember seeing how tall they were. *Mbuh ha haa!*
      The father was somewhat tall, but he was the smallest of the
      three.
      He wasn't as tall as the others.
      So much more than he *mbo hoh hooh*
         was his son.
      elefa tohongogehale wãke,
      And I remember seeing that the other one with them,
         buh! kapehelatsahambe wãke,
         buh! I saw that he was even taller than the other two.
            Shiku agagehale wãke, Dyo hale, Shiku kapohondua,
            No less than Chico, I remember, that's what Joe looked like,
            even as tall as Chico.
            Dyo wãke, Dyo.
            Dyo, I remember that's what Joe was like.
      engïlefa, engïlefa wãke ike, igele.
      This is what happened next, I remember this is what happened
      next, think of it.
   After they left,
      three days passed.
         three days passed.
         After three days passed, that was all.
         This is what happened, I still remember this is what
         happened, think of it.

When that was over, they came.
    They came.
  Yanuwa's father was the person who guided them.
  He was different, a member of the Dyagamï community.
  Kafusala.
  Think, Angafu's husband's name.
  What I'm saying is that he wasn't Kanugidyafïtï.
  He was Dyagamï.
  Angafu's husband.
His wife was, though, his wife, Kafundzu.
  efitsu feley wāke.
  I remember that's who his wife was.
  His daughter, that's what they came to call Yanuwa's daughter.
    That became his daughter's name.
  That's the name they came to use for talking about Yanuwa's
  daughter.
  He had another wife, a co-wife,
    who was Kutsami.
    Kutsami was the co-wife.
  Kafusala's other wife.
    Yes.
He was the man who guided those people there.

Here, Kambe is using a common device for linking the contemporary
knowledge of a listener—in this case people I knew well—to the details
of a story, thereby enhancing the listener's appreciation of those details,
however trivial they might seem to be. Moreover, letting me know that
there were still living descendants of eyewitnesses to the events he was
describing was also a good way of telling me where I might corroborate
his story.

  "*Kaah,*" he called out. "*Kaah.*"
    As for the time of day, the sun was over here.
    They were beside the riverbank.
    They were tired from all the walking.
    The boots they wore were eating into their feet.
    "Don't worry, you won't walk any longer. It's only a short way
    from here."
  So then, I guess they went on, after they had rested.
    They rested,
    until the sun had almost set.
    The boots they wore were eating into their feet, that's why they
    rested right there where they had been guided.
    And because they were so tired.

They were tired from carrying those tall packs of theirs.
Each man carried one. Their packs were worn on their backs.
Their packs were big, like this.
Inside them were knives like this kind.
    All kinds of fish hooks,
        that's all.
"*Kaah*," he called out.
    "Let's do it." We came canoeing to them. ["On the river?" I
asked.]
    Pupupupu, we paddled until we reached them. The river.
    Pok, we came to them on the other side, from the other shore,
    pupupupu we paddled until we came near to the shore.
    To where those people were, sleeping outdoors.
    Across the river.
Since the sun was at its height, ouch! they were suffering from the
heat.
    How red their faces were! Being fair of skin, the heat of the sun
    had burned them.
Father and the others came back. They drank something, and
when they were ready,
    "Where will you stay?"
    "I want to be over here."
    Underneath the trees, they wanted to be under the trees.
        In the shade.
"Let's do it," they worked to set up camp. "Set up camp next,"
they said. Father and the others spoke.
    People of my own group spoke.
    "Set up camp next," they said.
    As they cut branches.
    While their companions went to do that.
    They worked to set up camp, until they were finished.
Next came something like that thing you brought me, look, the
black plastic thing, something like what you brought me,
    they covered them, they covered them, three did.
    "Let's do it," so Father and the others hung up their hammocks
    for them.
That was done.
Next they brought food to them.
    Fish were brought to them.
    They ate some manioc bread there.
So they stayed there.
    "You should toast some manioc flour for me next,
        I want you to toast some manioc flour.

I want you to do that so I can carry it with me when I travel to
that far place."
"Very well."
So Mother and her companions were making it,
   day after day,
    they toasted manioc flour.
They put it into sacks, they put it into sacks, into sacks, three of
them.
   These were their containers, each one of them had one.
   One for each man.
They put it inside each of these.
Toasted manioc flour was inside.
Their food was inside, toasted manioc flour was inside.
aikugumbekudya! telïko wāke.
There was so much of it inside those sacks.
When they left, I remember.
And their hammocks, and also their guns, muzzle-loaders.

After staying in this dry-season settlement for several more days, the
foreigners decide to leave. Presents are distributed, including fish hooks,
an umbrella, blankets (which the Kalapalo had never seen), and, most
valuable of all, knives. Once again, the leader of the foreigners tries to
persuade the Kalapalo men to travel with him. They refuse, with the
wāke sentences ending this argument in an extremely conclusive way.

  They slept, and they were drinking hot manioc soup there.
    They were eating manioc bread.
  They were eating fish, and they were throwing fish hooks.
    Those people, the Christians would do that.
  Two of them would do that.
  One of them remained by himself.
  While he sang, he played a musical instrument.
  His musical instrument worked like this, like this. [He mimes
playing a harmonica and hums "God Save the Queen"!]
    He went.
  His musical instrument was black.
    That was just what it was like.
    What's it called? ["Harmonica," I told him.]
      That's what it was.
        He sang and sang.
  He put his arm around me this way.
  While he was playing we watched the Christians.
    While he was playing.
    Father and the others.

Then, "I'll have to be going," he said.
> They slept this many, look, they slept five more days.
>> Five.

"Captain, I must be going now," he said.
> "Here are some fish hooks, take them."
> He gave some fish hooks to Father and the others.
>> That's all.
> He gave them some fish hooks.
>> That's all.
> They were still very difficult to get.
> When he had given them to us, we were the only ones who had them.
>> To us, little ones,
>>> to the children.
>> This kind, look.
> The black thing we use for moving through the rain, to Father.
> To his younger brother also, to Lafati, Dyafu.
> They were his sons, my other father's sons.
> Kapi's sons.
> *Moh hoh*, that father of mine was huge.
> To him as well, the same thing.

Then, *boki* he gave a blanket to Agifiga, something different.
> A blanket. He didn't know what it was. He didn't.
> "Here, take it."
> This time it was a blanket!
> We had no idea what it was, none.

To Grandfather, to my grandfather, to Uwafu.
> To Grandfather, he was my grandfather.
> He was their uncle, Father and the others.
> "Uncle" was how they talked to him.
> One of these, a knife.
>> One of these.

That was all, look, that was all.
"Tomorrow I must be going," he said.
> "I will go in that direction over there."
> "Come with me," to my father.
> "I can't, no.
> I don't want to be clubbed by the fierce people.
>> I don't want to be clubbed by the fierce people."
> "As long as I have my gun no one will kill you.
>> As long as I have my gun."
> He would go alone ahead of the others.

"Let it be," my father answered.

"Don't mistake what I'm saying. I'm afraid of the fierce people,"
he told him.

ule atani tsingapafa wāke idyufeke tuefolï wāke.

Believe me, if he had perhaps done differently, a fierce person
might have killed him.

ifïgi tsïgïi dyalefa wāke.

That same man only had one gun.

"So take us there," he said.

"I want your followers to guide us.

I want your followers to guide us."

"All right," he answered.

"Let's do it." He who went by that old man's name, Kafukwigi.

[Here again he refers to a living contemporary of his.]

He was that man's own grandfather, his grandfather.

He. And also his son Dyagefiga, and also his older brother Agafu.

Also his older brother.

And Kagafi, and Father and his companions and their other
brother Kiñue. This boy of mine here came to have his name.

He was another brother of Father and his companions.

Their cousin.

He himself.

That was all, look, that's all.

"*Hoh, hoh!*" take this with you.

He gave them the manioc flour.

To each one of them.

So they could carry it.

And they walked to where the manioc field was located.

The other men.

With the other men.

They were still close to some water.

Still near a creek.

They slept.

The time was still about when people light their fires.

"I'll stay here," he said.

By the water, by the water.

Then, *kwa kwa kwa*

monkeys were calling,

monkeys.

"Shoot at them," he said. He wanted them killed.

He did, Kafukwigi did.

"Kill them for my food."

They came closer, *kwa, kwa*, they came closer.
That man did it.
"Shashashu" did.
  "Shashashu."
He shot them with his muzzle-loader.
  Bok, bubububu,
    The bullet that he shot broke this part of its body.
    When that happened to its flesh, it was done.
      One of them.
"Here it is, eat it."
  And so he brought it to him.
That was all.
"I must go now," he said.
"Then go," they answered.
"I'll sleep here, and then I'll leave tomorrow."
"All right."
When they had finished sleeping some more,
  they came back here, arriving late in the day.
    They had the monkey that had been shot.
  Then while we were eating it,
  "Where are they?" "They're still around here."
  They were saying the others were, they were.
  They slept there.
  At dusk,
  nduk! the sound of their shooting.
  Late in the day, when the sun was over here.
  Nduk. They were shooting oropendolas.
    Oropendolas.
The next day, very early at dawn they were doing that,
  the sun was still very low on the horizon.
  Nduk! Nduk! they were shooting.
  They were doing that as they walked away.
  They were leaving.
  Father and the others were in the manioc fields.
    "Let's go look for them!"
  "Let's go look for them!" he said.
  So they went again to see them again.
  But they had already gone far from where they had left them
  before.
  There were so many oropendola tails lying around!
    Oropendola tails.
    The ones that had been shot.
    That was their roosting place, where they had their nests.

Because Kambe is uncertain what happened to the Englishmen next, *wāke* is no longer used in his descriptions of events. Instead, his comments begin to be strongly marked by the evidential *koh* (which expresses his own ignorance) and the probability or suppositional evidential *ngapa*.

> Since they had walked around shooting at the birds' nests, there
> wasn't a clear trail, none.
> Just a few footprints here and there.
> *engikonangapafa pangia igeta.*
> I don't know how they managed to carry the manioc starch.
> Those loads of manioc starch, tall, like this.
> Inside each one of their packs.
>   They were carrying heavy loads.
> Those portions of manioc starch, tall, like this.
> Inside each one of their packs.
>   They were burdened with very heavy loads.

The Kalapalo men come back to the settlement with the valuable bird skins the *kagayfa* had left behind, which reminds Kambe of another wasteful habit.

>   The others came back.
>   Then they arrived home.
>   "We didn't see them," they said, "they've left."
>   They had the oropendola tails.
>   The oropendolas that had been shot where they were nesting.
>   At their camping place.
>   *Tuk*, those they had been shooting at.
>   When they ate the meat,
>   they skinned the birds.
> *ñalï wāke kanga engelui wāke sitïgïpe.*
> I remember they didn't eat ANY fish heads.
> They didn't eat any guts.
>   They stripped the flesh from the bones, *tsiuuk!*
>   When they ate fish.
>   They didn't eat the heads.
>   We ate them afterward.
> *ñalïma wāke sitïgïpe engelï wāke ifekeni.*
> I remember seeing how they NEVER ate the heads.

On the fourth day, the Kalapalo could still see smoke from the foreigners' fire, but after the fifth day, no more fire was seen. The Englishmen had apparently moved too far away from the settlement. So after a few days, the Kalapalo decide to go look for their trail. Worrying about what they might find, they ask themselves rhetorically why the foreigners had gone that way. The authoritative sentences again conclude the segment.

The next day they slept some more.
    Then they slept, they slept, the following day, on this [fourth] day, look,
    butsïki, their fire grew up.
    We could see it from where we were.
    From where we were at Tefupe.
Butsïki, the fire rose up,
        right over in that direction they had gone.
    "There's the Christians' fire," we said to one another.
    That was going on as the sun set.
The next day as the sun set, again their fire rose up.
The following day again, just a little smoke, spread out in the sky.
On this day, *mbouk*, their fire had gone out.
They had left.
They had gone away, so their fire had gone out.
Maybe they went to the Tanguro, I don't know how.
    I remember they all used to swim.
So then after they had slept, on this day,
    "We should go look for their trail,
        look for their trail,"
        Father and the others spoke.
    "Very well."
    "Tomorrow we'll go."
    My father, Isagagi, his younger brother Kiñue, Kafukwigi, his son, his other son Kagafi, this many went.
"Let's go!" After they had slept many days,
    after they slept,
    it looked as if the Englishmen's fire was no longer alive, as if it had been put out.
"What a shame! Why did he keep insisting they go away?"
engikomundengapafa Tangugufeke etelïko.
Maybe they couldn't get across the Tanguro.
    idyeningolefa wāke.
    I remember they all used to swim.
    "There are Christians over in that direction!"
    "The Christians were over that way!"
    awïndakofungu mbedyembale wāke.
    I remember hearing that, they weren't lying to them when they told them that.

They told them they should have come up this way instead.
kagayfa ande, la, Kalapalo kita wãke.
"There are Christians over that way," I remember hearing the
Kalapalo say.
"There are Christians over that way, Christians."
"But there are lots of fierce people over that way, where you're
going."
"The Christians are over in that direction."

The Kalapalo prepare to leave, and after entering the forest they come
to the last camping place of the foreigners, where they see traces of
someone having cut randomly through the vines with a machete.

So they went on,
   others made their food,
   I mean, Mother and her companions did that.
      They made manioc bread.
So they went, they went on.
When the sun was here, they came to where the others had slept.
And they went on,
   there was no sign the others had used a machete to cut the
   vines, none.
   Once in a while, *tsiuk.*
engikonangapafa etegatïfigïko fesiñïfudya.
I don't know how they were able to go through that uncleared
forest.
   Once in a while, *tsiuk.*
   While their footprints, while their shoeprints, *tik* had made
   signs on the forest floor.
   Our men walked along those.
   While they hunted monkeys.
   Each man had one.
   That was probably when they returned, think of it.
   They turned back.
   They were far away, still in the forest when they did that.
   They were eating monkey.
   "The monkeys that were there! *Mbah,* so many!" they said.
   After they killed them,
   they ate them there, afterward they ate them with manioc
   bread.
   There was no water.
   How terribly thirsty they were!
   Far away in the forest, that's what happened to them.

After they had slept many days,
   engikomundelefa atanini mbambale.
I don't know where they were while they were traveling back.
They came toward home,
      and they must have come back when it was very late in the day,
      to where the others had slept,
      to that place I spoke about earlier.
   To that place where the others had fired the gun.
They came there to drink water.
   A lot of it.
Very late in the day, when the sun was here,
   they came back,
      on the trail.
Very late in the day they arrived home,
   it was at the end of the day.
Adya! "We were nearly dead of thirst," they said.
   "They went way over in that direction!" they said.
      "They went away."
   ifatalefa wāke ifekeni.
I remember hearing them tell us about it.
   engikomundengapa wāke ila, angikogokainga.
I remember how puzzled I was that they went in that other
direction, near the fierce people.
   tuelïkolefa wāke angikogofeke.
And so, believe me, they were killed by the fierce people.

In his excitement, Kambe forgot that he wasn't supposed to use the
word *angikogo*. He had forgotten to substitute *indyu* as he once again
asserted these Englishmen were killed by brutal foreigners, not his own
people.

Kambe skillfully wove into the narrative account of the Englishmen's
travels through Kalapalo territory other comments that bore on the current situation in his own community, long divided by unresolvable political disputes over leadership. While ideally leaders are expected to
have inherited their positions directly from active leaders who were
their fathers, severe depopulation caused by influenza and measles epidemics forced the selection of collateral relatives as leaders. In Kambe's
case, it was his father's brother who had actually been leader; Ahpïū's
mother had been a Kalapalo leader, but not his father, who belonged to
the neighboring Arawakan-speaking group called Mehinaku. Only the
children and grandchildren of Ahpïū and Kambe were considered "true
leaders," though in 1982 they were just beginning to learn the duties of
this office.

Thus Kambe sometimes "recentered" (Bauman and Briggs 1991) the narrative when after recounting events in a rather straightforward manner he commented on what he had told me. This practice kept reminding me of my own status in the community, someone who occasionally lived and worked with members of his rival's family (whom he politely calls "your own people"), traveled to places of historical importance in the Alto Xingu Basin, and had an understanding of certain events and people through direct experience or knowledge gained from other important *akiñotoi* (local narrators).

While bringing my own experience to bear in understanding the importance of events in his account, these contextualization shifts are important because they lend authority to the political matters that Kambe repeatedly emphasized when he referred discretely to his own status as hereditary leader and stood in contrast to what he and his wives (one of whom was herself *anetu*) had long felt to be the weaker leadership status of the other hereditary elder and his family. His own legitimacy, based on years of service to his community, stood in even greater contrast with the nonhereditary and makeshift status of Brazilian leaders, who weren't even permitted to hold office for a decent length of time before they were removed.

Kambe moved from a description of Isagagi, his father's brother and a revered hereditary leader present during the encounter with the Englishmen, to a discourse on leadership inheritance, contrasting Kalapalo methods with those of the Indian agency FUNAI. At the time he told me this story, FUNAI was repeatedly replacing the local administrative agent with increasingly incompetent individuals, for no apparent reason and without any notice. The Indians at that time had no say in who was to be the local agent. They became increasingly concerned as they came to realize that their interests would never be adequately represented unless an agent were allowed to live for a long time in the region.

In Kambe's narrative, *wãke* sentences interlard the story, thus contextualizing in many ways what he said as authoritative. The leader, while telling me about his childhood, also speaks for his people. His speech is a testimonial, at once documenting events he thinks might be of special interest to me that he experienced firsthand, giving contemporary meaning to those events, while also saying a good deal about his own concerns as a hereditary leader of an embattled people.

PART
2

CHAPTER

5

Warriors

At the center of certain Kalapalo stories about the past is the remarkable figure of the warrior. The *tafaku oto*, or "bow master," was a man who had undergone special training from an early age to become a perfectly skilled and deadly marksman. According to Kalapalo, before firearms became prevalent, many boys were trained to be *tafaku oto*. If a parent had dreamed about the sparrow hawk it was felt that the next male child would, if properly prepared, become a *tafaku oto*. Sometimes young boys were selected for patient and dedicated training in order to fight long-standing enemies. In any case, specialists instructed parents who had dreamed appropriately in the art of creating a morally and physically beautiful person, one whose intelligence was oriented toward war and whose virile presence surpassed that of other men. The novice underwent an arduous and lengthy period of ascetic training that went far beyond the usual activities of male puberty seclusion. During his early years, his hands and arms were scraped every few days with a gourd implement set with dogfish teeth. The leader, Muluku, was in the habit of doing this to his twelve- and eight-year-old sons during some months when I lived in his house; the older boy (who eventually entered seclusion two years later) welcomed the treatment but his younger brother screamed and wept at the anticipated pain. They were fortunate, for had they been trained to be bow masters, harsh medicines such as chili water would have been rubbed into the scrapings, so as to eventually impart strength and a lethal aim. Muluku's medicines were the innocuous leaves of cotton plants, crushed to release their soothing and fragrant juices.

Later, about the age of thirteen, the boy would be secluded in his father's house, where he would live for many years inside a chamber walled off from the rest of the living space. Here, he was from time to time scraped over his entire body and made to "cleanse his insides" by drinking and throwing up gallons of herbal medicines, practices designed to strengthen and purify the body. Other practices were supposed to ensure that his eyes remained focused but aware of subtle peripheral movements, while he remained invisible to enemies.

The future bow master also followed an extremely limited diet in which many things that were normally relished as food were avoided: hot food, the brains of monkeys, fish jelly, turtles, grilled flesh, fats, and sweets. And like all secluded youths, he was expected to remain strictly celibate, lest all his body work be undone and (like those unfortunates who were always pointed out to me as object lessons) he had to exit seclusion a weakling of no consequence. His food was made by a young girl or a woman past menopause, and he was supposed to have no contact (even through speech) with a sexually active woman. When he emerged from seclusion, his personal beauty, deadly aim, powerful strength, and visual acuity were all embraced by the dreaming symbol: the sparrow hawk.

Many bow masters are associated with the Ipa Otomo, "Lake Community," ancestors of the Carib-speaking Kuikuro who lived in several settlements around the big lake called Tafununu.[1] Kalapalo regard these people as having been especially adept at training bow masters. In the following excerpt from a story about those people, the narrator, himself a Kuikuro man, describes some of the motives and techniques for preparing warriors. In this particular story, though, boys are being prepared to kill jaguars, pets that have escaped their owners to rampage among the people and their possessions. But again, the actions of the jaguars are reminiscent of cannibal raiders, men who devastate settlements and indiscriminately "devour" their enemies.

A long time ago some jaguars ate our ancestors.
    Large ones,
        who were guardians of the water. [Especially monstrous
        jaguars are thought to live underwater.]
            They were in the habit of eating our ancestors.
    They did that at various distant places,
        where they made people's ancestors serve as their food,
            and they also used to swallow their cooking pots.
                After which they would swallow their manioc
                starch.
Because of what they kept doing, people began to talk about preparing some children.
    Some children began to be prepared.
    Their leader spoke:
    "Children,
    Most likely those monsters they created will come here to act against us, and we can't prevent them from doing that. As we are now,"
        their leader said.

So even though they couldn't prevent that from happening,
everyone was thinking about their children.
   The people were all thinking about them.
      They were all thinking.
   "All of you keep watch."
"We humbly beg you.
   Our group selects your son," they said to someone.
"Ordinarily I would agree with all of you," this person
answered,
   "but unfortunately my dreaming never took such a treasured
   image as that.
      I never had such dreaming."
"No, unfortunately you didn't.
   But even though he's just an ordinary boy,
      let's separate our child so that if we're lucky he will avenge
      us when the time comes."
"Very well," the father agreed.
"What shall be done with him?"
"There will be two of them,
   so they will stand on either side and help each other."
"All right," the man agreed.
Then and there the father began to prepare magical herbs,
   he prepared magical herbs.
As the jaguars came they kept swallowing the possessions of the
Waura people's ancestors. [The very large cooking pots made by
these Arawak speakers; he is unable to use the word since it is
taboo to him.]
   Ceaselessly they came there.
They would go to a certain place,
   and there they would eat the people's ancestors.
      And they swallowed their possessions.
         That was what they did as they walked about.
The people of Lake Community intended to kill them.
At that very place those children were being prepared to punish
the jaguars some time later.
So as to punish the jaguars at a later time, people had been
thinking what to do.
It had been planned so that when the jaguars walked around,
doing as they had been, something would happen when they
arrived.
   That was what the people planned for.
Some who knew went around telling the others about their
children.

And they came around in that capacity,
   by the time those two boys had grown up.
"We should try them out in some way.
   Let's do it by taking them somewhere,
     let's take them somewhere."
      "All right," they answered.
They were taken to kill a tapir,
   since that creature is unaware of us when we go to kill it,
   because it doesn't hear us.
     That's how that creature is.
Because of how it acts, those two were taken to a tapir's place,
   so they could try out their arrows.
That was done at the very start of the day,
   while it was still dark.
Pepper was boiled *kulu kulu*.
Next it was taken off the fire.
And another was put on *puk*.
The father took that one off as well.
Then he passed their arrows through the steam,
   and the pepper smoked them,
     the pepper smoked them.
The partner had the same thing done—the partner of the first
boy—while they sat together, side by side.
   He and his partner sat side by side.
Their arrows were placed on a frame,
   and the father had pepper smoke fall over them that way.
   So that the pepper would penetrate them.
When that was done they picked up the pepper water
   and washed their hands in it.
     So their arrows would be painful.
Their father scraped them at the same time.
He did that using medicine made from the roots of arrow cane,
   he did that with the roots of arrow cane.
He scraped them thoroughly,
   and he also did that with pepper,
     He scraped them,
      so their arrows would be painful,
       their arrows.
Then, after all that was done they killed the tapir.
   After all that was done they killed the tapir.
   After that they came toward it.
When they had waited there for some little time, it approached
the place where they waited in order to drink.

They planned to kill it while it was doing that,
   they planned to kill it while it was doing that.
You see, they knew it traveled about aimlessly.
   That creature acts without thinking.
Tuk, so everyone sat perched in the trees.
   All the ordinary people had done that there in order to watch.
Their children kept coming closer, side by side.
They were going to shoot their arrows, that's how they were going to kill it.
They were going to shoot the tapir while it quenched its thirst.
   They were going to shoot the tapir while it quenched its thirst.
"Here it comes!" one of them said.
   "Keep your eye on it, look sharp!" he called to his partner.
   "Our arrows must enter at the same time,
      at the same time.
        And our bows will be stretched at the same time.
   Our bows will be stretched at the same time,
      so our arrows will go into it at once."
They began to test their arrows,
      to test their arrows.
These were the kind that had been kept hot with pepper steam,
   from the time the children were still small.
With pepper steam,
   which was the infusion.
The tapir kept coming toward them as they waited,
   it kept coming toward them.
All the people sat watching.
While they all watched the two stretched their bows.
While they all watched their father stood nearby,
   their father.
"Let's go!" one said to his partner,
   and as they kept walking the other people sat in a tree above the tapir's trail.
      Below them was the tapir's trail.
The two came,
   they were coming while the other people sat above them.
They stretched their bows.
They were right beside the trail of the tapir.
They came toward it, side by side.
"Get ready," one of them said.

Then the tapir came,
    it was coming while they waited beside its trail,
      their bows stretched.
  Having done that *suk*!
    their arrows went in right here,
      pu pu pu pum!
  It died right after they did that.
"They really did it!" Their father clapped his hands.
  "When the others come you will kill them, my children.
  When the others come you will kill them."
And so, when they came to the tapir, that's what happened.
  It died.
  "Did they do it?" someone asked.
  "How many of their arrows did it take?"
  "They killed it with only one shot.
    Now we can be sure our children will avenge us."
Our ancestors were always afraid because of what the jaguars were
doing to them.
  They were coming to them, swallowing their possessions.
  They came swallowing their possessions,
    because they were insatiable.
  They came eating us all.
    They ate all of one group's ancestors,
      and then they ate all of another group's ancestors.
        That was how they came.
Because they kept doing that the Lake Community people planned
something,
  because it was a place of many bow masters,
    that lake.
  I really don't know why that happened there.
  We began from that same place,
    our own beginning.
Listen. This is a story about it.
  They were jaguars,
    created by someone to eat us.

Training and Morality

The successful bow master was a person who during training had paid
particularly close attention to what the Kalapalo consider the organs
of feeling: the animate body parts capable of independent motion, including the genitals, eyes, pulse, and stomach. They were, as I said

in connection with dietary practices, in fact acting responsibly in developing their own bodies by learning (as do young people today) to consummate insistent physical demands (for food, sex, sleep, elimination) only within strictly defined limits. Thus, they emerged from seclusion not only physically beautiful but morally beautiful as well, because they were able to avoid potentially destructive feelings that would otherwise jeopardize their families. These feelings were not entirely eliminated, but their potential danger to the community was held in check, insofar as the warrior's interests were supposed to be channeled outward in the direction of enemies. Both the family and local community at large looked forward to receiving a new adult dedicated to their social well-being. They expected moral judgment to focus inwardly, on family and community; the sphere of ethical understanding did not extend to people of other communities. Such was the morality of this particular South American asceticism.

Today, no one is trained to be a bow master. But in a less intense way, young men and women still undergo the experiences of puberty seclusion in all the Alto Xingu settlements. Young people just out of puberty seclusion are still cherished and respected. They dance at the head of the line of more mature people of the same sex when several Alto Xingu communities come together to participate in the impressive yearly collective rituals, serving as a standard of human beauty and an active icon of the community's moral worth—a public demonstration of the success of the shared seclusion practices.

In the idea of the bow master was concentrated all the community's suspicion and hatred of outsiders, the objects of all his potentially destructive feelings. The aggressive manliness of the bow master was expected to be directed outwardly, toward *angikogo* (and, later, toward *kagayfa*, the non-Indians or "Christians"). The bow master was held responsible for protecting his local community by cultivating fierceness so as to overcome a real, threatening enemy. Thus he served as a kind of scout and as a military guard, accompanying his fellows upon request to dangerous places. He also led people to take revenge on enemies after weaker persons had been killed. Not surprisingly, while still a youth he was distinguished by those very enemies as the special target for their attacks.

The ideal image of the beautiful, intensely capable young man, which the Kalapalo ascribed to their techniques of raising boys, resulted in some other inclinations that were perhaps unintended but which were certainly understood and remarked upon. These other qualities of the warrior's character that fall outside the Kalapalo image of the morally good person developed out of puberty seclusion practices became the focus of the warrior biographies. What happened to these boys under the strange conditions of training and the men they later proved to be is the central theme of the warrior biographies.

The Warrior as a Kind of Person

Since the warriors in these stories all share certain characteristics, it is clear that a special kind of person is being described, with particular configurations of insight and understanding that emerge from distinctive habits of speech. These are not stereotypic images, though. Through representations of their distinctive habits of speech in conversations and declarations, we learn about the unusual decisions and choices made by warriors that made them so interesting to their contemporaries and so able to engage the sympathies of interested modern listeners. In their emergent development through narrative, these speech-centered experiences are precisely what make warriors memorable individuals, each a unique biographical voice and a unique biographical experience.

A Reader of Signs

Many older Kalapalo remembered bow masters, the youngest of whom apparently died in the late 1950s. The Kalapalo now say that the bow master was very different from his peers by virtue of his special beauty—his enormous size and strength. Typically, when they talked about the beauty of these men, they held their hands apart several feet and gestured upward, well above their own heads, suggesting a well-built, rather hefty man who was unusually tall. The lack of bow masters in their settlement was a source of some pain to these older people, for the mention of their dead heroes (who had died of illness blamed on witchcraft) reminded them of early times when their much larger settlements had been filled with the finest examples of men and women who had been carefully raised in the old ways of seclusion.

When someone tells a story about such a hero, in a way that always lends cohesion to his story a bow master is distinguished by the fact that he is an interpreter of signs for the others. The bow master's physical condition and his constant activities with signs of all kinds are closely related, since they arise from the conditions of his training. In the stories, dreams and ominous occurrences not only constitute the messages he receives about his own life but the beginning and end of his existence are marked by them. It was from his parents' dreaming signs that he was selected to become a warrior, through reading signs correctly that his authority is firmly developed (so that neither his friends nor those who were privileged to listen to his story generations later felt like challenging it), and from his own dreams that the way he was to die became known to him. In the story of Tamakafi, it is through the signs of the fallen atanga flutes that others learn of his death (only a strong and virile man is supposed to be able to play the heavy ceremonial atanga flutes while dancing continuously around the settlement).

The story of Tamakafi is in fact filled with signs whose messages are clearly understood but deliberately and self-destructively enacted upon by the warrior. In "Afuseti" (a story about the abduction of a woman), warriors are able to trace their sister's abductor by noticing and interpreting a series of clues she has deliberately created in the expectation that they will search for her. These heroes often interpret signs correctly while their companions misinterpret what they see or cannot interpret signs at all.

Sign-readership typically has a developmental quality, occurring periodically in stories and contributing in some way to a change of status or to a powerfully intensified or utterly different point of view. It is as if these pragmatic skills were developed in puberty along with the more expected moral and physical qualities. I propose that the elaborate preparation of a warrior from childhood resulted in a "reader of signs," an interpreter and teacher who could readily anticipate the course of his own action, a man who could project forward in his dreaming and in his day-to-day experiences so as to give meaning to his future experience. The many episodes in warrior biographies that involve sign readings and the creation of what might be called "personal signs" may suggest this more general aptitude.

Distancing His Relations with Others

The voices of warriors are ironic and embittered, their speech coming in tones of defiant assertion and disgust with the stupidity or incompetence of those around them. This somewhat arrogant manner of objectively evaluating social relations is an important element in the bow master character. It is closely connected to the fact that even before his training was finished, both the warrior and those around him considered him to be personally unique. As his training continued, and especially upon his exit from seclusion, the terrible responsibilities imposed upon him as war leader reinforced this sense of being different. Awe and fear and shame respond from all sides: Tamakafi's mother knows that he will die and suffers from that knowledge; warriors have older male relatives (fathers or uncles) who really have no regard for them at all, defiantly acting against the good judgment and strongly worded requests of the bow masters. (The fact that these men are never of the same status suggests we are not dealing with a "structural shift" in the warrior's htusehold affiliation, from loyalties toward father to those due a

Atanga flute players.

father-in-law, for example, but rather a more generalized sexual jealousy developing in the relationships between older and younger men.) Friends are lesser men astonished by their power, cowed by the apparent single-minded dedication of the bow master. The warrior Tamakafi is remembered as an arrogant and contemptuous person who (even as his friends were dying) sneered at the lack of care they had taken during their own training. And even more fatal was his deeply insulting disdain for the mutilated remains of his former father-in-law, whose sons, themselves bow masters, might have helped him during his battle against fierce people. Following the death of his father, Tapoge never weeps but brutally takes revenge in a way that is reminiscent of executions by the relatives of witchcraft victims. This arrogant detachment from social relations is an important element in the bow master character, one that I believe assisted him in killing and in making the kinds of decisions to separate from his own relatives that we see in the stories. This detachment does not mean he is incapable of emotional action: on the contrary, there are numerous references (made by quoting the warrior's speech) to his anger, grief, and guilt at the death of his friends. Also, he is clearly capable of taking responsibility for what happens. The point is that the warrior can simultaneously act as if such emotions were not being enacted: in "Wapagepundaka" and "Tamakafi" warriors lead their friends to their death, and in the case of Tamakafi, when his jealous uncle insists that they go to cut arrow cane in a dangerous place, the warrior acts against his own dreaming and his mother's urging that he remain at home, in effect committing suicide.

His Life a Lesson for Future Generations

At moments of the most intensely painful decisions to act, "trembling with grief" (as one storyteller put it), the hero charges his friends to "let my life be a story to tell," or cursing themselves, declare, "Let us be as we are" and "Let our lives continue in this way." These public, self-conscious declarations lead us into the most climactic or concluding dramas of the stories. (Such a peak may occur toward the beginning of a story, as in "Tamakafi.") These declarations seem to be a way warriors assert responsibility for fatal actions that involve other people. The heroes thus seem to achieve insight into the ambiguities and difficulties of their warrior status during these decisive moments. In the story about Tapoge, for example, the young bow master decides to ally himself with a group that is about to attack his father's own people. This desire to witness occurs toward the end of the awful slaughter of his father's relatives, when Tapoge spares five of them with the words, "Let them go away to tell the others what happened."

Similarly, the bow master Tamakafi has a developing sense of being irrevocably drawn toward a terrible death first anticipated by his dreamings. This is not simply fatalistic, however, but governed by his own repeatedly stated conviction before others that he has elected to die that way. Each of his statements occurs at a moment of decision when he chooses not to save himself and his companions and involves a variant of the curse, "Let us remain as we are."

When warriors declare their lives should be known to future generations, they are hoping that the full thrust of their decisions to act in morally significant ways will be carried out to the expected, anticipated conclusions, thus leaving behind a reminder and a warning. Since the warriors are telling stories about themselves through the actions they self-consciously perform and comment upon before others, thinking, it seems, of the importance of their lives for those who are to come after them, there is an autobiographical quality to them.

A Performing Presence

The Kalapalo title "bow master" stands as much for action in a "body-technical" mode, a constant active agency, and a kind of acutely alert yet calmly focused, murderous intelligence as it does for a "status" or a "role." One way of describing this is to say that bow masters perform continuously by being present in many of the senses of that word. Their sheer strength, size, and beauty create a presence, a feeling in lesser men that they face a model of what (and how) they should have been; bow masters are present in their constant signaling of their presence to others; they are present in their alertness, their palpable activity. But the bow masters are present in other ways as well. They offer themselves to their people as leaders in battle, protectors, advisors, men who avenge the murdered, devoured dead. And they are present in their indictment of the life they must lead, always aware that they might die, be mutilated and eaten, always on guard, never at peace, never able to fully enjoy the love of women, and forced to constantly persuade people around them who doubt their sincerity or good judgment. Although often an isolated actor vis-à-vis his own people, a bow master's decisions have the potential for dissolving this isolation and reconstituting new ties of affection and responsibility.

Ideological Shifts

More positively, then, it is from this subjective situation of detachment and continuous performance that the warriors expanded the locus of ethical judgment beyond their own group. They seem to be pragmatically more flexible in this particular way because of their "sign-readership," because they have learned to pay especially close attention to their own role in giving meaning to external events. This becomes of utmost importance when the warrior finds himself with unusual insights into the character of those events which others around him do not always find easy to share.

The day-to-day relations between people in the settlement were at least in part defined in terms of the opposition of the community as a whole to outsiders, who were understood to be dangerous, potential (if not actual) murderers. However, the warrior (although trained to be a leader in this aggressive orientation to the outside) came to see the possibility of peaceful contacts—especially marriage, but also ritual and trade—with strangers. He thus stood in contrast to his inflexible relatives, for whom strangers were by definition enemies outside the sphere of socially acceptable unions. In the Wapagepundaka story, there is a clear progression from an initial state of affairs in which the community of shared ethical judgment remains within the local settlement, to one in which the bow master Wapagepundaka has successfully expanded his community of personal ethics to include people he had earlier called "strangers." These people initially feared him, thinking he had come to kill them all. Similarly, in "Afuseti" (chapter 11), a woman's bow master brothers anticipate they will have to return their sister by force but ultimately resolve to accept her abductor's payment, leaving Afuseti behind in the stranger's settlement. Stories of more recent encounters with fierce people tell of successful marriages between Kalapalo women and potential adversaries (the Dyaguma) who nearly became integrated (as "brothers" and as the sources of riches) into Alto Xingu society.

Evidentiality in Warrior Speech

In warrior biographies, speech-centered events are increasingly and variously indicative of conflict, building up to incidents of resistance, reinterpretation, angry or disgusted disagreement, bitterness, and sarcasm, constructing a sense of the opposed, persistent, and irreconcilably different points of view that characterize a warrior and his more personal enemies. This conflict in the warrior's speech is conveyed by an extreme presence of various forms of evidentials.

The persistent, repeated, and occasionally flamboyant use of evidentiality—especially in sequences of dialogue where the testimonial is coupled with irony and sarcasm—makes the speech of warriors virtually unique in Kalapalo narratives. In other stories, as in day-to-day talk, it is only during the most stressful conflicts (for example, involving witchcraft accusations) that anything comparable is heard: the voices of tense, estranged men about to take violent, irrevocable action.

The variety and explicitness of evidentiality coupled with the unresolved or poorly clarified moral identity of participants in Kalapalo warrior narratives may be related to the challenges those men made to an order that no longer worked, a situation of blood feuding in which the categories "we people" and "fierce people" concealed both the real ties between people who fought each other and the murderous tendencies among persons claiming close social ties. Such an order was apparently in need of replacement through a renewal of the interpretive motive. This need to interpret anew naturally led to recontextualization through shifts in the conventional uses of person-category labels and through the expanded use of evidentiality, both of which were involved in marking resistance to the old and an opening up of new ways of understanding. Thus the warrior, although trained to kill, through his attempts at clarification of self actually opened the way to formation of an entirely new society, such as we see today in the Upper Xingu Basin, where the value of *ifutisu* (peaceful, restrained, modest behavior) governs relations between local groups. (Modern fears of witchcraft, emphasizing evil within the local community, seem to be closely connected with this emphasis on politeness, which makes suspicious anyone who refuses to conform in this way during activities involving public cooperation.) The "warrior" became more of a skillful hunter and fisherman and less of a military figure, while the "fierce people" came, most recently, to be defined as Indians whose values and way of life are either unknown or clearly different from those of *kuge*.

CHAPTER

6

Ahpĩũ's Story about Wapagepundaka

The first warrior story I ever heard was told during my visit to the Kalapalo in 1967. I was staying in a big house belonging to one of the largest households in Aifa, led by Ugaki, her husband, Maidyuta, and her brother Agakuni and his wife, Kafundzu. Ugaki and Agakuni were the sister and brother of Ahpĩũ, one of two important leaders of Aifa community at the time. He lived in a house directly across the central plaza from theirs. Nearly every day in the dry season, the old leader would visit his relatives in the late afternoon to drink hot manioc soup. After he refreshed himself, there would be lots of talk about my own activities during the day, as well as the community goings-on. Since I was actively working with Waiypepe, writing down his stories as one way of trying to learn Kalapalo, Ahpĩũ realized my great interest in storytelling. One day, seated in the doorway eating a piece of fish his sister-in-law had just given him, Ahpĩũ asked me to show him the tape recorder and listened to some of the songs people had recorded for me. He asked me then if he could record a story. When I agreed, his sister-in-law Kafundzu (who was still scraping some manioc roots she had gathered in her husband's field late in the day) told her young daughter Kafuga to sit with the grandfather. Kafuga was to be the *tiitsofo*. As Ahpĩũ began, others began to listen, including Kofi (still unmarried and also resident in the house). Somewhere in the middle of the story, Kafundzu asked Kafuga to help her with the manioc work, upon which Kofi continued with the listener-responder's role.

Ahpĩũ's story of Wapagepundaka is about a Kamaiura ancestor, he told me, referring to the Tupi-speaking people living far to the west of the Kalapalo, on the other side of the Rio Culuene. Brazilian ethnographer Rafael Menezes Bastos claims that the word *Kamaiura* is Arawakan, meaning "smoked dead people," based (according to local Arawak speakers) on this group's former habit of smoking executed prisoners (Bastos 1984–1985: 142). There are intriguing parallels in this story

with descriptions of settlement structure and the practices surrounding ritualized cannibalism among the sixteenth-century coastal peoples
known as the Tupinamba and as represented in the engravings of the
time (Fernandes 1949, 1970; Hemming 1978).

Typically, Ahpïū represents this special understanding of Wapagepundaka in a subtle rather than overtly descriptive manner, using the conventions of quoted speech and segmenting devices to create a developmental pattern. As in other Kalapalo stories, speech-centered events
constitute much of the action of this story, and the extensive quotations
(be they conversations, declarations of leaders, or, more rarely, private
musings) realize ideas of feeling, planning, reasoning, objectification,
and reification of the character's self and, by how other people's utterances are being understood and responded to, the relationships between
characters. The narrator's comments about these ideas are brief at best,
always taking second place to the quoted material.

Ahpïū's many references to time (as experienced by people through
sequences of events, in terms of duration and cumulative effects engendered through repetition) play an extremely crucial role in the narrative.
The changes in Wapagepundaka's decisions, choices, and responses to
others are made to seem inseparable from images of sleeping (as if certain ideas emerge during dreaming that takes place at this time), from
the motion of the sun across the sky as he travels from one place to
another (persisting stubbornly in the face of adversity), and from the fact
that he is made to repeatedly undertake certain activities (which lead to
goals being accomplished). It is important to emphasize the emergent
quality of this narrative structure. It is, in other words, not the result of
a semiotic analysis but results from how the narrator Ahpïū used conventional strategies for telling his story. Far more important than the
segmentation itself are the ways we are made to think about the people
in this story through the images of time.

    Listen:
      "Now, my children, my children.
        My children, my children.
       Perhaps we should try to go traveling soon,
         let's go traveling.   5
          Perhaps we should plan to go traveling soon.
      Comeheretomecomeheretomecomeheretomecomeheretomeee,"
      to his cousin.
        "Comeheretomecomeheretomecomeheretomecomeheretome—
        nowww," he said to him.

These lines are uttered in the style of a leader formally addressing another leader inside a house. This style involves rapidly and (as appears

here) continuously repeated words, with the urgent "must" (*fetsange*). The "cousin" (*ifaũ*) may have been the leader of a group that was allied by marriage and ritual obligations to Wapagepundaka's people, as in a moiety system.

> "All right," his cousin agreed.
> He himself came outside. 10
> "What is it? Why were you speaking that way?"
> "Why, I'm out here because I want us to travel with our older brothers," he answered.
> > "Why, I'm out here because I want us to travel with our older brothers."
> "All right," the cousin answered. "Why?" he asked.
> "Now, I'm going somewhere to perform the *takwaga*, 15
> > to perform the *takwaga*."

The *takwaga* are single-tone flutes, about six feet long. They are played in groups of five by men who dance in a circular manner around the inside of each house in the settlement.

> "All right, go if you wish."
> "Let's go together," he said. "Let's go together."
> "Well, no. I won't go, I won't go.
> > You can take our brothers, you. 20
> > > You take our brothers.
> Why, after the club people shoot you through and through with arrows, I'll be alive to avenge you all," he continued.
> > "After the club people kill you I'll be alive to avenge you all.
> > You take our older brothers.
> > > You."
> "We'll go together without you, our older brothers and I, we will." 25
> "Take your people," he said to him. "Take your people."
> And so Wapagepundaka and his people went away, it's said they went away after that.
> So then, "Let's all go, my brothers, let's all go, let's all go," he said to them.
> > "Let's go, let's go, we should go right now!" 30
> > They all went away.
> They all went away, he and his followers, they all went away.
> > Yes. They all went away.
> Then, so, at dusk when the sun was here, they came to the others.
> > "Yes, the *takwaga* performers are here. They really are." 35
> > > "The *takwaga* performers are here. They really are."

Performance of *takwaga*, Aifa, 1980.

"*Ah hoh*," so they were all there to perform the *takwaga*. Yes.
Lots of them!
"I can see you people are here now."
"As you can see, we people are here now. 40
We've just come to perform the *takwaga*, our brothers
and I."
"All right," he answered. "Stay here regardless of your reason for
coming."

This dialogue represents the greetings of the hosts and the reply of Wapagepundaka. It suggests a friendly relationship between the two groups.

So, they took them all into their houses,
Right away they took them all into their houses after that.
Right away they took them all into their houses, until they were
all housed. 45
So afterward they performed the *takwaga*.
They performed until they felt the darkness fall.
After that they all slept, I'm told.
All the while a stinking person must have accompanied each one
of them.
A stinking person accompanied each one of them. 50
So then the song masters went out to inform the people in their
other settlements.
They went.
Then they went to their other settlements, to their other
settlements.
"Some *angikogo* are here, some *angikogo*," they said.
"They're here." 55
"Oh. They are, you say?"
"What kind of people are they?" he asked.
"Wapagepundaka's.
He came to perform the *takwaga*, that's why he's here.
They've come to dance." 60
Then the next day at the beginning of their dawn, this time the
people of that settlement went around performing.
The following day the others performed the *takwaga*,
they danced and danced, they performed the *takwaga*, they
performed,
they performed.
They all slept. 65
They all slept.
They slept these many days, five days.
They slept five days.

"Well, perhaps we should leave right now, our children and I," he
said to the others.

    "Go then, go then.   70

So, what do you want to take back with you as a gift from your
seating place?" they asked. [The speaker refers to a gift given to
a leader who is formally "seated" during a ceremonial
performance.]

    "What do you want to take back with you?"

"Oh, some manioc starch."

Because they had left without food, they didn't have any food,
because those people never took food.

    Wapagepundaka didn't take any food.   75

Next they left for their own place with *timbuku*, balls of dried
manioc starch, Wapagepundaka left right away with *timbuku*.

        With *timbuku*.

    So much of it!

"You'll go now.

    You'll go now."   80

But before they did that they took up the manioc bread that
was cooked, because those *angikogo* had made some manioc
bread,

enough for everyone.

    Manioc bread was made, manioc bread was made, manioc
    bread was made, until they finished doing that.

When that was done they lifted it all onto their backs, they put
it all on their backs,

    timbuku was put on their backs.   85

    They packed it all inside baskets.

Pok pok pok pok pok, oh so much of it!

    That person's back, that person's back, that person's back, that
    person's back, that person's back, oh they were carrying so
    much!

        [Kafuga: "Only in the beginning did they go so
        nicely."]

    Beautifully.   90

Well, they were carrying away the manioc flour.

    Oh, there was so much of it!

"As you see, I'm ready to leave now," he said to them.

"Go as you wish, gonow, gonow, gonow, gonooow." [Again, the
rapidly repeated phrases indicate the speech of leaders, this time
a host's farewell.]

So they all came back.   95

    They were coming back then, I'm told.

Then while they passed through the open country,
  for some reason they sat down to wait for the others.
    Well, for the stinking people to do something, the stinking
    people.   100
The first ones came, the first ones came,
  the first ones came up to him *tiki*,
    and then they passed by him, they passed by him, they passed
    by him, they passed by him, they passed by him, *keeh!*
      So that by then he himself was right in the middle of them
      all,
      Wapagepundaka was.   105
        In the middle of them all after they did that.
Until every single one of them had passed by, until there were
no more.
"Come on, come on!
Come on!" Why, they were catching them *puuh*,
  and so the stinking people caught them all.   110
      They caught them all.
    That was done.
Then, so, it was all over for them after that happened. *Puk.*
  The others dumped out all of their supplies.
    Everything they had put inside their carrying baskets, all the
    manioc starch they had put inside them.   115
    Puk puk puk puk, and they scattered it all around.
      And they scattered it all around.
They took hold of them, the stinking people did that to them.
  Taking each one by his wrists, they pierced them *tsoduk.*
    On this side, too, they pierced their ankles.   120
    Their ankles were pierced, and that was done.
On each and every man's back,
  well, they carried them all on their backs,
  and they came back to their settlement, to their settlement,
  they returned finally, to their settlement.
They arrived after they came back. In that house, in that house, in
that house, in that house, in that house,   125
  So, they divided them up among all the households.
  This one was given a share, this one was given a share, that was
  how they went about doing it.
When they finished doing that they hung their arrows alongside
the bird-skin hats they wore in battle. These things were hanging
along the entire length of the main rafter, end to end.
So then, "What will happen to them now?"
  "What will happen to them now?" he asked. "What?"   130

"They will sleep for five more days, five."
"That's right."
"They will sleep for five more days."
"All right."
"That's right," they agreed.   135
"Why, they will sleep for five more days.
    They will sleep for five more days.
Their stink will be gone by then, their stink will be gone by
then." [When he heard this, my assistant Maidyuta laughed and
said: "Their stink never went away."]
"All right," they answered.
"In the meantime we'll be preparing the bread and soup that
we'll eat with them."   140
    During that time they were preparing the starchy things they
    ate.
        There was so much of it!
Then the next day they went to their manioc fields to get that
starchy food.
    They went, it's said, they slept, it's said, they slept, they kept
    sleeping.
        When they awoke on this day, they went to get bark to fuel
        the fires.   145
"All right, that should be enough, that should be enough.
Their stench is probably gone by now.
All right all right all right!
Tomorrow tomorrow tomorrow it will happen!
Tomorrow we'll go get our firewood!"   150
"That's right!" How excited they all were!
Then someone came inside the house where they had put him, he
was going to question him.
    "Well, so Wapagepundaka.
    You're Wapagepundaka, aren't you?"
    "*Anite*," he said. "*Anite*."   155
        "*Tufadya idye* . . . I'm Tufadya," he answered.
        (Tufadya was their nephew, their nephew.
    That was what they kept asking him about, what they had
    wanted to find out from him.) [These responses are supposed to
    be in the language of the fierce people.]
The next day they were ready.
    "All right, let's go, let's go, let's go."   160
In that same house was a secluded maiden whose hammock they
had hung by itself, close to the entrance.
    She was one of their secluded maidens, a secluded one.
        One of their maidens.

So they had all gone away, all of them.
    They went, all of them went.   165
  Then, they were ready.
  "Let's all go let's all go let's all go let's all go," and they all left.
    It was still fairly dark outside.
Then, that was all.
Well, she hurried over, the maiden hurried over to look at him. 170
  "You're Wapagepundaka, aren't you?" she said to him.
  "Look, see if you can cut this off me,
    cut this off me," he said to her.
      "Cut this off me."
  "I can't.   175
    I can't.
      I'm afraid if I did some relative of mine would kill me.
      I'm afraid if I did some relative of mine would kill me."
  "No, they won't," he answered.
    "In fact, I'll come back later to make you my wife if you
    rescue me. That's what will happen to you." 180
    "All right," she said.
Then she cut the chords from the holes in his wrists *tsukatsuka*
tsakitsaki.
  "Do this next," he said.
  He had been pierced through his ankles, too. *Tsiki tsiki tsiki*
ndik, finally she did it.
  Next he stood up, and then he made love to her. 185
When he had finished, "Be sure to wake up.
  Be sure to do that quickly when I come to get you.
    I'll be in a hurry when I come to get you.
  When I suddenly shake your hammock, you'll wake up, you'll
  wake up."
  "All right," she said. 190
    "All right."
Then when the sun was here, high in the sky, someone else came
to where he was. *Pok* an elderly person, an old woman.
  Bum that old woman dropped her firewood to the ground.
  "That man's still here, isn't he?"
    "He's still here." 195
  "Wapagepundaka," she addressed him.
  "Look at this, look at this. When I eat you
you'll come out from here," and she spread apart her buttocks.
  "From here, you'll come out from here." [This persists as an
insulting gesture used by young boys to one another.]
  "I've already come out from somewhere," he answered. 200
    He grabbed her, *tuk*. *Bok*, and he threw her down.

Once again someone else came to him.
    "Wapagepundaka.
    You're really Wapagepundaka.
    Look, you'll come out from here," she said.   205
    So, she spread apart her buttocks.
    "I've come out from somewhere," he said to her. *Pok* so he
    threw her down also.
        And this time he beat her with his fists.
    That was all, there were two of them.
Well, the others all arrived home with their wood *pom
pom pom.*   210
    They went to the plaza to pick up their firewood, to the
    plaza.
            To the plaza.
    Then they prepared their food, they made their manioc bread,
    and all of the starchy things they ate.
        The women made the starchy things they ate.
            They made it, they made their manioc bread.   215
                It was ready.
"All right all right all right the next thing to do!
    We should make manioc bread we should make manioc bread!"
    he said to them.
    "Manioc bread with which to eat them, manioc bread for eating
    with them," he said to them.
    "That's just what we should do," they said to their leaders. 220
        Well, they made manioc bread.
    Well, they sang about it.
        They sang about it.
    "*Huu huuh huuh heh heh,*" they sang about it.
    They sang about it, they sang about it, they sang about it.   225
    "They'llreallybeexterminatedexterminatedexterminatednowww!"
    they went.
    "They'llreallybeexterminatedexterminated."
    [He begins to sing:] "*Eh, kutsiwewe kutsiwewe kutsiwewe.*"
    Oh, how they sang about it!
    "Yes, howtheywillbeexterminatedexterminatedexterminated.
    Yes, after all this is done they will really die.   230
        They will really die after all this is done!"
    [Sings:] "*Kutsiwewe kutsiwewe kutsiwewe.*
    Eh, gikufutigihe, kutsiwewe kutsiwewe kutsiwewe,
        kutsiwewe kutsiwewe kutsi . . . hetuhetuhe heeee . . ."
That's their song.   235
    They sang, they sang. "They'llreallybeexterminated,
    they'llreallybeexterminatednow!"

"Goaheadgoahead.
Youshouldgogetthemgogetthemgogetthem."
As soon as he heard their leaders saying that, Wapagepundaka got
to his feet.
Well, he grabbed an arrow of theirs when he heard that, one
that had been stuck in the thatch of the house.   240
He grabbed an arrow when he heard that, he took a white
feathered bird skin,
and then he flew up and out the top of the house!
He flew out the top of the house to a place nearby after that.
[Like all warriors in these stories, Wapagepundaka is able
to fly.]
He flew farther on *pupupupu*,
To where they had surrounded themselves with a stockade. 245
And there he stayed after that.
Well, some others came after him, some of the stinking people
did that. *Pupupupu*.
Four of them went.
Tuduk! They leaped up and ran after him.
They went on, while Wapagepundaka kept running.   250
When he came to a giant armadillo's burrow, he went inside it.
The others passed around it.
Nearby was a deer.
When they ran by it they saw it and then they ran after it.
And they lunged right at it, they lunged at the deer!   255
"Why, this is just a deer!"
How surprised and angry they were!
Then they came, they came, they came, they came, until they got
back.
When they finished coming back, "Nothing at all," they said.
I mean they carried nothing more in their arms than that
deer.   260
They carried nothing more in their arms than that deer.
They carried in their arms.
"All right! Now!"
"We should do something now," and so they brought the others
out from the houses, I'm told.
While they were bringing them outside, Wapagepundaka ran
back.   265
"I'll watch them kill my brothers." He came toward that place
and perched on top of a tree, on a tree.
Then the others brought them outside.
They brought them out of this house, they brought them out of
the next house, they brought them out of yet another house.

And after they had brought them out of all the houses, the
stinking people clubbed his brothers *tok tok* they clubbed them
all to death.
The ones who had been in that house, the ones who had been in
the next house.
And while he watched them there, they danced, and then they
clubbed the others, they clubbed them to death *tok*, they were
all done away with, they died. 270
They clubbed them, and clubbed them, and clubbed them.
Until they were all dead.
    Until they were all dead.
And then they ate them all, the stinking people did.
"I think I'll go now," Wapagepundaka said. 275
    "I'll go now."
Then while they ate them all,
    while the stinking people ate them all, while they were eating
    all his followers,
    the only one remaining went away.
They were eating them all. That's what they did after the others
died. Yes. 280
After that he came back *titi . . . iii,*
    to what they had left behind, he came back to what they had
    left behind them.
What they had taken with them was lying scattered on the
ground.
"Oh, it's true, isn't it, my poor brothers!
Their older brothers will discover this very soon when they
return with me to take revenge." 285
    He was talking about their possessions, the things they had
    puk puk carried on their backs.
After that he finally came back, using a fire to signal his return.
While his cousin was coming toward him, watching for his fire,
he was coming toward Wapagepundaka, watching for his fire.
[That is, they have agreed to do this beforehand, a customary
practice when men carrying food returned from visiting a
ceremony; this way, they were correctly identified and not
mistaken for enemies.]
"Oh, they're right in sight over there. Well, I'll go see them right
away," and he went off to meet them all.
He came searching, he came searching, he came searching, he
came searching until he found him. 290
Well, he kept coming.
    Well, he kept coming.

But now he came differently.
He came differently now.
This time as he came he concealed himself. *Keh*, that was how
he was doing that. 295
That was just how he was expected to do that.
Next he went on *tititi tititi*, well, he was tracking
Wapagepundaka.
I'm thinking that he came with his bow aimed at Wapagepundaka.
And he shot him between his legs!
"My cousin, I see you're still very much alive." 300
"As you see, my brothers and I are still very much alive." [A
ritual greeting after men return from war.]
"Where are our brothers?" "As far as I know they're still back
there.
Because they're all loaded down with manioc starch
back there."
"I see," he answered.
"Go then," he said to Wapagepundaka. 305
"Go then."
"We have to make arrows for ourselves.
We have to make arrows for ourselves. My brothers have to
make some arrows for me."
"All right," he answered.
After that he came right back. 310
Then, well, he came back after all that, I'm told.
Then, well, when the sun was here, it was dusk, he arrived home.
"*Huu!*" how he called out!
Others were hidden, they were hiding. As he was came back
onto the entrance path, close to the settlement, the ones who
had hidden themselves stood ready to do something to him.
"I'll try shooting him now!" *Bok!* the arrows went between his
legs. 315
The next man in line also tried, *tok*, the next in line as well,
tok, and the next in line, *tok*, and the next in line, *tok*, and then
the cousin in the middle.
"I'll try shooting him once and for all!" but none of them could do
anything to him at all.
Tok tok, when he came very close the last one who stood on the
edge of the group shot at him. So, he came after they had done
that to him.
"Why were you all trying to kill me? Why did you all try to
kill me?"
He came after they did that to him. 320

"I see you're still very much alive," was how they greeted him.
"I suppose we still are. "
"Where are your brothers?"
"They're still back there. They're still back there.
They're still carrying some manioc starch back there."   325
"All right," they answered.
When they saw the sun move, and move, until it was way over
here, low on the horizon,
    the wives of the dead men really began to weep. Those wives of
    theirs.
    "How can your brothers really be where you said they were?"
    "Your sons are no longer alive," he answered.   330
When the men learned that their wives were weeping, they
said,
    "You'll weep later on. After we men have gone back there and
    taken revenge."
    The women stopped weeping when the others said that, they
    stopped.
When that was all over, he slept, he slept, he slept, he slept, he
slept, he slept.
    He slept five days.   335
    He stood outside.
        He himself stood outside.
"My cousin my cousin my cousin!
    Come out here, come out here to me!"
    "All right," he answered. He stood outside.   340
    "Why must I do this?" he asked.
"Look, the next thing we'll do is return to our brothers.
I saw our brothers serving as morsels of food for them. The
fierce people were feasting on our brothers."
    "Unfortunately you did.
    Unfortunately you did.   345
Where?" "Far from here!
They captured us so quickly! And I was almost wiped out then
and there."
    "You were, you say?
    I see," he answered.
"Let's go as you say," his cousin continued.   350
"How many days should we spend making arrows?"
    "In five days we'll feather the arrows."
    "That's fine with me," he answered.
The next day they made their arrows,
    the next day they made their arrows,   355

the next day they made their arrows,
the next day they made their arrows,
they spent four days doing that.
So then they were ready.
"Let's go, let's go, let's go now!" they went.   360
Every one of them left.
                    [Kafuga asked: "The women?"]
[Tightly, in disapproval:] Not the women. Only the men did
that,
          that's what you should say.
                    [Kafuga, shyly: "Without any women."]   365
"All right everyone, let's go now," so their older brothers left
before anyone else.
     "*Hum, hoo!*" they all left together before the others.
Then those who were born after them came together.
And also those who came last, for they left in three groups.
[These may have been age sets or grades.]
     How they went on after that!   370
Then, they came to the place of their capture.
     "Now look. Look, my brothers," he said to them.
     "You can see for yourselves, this is where we were captured.
     You can see for yourselves the remains of what we had
     with us.
          You can see just what we had with us right here.   375
       Here is where they captured us. Right here.
       Right here is where they captured us."
     "All right," they answered.
   "Look at what our brothers had with them. It's just as he said."
     What they had with them was still there, it was still all
     there.   380
     It was all in the carrying baskets just as they had left it.
     "All right," they said.
     They all stood there together.
   "This was what I saw happening to us here."
     Well, they went on.   385
Then, just as dusk fell, when the sun was right here, they came to
the edge of the settlement.
       The edge of the settlement.
   "There they are.
     Yes, here was where those men mercilessly ate our people.
     I saw each and every one of them eating our brothers."   390
All around their houses they had built stockades. Their houses
were surrounded by stockades.

"We'll wait here, it won't happen just yet," he said.
    "We'll wait here for a while.
      We'll wait until it gets dark."
Then they saw the sun set.   395
      They saw the sun set.
    And as they saw the sun set, they got ready.
    "All right. Let's listen to them for a while, children," their
leader said to them,
      "Let's listen to them for a while."
    "We will." A pair of them came toward the houses.   400
    "*Uwaaa!*" "*Ho ho ho!*" they answered.
    "Wapagepundakaaa! Wapagepundakaaa!" they called out to him.
    "Listen, they're going to be listening for us."
Then when they got back, "Anything?" "Yes, they've all just
answered us.
      They'll be listening for us now."   405
      "They're done for!"
Then, around the time when we're asleep,
    "Let's listen to them again, right now."
    One called out again, *isogoko*, the maned wolf.
    "*Waaaa ho ho ho.*" "Wapagepundaka, Wapagepundakaaa!"   410
    "Listen! Someone's still up!"
    "They're listening to us, that's for sure."
As the night deepened, in the darkness they did as before.
    "*Kah kah ko kah kah ko,*" they called out. "*Ho ho.*" "There are
still lots of people there, isn't that right?"
    "None of them are sleeping yet, are they?"   415
Then even further into the night, not long after they had been
talking,
    so *pupu*, the great horned owl, was calling out.
    "*Pupupupu.*" "Ah haa!" "Lots of them are still listening to us
over there."
    "Not all of them are listening. They'll have to stop soon.
    If we wait awhile longer they'll fall asleep."   420
So an old man put the urge to sleep in their eyes,
      to make them go to sleep.
Then after he had finished,
    "Go listen to them again this time. Go ahead, go listen now!"
    They got ready.   425
    "*Waaa.*" "*Ho ho,*" they answered.
    Only a few of them answered.
    "There are only a few left," they went.
    "Let's wait until they fall asleep."
    It was over.   430

Then only when it was dead of night did they call out to them
again. Only when it was dead of night did they call out to them
again.
"*Kugukaga.*" *Kugukaga*, the dove, called once again.
"*Ho ho ho,*"
    only a very few were left, here and there, that was how they
    were.
"Only a few left, it's all over. 435
They're sound asleep."
"*Waah!*" so now it was in the dim time before dawn.
Then "*pupupupu,*" the great horned owl calling.
Pupupu. The great horned owl calling. Nothing.
Again, "*kugukaga.*" Nothing. 440
Again "*waaa.*" Nothing, no answer.
"They're sound asleep," they said to each other.
"Is it all right?" "They're sound asleep!"
"Let's hurry then," they answered.
    "Let's go now," they told each other. 445
So they continued on.
"Stay here for now.
    Wait until I see my wife," he said.
    He went to get the woman who had cut him free.
"She's sure to be over there," that's what he said. 450
    He stood beside her hammock.
Kï kï kï kï, he shook her hammock.
"Come along now," he whispered.
    "As you see, I'm here to get you."
"All right!" 455
And, to his father.
"Father," he said.
"What?" "This woman who stands before you is my wife.
    This person you see here is the one who saved me before.
This person you see here is my wife. None of you must kill
her," he said to his father. 460
    "All right, bring her here."
Teh, she was a beautiful woman!
Then, "You can go ahead now," he said.
    They all went into the houses.
"You go on this side, I'll go on the other side." 465
They did that with sharp weapons, they did that with sharp
weapons. The things they used were tall, like this.
    Tall ones. [Ahpïũ uses the word *taho*, "bladed instrument,"
    used to refer to knives and machetes; he is apparently
    thinking of the weapons called *tacape* (see Fernandes 1970).]

[Kafuga: His wife was still with them.]
Tsiu, tsiu, tsiu, tsiu, tsiu, tsiu.
When the people who slept on one side of the house were done
away with,   470
 then they went to another house to do the same.
His cousin was also doing the same thing across the way.
When one household was slaughtered, he went next door to do
the same.
 And when that household was slaughtered, he went next door
 to do the same.
His cousin worked in one direction,   475
 while Wapagepundaka came toward him from the other
 direction.
Their followers had surrounded the settlement, they had
surrounded it until they came together after they had gone all
around the house circle.
They had surrounded it *tsiu tsiu,*
 while they had slashed at the people,
  in each of the houses.   480
The cousins came right toward each other from opposite
directions,
 he and his cousin coming toward each other from each side.
  [Kafuga: Wapagepundaka on the other side.]
 Yes, Wapagepundaka on this side,
 Tufadyaga on that side.   485
But two of the households were still alive.
Because Tufadyaga had cut them only slightly behind their ears.
Tsuk they were cut here beside their ears just a little, *tsuk.*
"*Ahaaah!*"
"*Hooo ho ho,*" two houses of people were still alive!
 There were two households left alive.   490
 "*Hooo ho ho ho,* that's not right," they said.
  "Their relative just injured them slightly." *Tuk tuk mbiii,*
 until the others were all dead,
 until the others were all dead. The others were all dead.
"*Ho ho!*" Now they were all celebrating what they had done.
"Where's my wife?" he asked his father.   495
 "That's her body over there," he answered.
 "Oh, why are you eating her?
When we were here before, she alone saved my life, you know.
Not like what we did here today.
You'll see. I'm leaving right now," he said to him, and he went
home then and there.
 He went back home.   500

He came back,
   Wapagepundaka did, right away.
      While the others stayed behind
         until the dawn came.
There they were, eating those poor people,   505
   right away they ate those poor people.
Then he came back to his mother while the sun was here.
   "I see you're still all right."
   "As you thought, I'm all right," he answered.
   "And where is your father?" she asked.   510
   "He's still back there doing what he usually does," he
   answered.
      "He's still there."
   "All right," she answered.
Then the next day, they were still sleeping back there,
   because they stayed there while they smoked those poor
   people,   515
      they had been smoking those poor people.
         They had been smoking them.
   "Everything's ready," they said.
   "It's all ready," they said. "It's all ready."
   "Everything's ready," they said.   520
They came back to that same place where those who had died
had left their food.
   Then they carried all that the victims had left behind.
   Each man had some of it, since they had shared out among
   themselves all that the victims had left behind.
      They distributed among themselves what those poor people
      had left behind, the remains of the manioc bread that had
      been prepared earlier.
         And so they ate the enemy.   525
After they had eaten everything they came back home,
   and they arrived home.
"Mother," Wapagepundaka said,
   "Father really betrayed me," he said to her.
      "Father betrayed me."   530
   "Why? What did your father do?"
   "He ate my wife!
      He ate my wife."
   "He did, did he?"
   "I must leave, Mother, I'm going.   535
      Far away from this place.
      Perhaps that way I'll find a wife."
   "Go if you wish," she replied. "Go if you wish."

"Make a supply of bread for me now," he said.
   "Make a supply of bread for me."   540
   "All right," she answered.
Then his mother worked at making a supply of bread for him,
   his mother made a supply of bread for him.
"I'm off!" He said that as he stood beside her.
Then, well, he went to a poor little settlement of some strangers
who lived nearby, where he had once seen someone.   545
   She must have been a child when he had first seen her.
     She must have been a good-looking girl.
   She was the one he now went to see.
Then, I'm not sure what kind of game he had with him,
     the game he had with him.   550
   He had two baskets filled with game,
   which he carried with him as he walked on.
Toward dusk he was still walking. The sun was still just barely
above the horizon when
   tiki he came to a place from where he could see the houses.
   He moved forward, but as he was still far from them, he moved
   forward again.   555
Then he arrived, he arrived at that very place where he had
seen her.
   There were only a few people left around those houses.
   Most of her relatives had gone to their manioc fields. Her
   brothers and people who lived in the other houses were in their
   manioc fields.
   She was practically all alone.
Someone was standing outside the house.   560
     Her mother.
"Child," she went.
   "You should bathe yourself out here," she said to her.
     "Come bathe yourself."
"All right, bring the water in my gourd jug."   565
   Her mother took out the gourd jug.
     She went to get some water.
And when she brought it back, she said, "Here it is, child."
   "Put it over there, outside," her daughter answered.
     "All right," she said.   570
       She put it outside.
"Here it is, go bathe yourself." "All right," her daughter said.
She untied the wrappings around her knees, *pupupupu*,
   she untied the wrappings around her knees.
Then she was ready.   575

Then she walked out of the house to bathe herself.
  He was outside, watching,
      outside.
  She saw him standing there.
  "Oh! Who can that be?   580
  Who can that be?"
  She came up to him.
    "Who can that be?"
She came to where he stood to see who it was.
  "Who are you?"   585
  "I'm me."
  "What are you doing here?"
  "I've come to be with you,
    to you.
    Just as you see."   590
  "All right," she answered.
  "Wait for me. I'll go get Mother."
  She went up to her mother.
  "Mother." "What?" she answered.
  "Wash me here on my back," she said.   595
    "All right," her mother answered.
  Her mother came toward her.
  "Mother," she whispered softly,
    "I asked you to come out because there's someone here.
    Someone.
  I'm not sure what kind of person he is," she continued.   600
  "That's strange. Where is he?" her mother asked.
  "Right here. 'I've come to you,' that's what he's been telling
me."
    "We'd better go see him, then," her mother answered.
She walked over to see him until she reached him, standing by the
rear doorway.
  "Didn't I tell you?" her daughter told her.   605
  "Well, my young relative," the mother addressed him.
    "You are certainly here, aren't you?"
  "As you see, I am."
  "Yes, but why are you here?"
  "Please, as you see I've come to be with your daughter.   610
      To be with your daughter."
    "You have, have you?
      You have, have you?
  Think carefully," she said to her daughter.
    "We're done for," she said to her.   615

"It's all over for us.
   Why, that man's a real warrior,
   that man's a real warrior," she continued.
"He could kill us any time now."
"She really shouldn't be afraid of me," he said.   620
   "She shouldn't be afraid of me," he said to her.
      "I don't know why. She shouldn't be afraid of me.
      Because I didn't come here to kill you," he answered.
"All right," the maiden answered.
"Go get him," her mother said.   625
   "Get your younger brother."
"All right." So they all came back with him walking behind them,
they all came back, and she hung his hammock over at the side of
the house.
   They were very excited.
To their people, "There's a real enemy right here among us,"
she said.
   Her mother said that as she went outside to tell the others.   630
      "Now we're done for.
   He's a real warrior.
      He's a real warrior.
That's the only reason he's here.
   Look at what he's doing, why else should he be doing that?"   635
   He still clutched his arrows close to his chest.
"It's all right to put your arrows down,
      put your arrows down.
That makes my relative terrified of you.
      You're frightening my relative.   640
'He's come to wipe us out,' that's just what she told the others."
"But why should I want to come here to kill her?" he answered.
"The only reason I came here was to be with you.
I'm not going to kill you,
      I'm not."   645
And *pok* he set his arrows down behind him, *pok*
   he put them down behind him.
As the sun moved farther and farther, her father came back from
working in his manioc fields,
      and her brothers arrived.
      The neighbors finally came back home.   650
"A warrior is here right among us. We're finished once and for
all," her mother said to them.
   All the neighbors were frightened of him.
"We're certainly done for.
   We're certainly done for."

"These people are terrified of you," she said to him.   655
    "But there's no reason for them to be frightened of me.
    I didn't come here to kill you, but with something else in
    mind.
    I came here just to be with you.
    There are a couple of things I'd like us to go see," he said to her.
        "I want us to go see those two things."   660
They walked until *tiki* they reached his carrying baskets.
    His two carrying baskets weren't very far away.
    "Go ahead," *mbuk*.
        "These are they," he said.
    "All right," she answered.   665
    She put one on her head.
    Mbuk he lifted the other one onto his back.
    When they returned they put them down in the center of the
    house.
This is what he had brought for her father.
    "Father," she said.   670
    "This person's game is right here. Here it is," she said.
    "All right," he answered.
        "All right."
        That man was their most important leader.
Then he carried one of the two baskets of food outside right away
to give to his followers.   675
        He kept the other carrying basket.
By now the others were beginning to hide their things,
        they were beginning to hide their things.
    They were beginning to hide their things because they were all
    frightened of him.
After the food was carried outside, over there in the plaza they
divided all his meat among themselves.   680
    They divided it among themselves in the plaza.
Then that foolish mother of hers untied her hammock.
    "Why is our parent leaving now?" he asked.
    "You're frightening her, you're frightening all of them."
    "She shouldn't be, I didn't come here to kill them," he said to
    her.   685
    As I said, he still hadn't put his arrows down, that's why they
    were still frightened of him.
    "I won't," he went.
    The others were dividing everything he had brought out to the
    plaza, while the mother began to leave.
Well, after her father had gone outside, the others all went off.
    They all went off after that.   690

His sons all left, her father was the ONLY one who didn't run
away.
"If he's going to kill me let him do it here while I'm with my
daughter," he said to the others.
    While the others left.
"Why is your family going away now?" he asked her.
"Because they're all so frightened of you," she answered.   695
    "They're worried you will kill them otherwise."
    "But I didn't come here to kill you."
      That's what he kept saying to her, over and over.
They were lying about his wanting to do all that.
"I mean it. I didn't come here to kill you," he said.   700
    "I mean it. It wasn't to kill you."
But the others had gone out among the manioc while all that was
going on. By now all the people had gone away, though they were
still nearby.
    Inside the house the two stayed together, in their father's house.
    They sat together pitifully by themselves inside their house.
    "How could I alone ever kill them all? It's all a stupid lie."   705
That was over.
They slept, they slept,
    after he had slept three times there,
      five times.
        He had slept five times.   710
"Let's go some place far from here.
    Is there some dense forest around here?" he asked her.
"There's some at a place far from here, that's where it is," she
answered.
"Let's go there," he said.
"We'll look for some game for ourselves there," he said to her. 715
"Let's go if that's what you want to do," she answered.
"Father," she said to her father.
    "Tomorrow we two are going to search for some game for
ourselves.
    We'll be spending one night, one."
"All right, you two should go if that's what you want to do." 720
("This could be the end of my daughter. I think he's going to kill
my poor daughter," he said to himself.)
Despite what he said, that same day she prepared a supply of
bread for themselves.
The next day after all that had happened, they got everything
together after all that had happened. He went off with their food,
he left the settlement.

First he took their food over there, to a place where they were
going to stay.
When he finished with that he came back to get his wife.   725
They both came back together after that.
They stayed there together, well, they stayed there together after
they had done all that.
When they had finished *tiki* they stopped at their camping place.
They cleared a space for themselves there. When they were
done,
"We should go hunting now."   730
   But first he cut his wife's club, a long one.
He cut something long for his wife to use as a club.
"When one of them comes toward you you'll club it,
   you'll club it."
      "All right," she said.   735
They looked for them, and finally after that they found them.
   "If you watch very carefully you'll see which way they go."
      So the peccaries began to run by them after that,
      "*Um um um.*"
"Here they are," he went. "Be sure to watch them carefully.
Be sure to watch them carefully, don't fail to club them with
this if they come toward you."   740
      "All right," she answered.
They stood right next to each other this time.
Tok tok tok tok tok tok,
      as they came toward his wife she clubbed them.
      She clubbed them to death.   745
He shot arrows into the ones who scattered,
and afterward he was clubbing them *tok tok* until they were
all dead,
until they all died after that.
After that they began to smoke them on a grill.
When the sun was over here,   750
      they smoked them on a grill,
         they began to smoke them well. They began to smoke them
         on a grill.
Yes, they skewered a few scraps of intestines,
      some small pieces for her father.
         "Let's take these few pieces to Mother." He spoke about a
         portion of what he was planning to bring out to the plaza. 755
         I'm talking about those bits of stomach.
By the time they had finished it had become dark for them.
      So they slept.

He had already made a carrying basket, a single carrying basket.
Then the next day, "Let's go." They stood together.   760
   "Let's go," and they went until her husband returned, carrying
   his game on his back *tiki* and walked up to the house where he
   left the basket.
   Then he went back to get her, to get his wife,
      so he came to her, and they got ready.
Pok she put the basket on her husband's back
   When that was done, they both came back and they came inside
   the house.   765
   The sun was here, low on the horizon.
"I see this time you've brought something more for us."
This was her father speaking.
   "Yes, as you see we've come back again, Father," she said.
   "There's something we found for you over there. You should go
   ahead and eat it," she said.   770
   And so her father ate a little of it,
      he ate a little of it.
When he was done,
   he put some on the central platform of the house, on the central
   platform,
      he put it on the central platform.   775
   While he left most of it on the grill,
      he ate a little of what those two had brought him, he ate a
      little of it.
That was all.
Then the next day, "Go get your mother," he said
      to his daughter.   780
   "Go get your mother," he said to her.
      "All right," she answered.
   But first she made some manioc bread.
   When that was done, she wrapped the manioc bread around a
   piece of meat *pok*.
      This was a hindquarter she had cut off. *Ngiuutok*, she had cut
      off a piece of the thigh.   785
   Then *mbok* she wrapped it with the manioc bread.
"Let's go look for Mother," she said.
   "All right," he answered,
      and they walked on.
Then when they came to the manioc,   790
      the others were beginning to talk to each other,
         the others were beginning to talk to each other.
   Finally they saw the two coming. "Your daughter is coming
   right toward us," they said.

"Don't take more than one arrow with you," she said.
"Don't take more than one arrow with you. That way they
won't be frightened of you."   795
"All right," he answered. So he only took one tiny arrow with
him.
"Mother," she said. "What?" the other answered.
"I see you're here," she said to her daughter.
"I'm certainly here as you see and I've come to get you," her
daughter answered.
    "To get all of you."   800
"You have, you say?" she said.
"'But despite what they say about me, as you see I didn't plan to
come here and kill you. Not at all,' he told me."
"All right. It's all right for all you people to come with us," she
said,
    as she gave her mother what she had, as she gave her the
    manioc bread.
While her mother ate the food she shared it with the other
people who were there, and they ate it.   805
"All right, let's all go," and they walked until they all came back,
they all came back.
It was over.
It was finally over and everyone came home.
    "But despite what's being said about me now, I didn't come
    here to kill all of you," that's what he had been telling her all
    along.   810
That ended it all.
    When those people arrived home,
        they went into their houses,
        into their houses,
        into their houses,   815
        taah, into their houses, into their houses, into their houses,
        into their houses, into their houses . . . teeh,
            into their houses after that.
That's all.
    Those people came back home.
    Everyone came back home.   820
        So then that was how he came to live with a wife.
        He lived there.
That's all.

Wapagepundaka's story is unusual among Kalapalo stories about warriors because in it there is so much resistance to local values, and an
attempt is made by the hero to reformulate those values. In addition,

the warrior himself changes profoundly. At first, his entire bearing suggests aggression. When Wapagepundaka first arrives among his young wife's people, he stands about clutching his arrows to him, as if he were about to attack the very people he is trying to persuade of his peaceful intentions. This sign of his earlier disposition toward violence terrorizes the people of his wife's community. He is repeatedly urged to put down his arrows, but it is only toward the very end of the story that he finally manages to behave convincingly. It is as if he himself is uncertain about how his relatives will behave; he suspects that he will be ambushed even as he repeatedly maintains his own good will. All the while, he concretely demonstrates this good will by providing food for his father-in-law.[1]

Everything Wapagepundaka does results in an expansion of his field of ethical judgment as experienced in the earliest episodes of his story, when sympathy and support, the desire to revenge his friends who have been killed by enemies, were maintained within his family, that is, the people of his settlement. The warrior was able, however, to see the possibility of peaceful contacts, especially marriage, with strangers. He stood in contrast to the inflexible attitudes of his father, for whom all foreigners were by definition enemies. And he stands in contrast as well with the only other named warrior figure in the story, his "cousin" Tufadyaga, who, it develops, is a relative of the enemy. Tufadyaga, it might be said, voices an entirely different point of view from Wapagepundaka, though like Wapagepundaka he is ambivalent about a good deal that goes on. Initially, he seems to be sarcastic, telling Wapagepundaka that he will take revenge after Wapagepundaka's people are killed. Later, right in the midst of the preparations for the cannibal feast, we are told that Tufadyaga is actually a relative of people in the enemy settlement. Therefore his response to Wapagepundaka's invitation is not sarcastic at all but deeply ironic. For he must, in the end, see his own people killed. For him, slaughtering that community does not come easy, and he is discovered leaving his own people only slightly wounded. Tufadyaga's ambivalence, then, is a pragmatic one, whereas Wapagepundaka's is ideological.

In the story, there is a clear progression from an initial state of affairs in which the community of shared ethical judgment remains congruent with the local settlement, to one in which Wapagepundaka has successfully expanded his community of personal ethics to include strangers. This contrast is developed through a series of descriptions that repeatedly and cumulatively reinforce the lack of support, or suspicion, or even outright resistance to Wapagepundaka that comes from those surrounding him. The first time this happens is when his cousin Tufadyaga (anticipating that Wapagepundaka's men will be killed by enemies although their intent is to peacefully perform music) declares that he will remain behind so as to take revenge later on. A second act of opposition to Wapagepundaka is seen when members of his own settlement shoot at him upon his return from the fierce people, because he is a lone survivor, a dangerous person. (In this connection, such aggressive greetings in South America seem generally to assert a temporary abatement of an existing potential for mutual aggression. In the Alto Xingu, wrestling contests between visitors to a community and their hosts occur prior to trading ceremonies, or when a few men come to visit a community in which they have no close relatives who might justify a visit. On these occasions, these contests seem to be designed to effect such an amelioration of the usual suspicion between communities.) A third occurrence is seen when Wapagepundaka's cousin's own people (having returned to the settlement of fierce people to take revenge for their killing and eating of Wapagepundaka's men) slaughter the wounded because they do not wish to see anyone spared. The fourth occurrence involves the failure of Wapagepundaka's father to prevent his wife from being killed and eaten; when Tufule told me this same story, he had the father say, just before clubbing the woman: "We can't marry enemies." Finally, a fifth occurrence involves Wapagepundaka's need to convince his hoped-for wife's mother of his sincerity. Once he has convinced her, he has successfully created the conditions for the active expansion of his ethical field. What ensues is a radical restructuring of his personal ties, not an inversion but a reordering or redirecting: his enemies are now his family—his in-laws—but his original family are not now his enemies. His local allegiance is to his in-laws, rather than to his own father and brothers. We are left uncertain, however, as to whether or not he must fight against his original family. In other words, Wapagepundaka ends up a very special kind of individual thinker, standing apart even from the residents of his new community. He is the sole person for whom personal ethics has replaced a morality in which family or community relations are the locus of ethical judgment. But to gain this unique status, he must discard a crucial emblem of his warrior status: he must put down his arrows.

This important shift in relations is marked by the image of Wapagepundaka's traveling. At first, Wapagepundaka travels to the fierce people to perform a musical ritual (where his people are killed and eaten). After this, he returns home to begin preparing for revenge. Then, he goes back to the fierce people a second time, takes revenge, but, disappointed by his father, returns for the last time to his own settlement, from whence he leaves alone for a distant settlement of foreigners. There he remains. His travels with a group of supporters is always followed by a solitary trip in which (in one way or another) he is contrasted with the rest of his people. In general with Kalapalo narratives, traveling between two places suggests a contrast between two different states of mind or consciousness. Thus, Wapagepundaka's troubled movement back and forth between his own and the fierce people's settlement suggests anxiety and confusion between his wish to get away from the slaughter, his obligation to avenge his dead brothers, and his desire to affirm his marriage to the woman who saved his life. His more purposeful departure for his future wife's settlement is clearly related to a more committed desire for domestic harmony—it is a higher goal that subsumes all action in the second part of the story. This is persuasive, focused action, in contrast with what occurs in the first part of the story.

In "Wapagepundaka," as in other warrior biographies, the persistent use of evidentiality contributes most strongly to a sense of the conflict between the hero and his most personal enemy. As elsewhere, the particular emotional experience of contact between persons, represented in Kalapalo narratives generally by quoted speech, is made most personally salient through the manner in which reasoning about past events occurs in these quotations. Thus, the meanings of Kalapalo evidentials in the story involve not only epistemological processes but the psychological processes that are created from shared or disputed conclusions.

As a first step, we can see how this works by comparing two major sections of the story. The first section concerns the hero's return to his people as the lone survivor of the cannibal massacre, during which he ties himself back to his group and describes what happened to his followers (lines 300–385). The tragedy is revealed only bit by bit, the terrible details being disclosed only at the very end of the narrative segment, when the remaining men are on their way to take revenge. The following sections in which evidentials appear are excerpted from the full text of this segment; I have, however, tried to preserve as much of the conversational activity as possible, since I am concerned as much with the responses to conclusive statements as I am with grammatical features themselves.

The first instance (a) occurs when Wapagepundaka is met outside the settlement by his cousin Tufadyaga, to whom he has signaled his return. The section opens with a conventional greeting:

(a)   *ah, ufaū, wegegele aka fegei.*   300
        "My cousin, I see you're still very much alive."
        ah, ugegele taka upidyaū ake.
        "As you see, my brothers and I are still very much alive."
        undema kupidyaū? atikokagele.
        "Where are our brothers?" "As far as I know they're still back there.
          ah, timbukufeke itamitako fegey
          Because they're all loaded down with manioc starch back there."

eh he, nïgifeke.
"I see," he answered.

In the first three lines are the evidentials *aka* and *taka*, referring to firsthand, especially visual evidence that the speaker confirms. This pair occurs most often in greetings and other routinized activities that open important events, often followed by discussions of plans or on-going activities, which are then validated. An example of this kind of discussion and validation (by the expression *eh he*) is found in the last two lines. After Wapagepundaka arrives home, a similar greeting pattern occurs, as in (b), but here an interesting thing happens. Wapagepundaka cannot accept the conclusion of his friends (that he is still alive) after having seen all his followers killed and eaten. In response, therefore, he uses the form *laka*, which marks puzzlement, a strong inability to understand. Although he doesn't contradict his greeters (he is, after all, still alive, as they say), he begins to suggest there might be something wrong:

(b) *ah wegegelekafegey nïgifeke.*
"I see you're still very much alive," was how they greeted him.
ah tisugelakagele.
"I suppose we still are."
undema fidyaü?
"Where are your brothers?"
atikogele. atikogele.
"They're still back there. They're still back there.
ah timbuku tafitako egele.   325
They're still carrying some manioc starch back there."
eh he nïgifeke.
"All right," they answered.

This confused voice is reinforced even more as the people wait in vain for the arrival of the traveling party, (c). The women who speak use the evidential *male*, which indicates strong doubt (even rejection) of hearsay evidence. Wapagepundaka is forced to admit openly that the men are dead. The women are actually expressing more than doubt; they are separating themselves from the men remaining at the settlement, and from Wapagepundaka in particular:

(c) *unago, unago, inde inufokinïngo*
When they saw the sun move, and move, until it was way over here, low on the horizon,
ah, ifitsaükopetsï tïfonï, ifitsaükopetsïfa.
the wives of the dead men really began to weep. Those wives of theirs.

undemale fidyaū anïgï?
"How can your brothers really be where you said they were?"
ah, afïtïfa elimokola nïgifeke.   330
"Your sons are no longer alive!" he answered.

Later, Wapagepundaka tells the men who did not originally want to visit
the fierce people that they must all return to take revenge. In order to
do so, he becomes very explicit about what happened to the victims,
speaking of them as having been insulted in the worst way: by having
been reduced to morsels of food.

(d) *inkefofo, kupidyaū opidyïña kutelu.*
"Look, the next thing we'll do is return to our brothers.
*kupidyaūfeke wūke tuiñambafo wāke. tiñambalefa kupidyaū
enïgi angikogofeke.*
I saw our brothers serving as morsels of food for them. The fierce
people were feasting on our brothers."
eh he kingi.
"Unfortunately you did."
   eh he kingi.   345
   Unfortunately you did."
undema? laa!
"Where?" "Far from here!
ah tisifenïgï wāke. afïtïngo itsopïgïlefa ugelefa.
They captured us so quickly! And I was almost wiped out then
and there."
   eh he kingi.
   "You were, you say?
   I see," he answered.
kigeapa nïgifeke.   350
"Let's go as you say," his cousin continued.

As he describes what happens, Wapagepundaka uses the evidential
form *wāke* together with the exclusive "we" (*tisuge*). You will recall
that *wāke* marks a conclusion of utter certainty with reference to firsthand, distant past experience, with a sense much like the English "I
bear witness." The speaker stands as an individual voice against any
possible others. In the present example *wāke* suggests a necessary and
unopposable fusion of speaker and all listeners. His cousin replies by
using the expression *eh he kingi*, thereby saying he believes Wapagepundaka's version of events but cannot validate the actions of the enemies
that are being described; see lines 344–345 and 348. (Instead of translat-
ing the expression by the English "They did, did they?" and similar responses, I sometimes use, "Too bad" or "Unfortunately that had to hap-

pen," thereby giving more emphasis to the speaker's reaction to the events rather than to the original actors.) Wapagepundaka hardly needs to convince his listeners of the truth of what happened, since they can see with their own eyes the remains of the food that was thrown about where the men were captured:

(e) *lepene, tifetïfïgïkoiña.*
     Then, they came to the place of their capture.
     inkefa, inkefa, ufisï, nïgifeke.
     "Now look. Look, my brothers," he said to them.
     tisifetïfïgï akigey wāke.
     "You can see for yourselves, this is where we were captured.
         tingipingope akigey wāke.
         You can see for yourselves the remains of what we had
         with us.
         tingipingotsïfa akigey.
         You can see just what we had with us right here.   375
     inde fegey tisifeta ifekeni, inde.
     Here is where they captured us. Right here."

Elsewhere in the story (as in the fourth line of [f], below, taken from a later segment) the evidential *wāke* can also suggest the situation of opposed and irreconcilable voices, as when Wapagepundaka discovers that his wife has been killed while his men take revenge in the enemy settlement:

(f) *ho ho ailitalefa ifekeni.*
     "*Ho ho!*" Now they were all celebrating what they had done.
     undemufitsu nïgifekeni.   495
     "Where's my wife?" he asked his father.
     ngele felei.
     "That's her body over there," he answered.
         ah, tïtomi engetaefenkeni.
         "Oh, why are you eating her?
     ele ale wāke, winïgï tikunui.
     When we were here before, she alone saved my life, you know.
     Not like what we did here today.
     utelaketsigei, ah sinïgïmbelï.
     You'll see. I'm leaving right now," he said to him, and he went
     home then and there.

In the fourth line of (f) the evidential *wāke* and the taxis form *ale* (suggesting action having a goal different from a previous occurrence) are now used by Wapagepundaka to strike a particularly disjunctive tone, as he distinguishes the woman's own bravery and sincerity from his father's cowardly betrayal. While *wāke* here also marks firsthand, visual evidence, the interpersonal tone varies from what we understand it to be in (e). This voice is very different from the solidarity expressed by two people greeting one another that is constituted by *aka/taka* combinations, as in (a) and (b). *Wāke*, in other words, is used by Ahpīū to separate Wapagepundaka more and more from those around him.

Evidentials appear again in the second half of the story, when Wapagepundaka appears among strangers in the role of suitor. Then, he must convince the woman and man he hopes will let him marry their daughter that he has not come to kill them all, as they think, but has appeared among them in order to marry and lead a peaceful life. It is not easy to convince them. The daughter, on the other hand, seems from the first quite willing to marry him, agreeing to his request to be with her with the characteristic validation *eh he*. In part this response is typical of how young girls receive their suitors in Kalapalo stories, but it is also in keeping with the way women in general tolerate the motives of men in these particular narratives:

(g) *uwamale itsa?*
     "What are you doing here?"
       eiñadyeta weta,
       "I've come to be with you,
         eiña.
         to you.
         angoloka.   590
         Just as you see."
       eh he nïgifeke.
       "All right," she answered.
(h) *ama, nïgifeke,*
     "Mother," she whispered softly,
         kuge mbangi. kuge.
         "I asked you to come out because there's someone here.
         Someone.
         ingkomungungapa kuge egey, nïgifeke.   600
         I'm not sure what kind of person he is," she continued.
         undeki nïgifeke.
         "That's strange. Where is he?" her mother asked.

The mother is very cautious. She greets him correctly, but despite Wapagepundaka's equally formal request that he be allowed to marry her daughter, she cannot agree:

(i) *eh, wamewama eitsa legey?*
     "Yes, but why are you here?"

eeh, endisïïñaka weta egey   610
"Please, as you see I've come to be with your daughter.
  eindisïña.
  To be with your daughter."
eh he kingi,
"You have, have you?
  eh he kingi.
  You have, have you?"

Fearful of what he might do if she refused, the mother invites Wapagepundaka into the house. Once inside, the daughter tells him of her
mother's fear. For the second time he tries to assure her that he comes
in peace:

(j) *eh tate afïtï, nïgifeke.*   620
     "She really shouldn't be afraid of me," he said.
       tatengaliko ufeke, nïgifeke.
       "She shouldn't be afraid of me," he said to her.
         um, tatengaliko ufeke,
         "I don't know why. She shouldn't be afraid of me.
       elïkoiñalata weta igey nïgifeke.
       Because I didn't come here to kill you," he answered.
     eh he nïgifeke.
     "All right," the maiden answered.

Later, when the daughter actually quotes her mother, Wapagepundaka
uses stronger language to try to persuade her:

(k) *ukwelïkoiña akigey sita taiketsange ifekeni.*
     " 'He's come to wipe us out', that's just what she told the
     others."
       tatiki elïkoiña wenalï, nïgifeke.
       "But why should I want to come here to kill her?" he
       answered,
         eiñadyetalefa weta igey.
         "The only reason I came here was to be with you.
       afïtïtifa elïkoiñala,
       I'm not going to kill you,
         afïtï.   645
         I'm not."

Further on in the story, the mother is joined by other people, who also
express their fear of Wapagepundaka. These people, too, are quoted, and
their fear seems even stronger than the mother's. Wapagepundaka, in
turn, replies with yet more forceful language.

(1) *kwapungukoketsigey.*
"We're certainly done for.
   kwapungukoketsigey.
   We're certainly donc for."
   ago engetakitsange efeke igey, nïgifeke.   655
   "These people are terrified of you," she said to him.
   tatila tengengalïko ufeke.
   "But there's no reason for them to be frightened of me.
   elïkoiñalataligey weta.
   I didn't come here to kill you, but with something else in
   mind.
   eiñadyetalefa wetïfïgï igey.
   I came here just to be with you."

Things don't get better, because everyone leaves the settlement, leaving
Wapagepundaka and the young woman alone in the house, with only
their father fatalistically remaining behind. For the fifth time, Wapagepundaka tries to persuade her that he is not going to kill anyone:

(m) *unanigey ukwoto teta nïgifeke.*
   "Why is our parent leaving now?" he asked.
   tengetalegey efeke, tengetako efeke egey.
   "You're frightening her, you're frightening all of them."
   tatiki elïkoiña lataligey weta, nïgifeke.   685
   "She shouldn't be, I didn't come here to kill them," he said
   to her.

But despite this, the people prepare to leave, fearing they will be killed
by the warrior living amongst them. Wapagepundaka protests for the
sixth time:

(n) *unamale ago teta fïgey nïgifeke.*
   "Why is your family going away now?" he asked her.
   ñengetundakotsaligey nïgifeke.   695
   "Because they're all so frightened of you," she answered.
   tuelïkofangamita igey efeke.
   "They're worried you will kill them otherwise."
   tatiki elïkoiña wenalï?
   "But I didn't come here to kill you."
   nïgiletsïïfeke.
   That's what he kept saying to her, over and over.
   awïndafïngï mbedyetsalefa.
   They were lying about his wanting to do all that.
   elïkoiñalataligey wetïfïgï, nïgifeke.   700
   "I mean it. I didn't come here to kill you," he said.

elïkoiñalata.
"I mean it. It wasn't to kill you."

And soon after, for the seventh time he must express his good intentions. But this time he begins to lose patience, which we know from the two evidential features in his reply: the doubt evidential *ma* coupled with a rhetorical question prefix *tï* juxtaposed with his expression *awïndafïngïsu*, a deeply pejorative word formed from *awïnda*, "lie" + *fïngï*, "a kind of" + *su*, "stubborn" (the suffix indicates compulsive action):

(o) *tïungufeke tsïma tuenalïko. awïndafïngïsu itsa fegey.*   705
      "How could I alone ever kill them all? It's all a stupid lie."

The situation is only resolved (typically after nine incidents) when Wapagepundaka takes his wife hunting. At first, the woman's people continue to anticipate only the worst. The father has remained entirely passive for the greater part of the story, in keeping with his own peaceful inclinations; we might say he is a model of peaceful leadership, in contrast to Wapagepundaka's hateful father. Rather than trying to protect his daughter, he quietly weeps to himself while the two others prepare for the hunting trip (line 721):

(p) *windisu apungufalakigey windisï elïfala ifeke kaaa nïgifeke.*
      ("This could be the end of my daughter. I think he's going to kill
      my poor daughter," he said to himself.)

It is only after Wapagepundaka and his wife return, with game, that the final two persuasive incidents occur. In each, food is presented to the parents, first to the father (lines 767–772), then to the mother (lines 797–805). And in presenting the food, only the wife speaks (as is appropriate in such a formal situation, when a new husband—who in any case refrains from speaking to his parents-in-law—brings food as proof of his commitment to the marriage). In turn, the fact that each of the parents ultimately accepts this food is a confirmation of the suitability in their minds of the union between their daughter and Wapagepundaka. The last conversation we hear in the story is that between the young woman and her mother. The daughter repeats for the last time Wapagepundaka's protest: "But despite what's being said about me now, I didn't come here to kill all of you. Not at all." And the mother confirms this with her "All right," in the end accepting the truth of the warrior's declaration.

7

Madyuta's Story about Tapoge

I first heard the story called "Tapoge the Bow Master" from the leader Madyuta, who told it to his wife, Ugaki, and me on a hot dry afternoon in the Kalapalo settlement of Aifa. Madyuta had recently heard this story from his sister's husband, a Kuikuro man descended from the Tafununu Lake Community mentioned in the narrative. For several years this man had gone during the dry season with his younger relatives to farm beside Tafununu. When he visited the Kalapalo just prior to such a trip, as a gift to his hosts Madyuta's brother-in-law told the story of Tapoge. (He may also have been occupied with the thought of encountering strangers there, since he asked me if I had seen any people as I flew over the lake on my way to Brasilia.) About a month later, Madyuta asked me to have him record it. My tape recorder was present because Madyuta, who had often helped me transcribe other people's stories, wanted me to have a recording of one of his own (very rare) performances. Ugaki's daughter-in-law Kefesugu and two of her adult sons (the leader Muluku and his younger unmarried brother Faidyufi, who had heard this story at the same time as had Madyuta) were also listening to his version of the story.

The setting was typical of Kalapalo occasions for storytelling. People were relaxing after a day's work, waiting for Kefesugu's husband (who had gone fishing that day) to return from a nearby lake. Ugaki and I sat together in the doorway while Madyuta drew up a wooden seat and began his story. While Kefesugu silently attended to the boiling manioc soup during the telling (she was extremely shy before her mother-in-law), the others frequently interrupted. Muluku even tried to take over the storytelling. Such interruptions and comments often occurred in such informal family settings, where listeners often prompted their relatives to add special details that had been passed over.

The story begins with the teller's separation of the narrative from some previous talk about where we are going to put the tape recorder,

when he says to me "Listen now." Unlike Ahpĩū, who entered directly
into his story of Wapagepundaka, Madyuta begins his narrative with an
introductory orientation, letting us listeners know who the main characters are, and why they are significant:

So listen.
There was a person called Januasi.
   Tapoge was still a youth.
     Still a youth.
      Tapoge.   5
Januasi had already taken a wife from the Lake Community
people.
     Yes, the Lake Community.
     That's all.
However, Januasi made his plantation at a place far from
there,
     his plantation.   10
      Yes, his plantation.
     Where he grew a lot of corn, manioc, and all kinds of plants.
So, his son was very beautiful.
     Beautiful
"Child of mine," he said to his son.   15
     "Child of mine," he said.
     "Tomorrow we'll go look at our crops, tomorrow."
"All right," he answered.
     "If you say so, we'll go."
      "Let's go."   20
But before they had a chance to do that, his brothers-in-law
spoke up:
     "Did we hear correctly you two are going?" they asked.
      "Did we hear correctly you two are going?" they asked.
     "That's just what I said," he answered.
"You must not go any longer," they answered. "You must not go
any longer. Since you need to guard this son of yours all the time,
this son of yours.   25
     Your son."
"You're wrong," he answered.
     "You're wrong.
Does anything like that ever happen to us?
I've never had any problem even though we always go there.
That's how it is."   30
     "You're wrong. Why do you insist in going against our wishes?"
"Now listen to me," he said to his younger brothers.

Tapoge's uncle spoke.
"Listen to me now."
"Let's go with our nephew's father.   35
    Be with our nephew's father."
  "Let's go," they answered.
    "Let's go."
"We always have to watch out that our nephew isn't murdered
by fierce people.
    We have to be careful."   40
  "All right," they answered.
    "If you say so, let's go.
      If you say so, let's go."

Januasi's brothers-in-law appear concerned about the fact that he persists in traveling to this distant plantation. Now that their nephew is
grown, they are worried that he will be captured and killed by *angikogo*.
But Januasi isn't worried and argues with them about the danger. Here,
early in the story, we hear his rude and unthinking voice conflicting
with the careful judgments of his wife's relatives. The Kalapalo is particularly forceful because Januasi rather coarsely dismisses the concern
of the others, placing his own experiences before theirs. Here are some
examples of how evidentiality (words of denial, coupled with doubt and
insistence evidentials) is used to such strong effect, in lines 28–30:

afïtï.
"You're wrong.
ungualekuguma tisiñalï!
Does anything like that ever happen to us?
tipakinafagitse tsitselï pokiti. la.
I've never had any problem even though we always go there. That's
how it is."

The brothers-in-law then reply with nearly equal force and discuss
what to do; the oldest proposes they accompany Januasi, and the others
agree. From the start, Januasi's argumentative, disrespectful voice com-
pares unfavorably with the casual ease with which the younger brothers-in-law validate their older brother.

Then when dawn appeared, food for their journey was prepared.
When it was ready, they all left.   45
  "Let's go," they said.
    "Let's go."
"We'll travel by canoe," he said. [That is, the oldest brother
spoke.]
  "By canoe.
    By canoe," he said.   50

"As for your nephew and I," the father answered, "we'll go in
that other direction. That way. By the trail."
   "No, it's too far that way. Too far.
   It would be better if we all went together in one canoe, all
together," they said.
      "All together."
   "All right," he answered.   55
      "All right."
So they went away, shooting many fish as they did so *tsik, tsik.*
   Now their spirits rose,
      they were smiling while they did that.
         They kept shooting fish.   60
   One of them went, tsik.
      Another of their party *tsik.*
         They were smiling at one another.
"Let's roast the fish right now, come on," their older brother
said.
      "Come on, let's roast the fish right now," he said.   65
   Tapoge was with them,
   Tapoge.
So they ate. "As soon as you get here you'll eat."
   Their nephew was still with them. Then as they all ate,
"Listen to what I say," he told them, the father spoke.   70
"Listen to what I say."
"What's that?"
"Since we're getting close, your nephew and I will begin
walking. We're getting close."
"No. We must all go together as I said before, all together.
   Your son does have to be carefully guarded all the time," he
   answered.   75
      Then that was all. "Why are you going against our wishes?"
      he said. "Why?
It's best that we stay together the way we started out. All
together.
Now we have to watch out and stop them if they try to murder
your son."
"All right," he said.   80
Then they all went on.
That was all. "We're going now," he said to them. "We're going
now."
   "Go then," the oldest answered. "Go then.
   You must come to us right away if they try to murder your son.
   They'll want to kill you both.
      They'll kill you both.   85

We certainly don't want them to do that to you and capture your
son," they told him.
"Nothing like that will happen," he answered.
   So he left ahead of the others.
They went upstream in that direction, while he followed the
path.
        Those two walked away along the path. Along the path.   90

When Januasi's brothers-in-law suggest the group travel by canoe, he
wishes to go by way of the trail. But he agrees when they tell him it is
too far that way. Later, in lines 70–79, Januasi argues again and more
forcibly with his brothers-in-law, even to the extent of anticipating disagreement. Januasi begins by saying, *tsatue ukili*, "Listen to what I say"
(line 70), a formulaic utterance that indicates deep sincerity and a commitment to the proposition in the statement that follows. This utterance functions as an appeal to validation by the listeners. Januasi tells
the others that he wants to separate from them now, since they are
"getting close." The brothers-in-law reply angrily (lines 79–80), and Januasi appears to agree they should stay together. In this segment, the
brothers-in-law seem to feel that by trying to go back on a prior agreement, Januasi has failed to commit himself to the best interests of the
entire group. But soon after (in line 82), for the fourth time he states his
wish to leave the brothers and go his own way, and so (this being the
fourth time), the brothers let him go, cautioning him to be careful and
to hurry back if danger threatens. Januasi, however, is (if anything) even
more smug than before, dismissing their concerns with the comment
"Nothing like that will happen," using the disagreement evidential *ata*.

   afïtïata nïgifeke
   "Nothing like that will happen," he answered.
   They walked on *tititi*, while the others kept doing as before, *tsik*
they kept shooting at fish.
      They were killing a great many fish,
         his uncles were.   95
Then they went on as before. As for that relative of theirs, the
father was up ahead when they arrived at the path that led to the
place where water was drawn,
at the path that led to the place where water was drawn.
      "It looks as if they were right after all." Being first, the father
      ran on quickly until he reached the path ahead of his son *tikii*.
         "Child of mine, I feel someone's here," he said.
         "Child of mine."   100
      "That must mean your uncles have already arrived.
      Your uncles have already arrived."
   "Have they?" he answered. "Have they?"

"Yes," his father said to him. "Yes, those men up there are
    your uncles.
We shouldn't wait any longer to go see," he said to him.   105
But his son didn't hurry at all.
    He didn't.
        He stayed some distance from his father.
So then they went closer to the water's edge.
    They could see some other men. "See what's there, my
        child.   110
I don't understand why you should feel frightened of that.
There's no reason. I assure you, what that is up there is the older
brother's bow, adorned with a piece of the tail of a yellow-
headed cacique bird. [These were trophies.]
    Adorned with a piece of the tail of a yellow-headed cacique
        bird.
And that's their younger brother up there, whose bow is
adorned with a piece of toucan's tail,
        the tail of a toucan.   115
That's what your uncles have done up there, with pieces of the
tail of the cacique with the red rump."
"You're wrong," Tapoge answered. "You're wrong.
    You're all wrong about this. These aren't my uncles, no,
        they're not.
        They're still far away.
            They're still far away."   120
"You're wrong. I'm not waiting any longer to go,
    I'm not waiting any longer to go."
                                    ["The father spoke," I said.]
    The father spoke.
        "I'm not waiting any longer to go."   125
His father glanced behind him.
    The path must have been clear and wide.
    He was like this [Madyuta showed us how the father walked
    with his head turned around, that is, very carelessly],
        he was looking behind him.
Finally, as it gradually widened into a place like this, he reached
the plaza.   130
    "Now, children, children," he said. "Children," he said.
    "Children, there wasn't any reason to take a share of what your
    nephew shot, was there? Since we haven't joined you yet," he
    said.
    Bok. The others stopped talking.
                                    [I said, "The fierce people."]
        The others stopped talking.   135

"Those who have come by the path are really hungry as they
join you, your nephew and I," he said to them.
"Fuuh, hoh, kaw kaw," they shouted out.
Tetutu, so, he ran away,
                              [I said, "His son ran away."]
    his son ran away,   140
        tututu. The father had not taken his bow with him.
        His bow.
Tititi tutututu so he was done for.
                              [I said, "The father died."]   145
        Tutututututututu. . .

When Januasi and Tapoge arrive at the distant settlement, the father
is surprised to find that people have arrived ahead of them. He rashly
identifies these people as his brothers-in-law, using both the introspective evidential expletive *um* ("it looks like") and the counter-expecta-
tion evidential *maki* in lines 98 and 101. The original Kalapalo:

um! andemaki. fotugui, isuwï itsakilï, fotugui tikii.
"It looks as if they were right after all." Being first, the father ran on
quickly until he reached the path ahead of his son *tikii.*
andemaki isoko etifïgïlefa.
"That must mean your uncles have already arrived."

Now, in line 103 Tapoge speaks for the first time, expressing uncertainty
about what his father has just said (using the uncertainty evidential
nika):

anika nïgï. anika.
"Have they?" he answered. "Have they?"

The father responds with more assurance, even impatiently: "Yes, those
men up there are your uncles. We shouldn't wait any longer to go see"
(lines 104–105). This tentative disagreement between father and son
becomes more fixed when, in lines 110–116, the father insists that
what he sees are the decorated bows of his bow master brothers-in-law.
For example, in line 112 he again uses the evidential *nafa*, insisting that
he is correct in how he interprets what he sees:

ekunafa elei, efiñano tafakugunafa egey kwi igoketïfïgïpi.
"There's no reason. Believe me, what that is up there is the older
brother's bow, adorned with a piece of the tail of a yellow-headed cacique bird."

In the lines that follow, Tapoge (who is beginning to take shape as a
distinct person) directly disputes his father's interpretation of what is

going on. By his caution and his responses to his father in this section, he shows himself to have the acute sensory awareness that, among other features of his character, indicates his potential to be a true bow master. Tapoge's father, on the other hand, continues to resist his son and stupidly advances forward, not only weaponless but actually trying to joke about their being late. He walks right into the enemy camp and is killed.

> When the sun was here, at its height,
>   "Ha ha ha," now he heard his uncles laughing.
>   "Here are my dear uncles." *Tuk*, right away he ran back the way
> he had come.
>   *Tututututu.*

With a shift in focus marked by Madyuta's reference to the sun being at its height, attention turns to Tapoge and his relations with his uncles, considerably more developed than his feelings toward his father. Tapoge's subsequent development as a warrior significantly takes place in the presence of these uncles. Tapoge's later actions seem less a consequence of his mourning his father's death than connected to his concern to serve his uncles when they decide to retaliate.

> As he went on, he saw that they walked with tightly drawn
> bows.   150
> With their bows kept drawn in his direction,
> with their arrows aimed at him.
> "There's a club carrier, a fierce person."
>   They looked at him,
>   and they saw his shell collar. "Oh. That's our nephew," they
> said.   155
>   "'Let's wait,' weren't we saying that to him?" he asked.
>   "'Let's wait,' weren't we saying that?"
> "Our nephew's right here. Let's go join him," he said.
> "Uncle. We aren't well with Father," Tapoge said. "Uncle. I'm
> certain Father is no longer alive."
>   "'Let's wait,' we were saying that, weren't we?" his uncle
> said.   160
> "Let's go." They left the canoe and entered the path.
>   They entered the path.
> *Ti ti ti ti.*
>   A short distance.
>   "We should paint ourselves here right now, we'll paint
> ourselves with charcoal."   165
> That was done. They were with Tapoge. Tapoge.

When they were finished, they walked to the path that led to
the place where water is drawn.
    To the path that led to the bathing place.
"I'll go first from now on." That was Tapoge speaking. "From now
on I'll be the first. So I'll be able to see ahead," he said.
        "So I'll be able to see ahead."   170
    "All right," his uncles answered. Then they came on the path,
tiki. From that spot the fierce people's footprints continued to the
house.
    Tapoge examined them. "This isn't what I thought. These look
like some of my own people," he said to them.
        "Our people, not yours."
                                        ["Who spoke?" I asked.]   175
        Tapoge spoke.
                                        ["Tapoge spoke," I said.]
        Yes.
    "These are people just like us.
        These are people just like us.   180
            My own people."
["Those were the fierce people, weren't they?" Ugaki asked.]
        Indeed they were.
        "See for yourselves. Their footprints go over from here
        up that way. Look at them.   185
            These are the stinking people.
                From now on you'll call them 'stinking people.'
        They are finished," he said to them.
        "So they will remain, I say.
        Even though they are my own people, I say, let us remain as
        we people are. Even though they are my own people.   190
        They should be made to chew on wild gourds and nothing
        more," he said. "Wild gourds.
            Until their stomachs are filled with wild gourds. They will
            chew hard on them.
        That must be what we'll eat,
            our food."
        "Let's do it."   195
            That was all.

Upon their arrival, the uncles mistake Tapoge for an enemy but correct
themselves when they see that he wears the distinctive shell ornament
used by men of their own group. From their point of view, he is different
from Januasi, whom they treated more as a stranger come to live among
them than one of them. Tapoge is clearly one of them. They all decide

to paint themselves with charcoal, a prelude to battle. Madyuta takes care to emphasize that Tapoge, too, painted himself this way, thereby declaring his willingness to kill. In what follows, Tapoge begins to more actively take on this warrior-killer identity by telling his uncles he will lead the way, "so I'll be able to see ahead." He does this even though they are experienced bow masters. In what follows his warrior agency becomes even more powerful.

But now the horror of his choice begins to become apparent. He identifies the footprints of the enemy as belonging to people of his own (that is, his father's) group; use of the exclusive "we" (*tisuge*) is strikingly apparent in this section, because he is clearly insulting and cursing that same "we." In lines 186–187 he uses the expression "stinking people," calling his father's killers enemies by use of a particularly insulting expression. In line 188 Tapoge first curses the enemy by declaring that they "are finished." In line 189 he curses them even more strongly, saying *latafa itsanini*, "So they will remain (as we know them to be)." (Here, the third-person pronoun is used.) In other words, they will die as they lived (without having a chance to change their ways). And finally, the grotesque business about wild gourds, in which the exclusive "we" appears once more. Madyuta suggested that the enemy corpses were to lie unburied with the wild plants twining in and out of their rotted stomach cavities.

"But who should be the advance guard?" one of them asked.
    "It would be best for you to wait here," Tapoge answered. [He starts to line them up in position.]
    "All right."
    "It would be best for you to wait here," he said. "All right."   200
    "It would be best for you to wait here," he said. To the youngest brother. "It would be best for you to wait here."
      To this one, to their fourth brother.
      The fifth one in their group, the last one, was Tapoge.
        Tapoge.
    "I don't think they ever come with their arrows pointed.   205
So don't cry out.
That's just how they trick people.
    Believe me, that's how we are," he said.
      "Believe me, that's how we are when we're on our way to murder people.
To another settlement, this way," he said.   210
"'*Hoh hoh hoh*,' we call when we go to drink [the utterance is an aggressive signal to enemies that they have been seen; this is the "trick"],

'*Hoh hoh hoh.*'
    When we do that we're moving about with our bows drawn,"
    he said to them.
"This way," he said to them.
    "This way," he said. "This way. This way. This way.   215
    This very way," he said to them. [As he speaks, Madyuta
    gestures to suggest a man deftly shifting his drawn bow in
    various directions.]
"So that way they can frighten you and me. It's a trick.
    They move very quickly.
    Very quickly."
"All right." One by one they agreed with what he told them.   220
    "All right.
    All right."
Then they waited, and waited, and waited for the others to come.
When the sun was setting, just as it is now,
    "*Kah kah kah koh,*" the others shouted loudly.
                        [Ugaki asked, "The fierce people?"]   225
    They did indeed.
    Now they were coming to drink.
                        ["All right, I understand," she answered.] 230
Once again, "*Kah kah kah kah koh!*"
Once again, four times.
"They're really coming now!" he shouted. "They're really
coming now!
    There they are!"
    Hum hum, one of them came out of the water. The first one
    came out of the water.
He came toward them just as Tapoge said he would, with drawn
bow, with drawn bow.   235
                        [Ugaki asked, "A bow master?"]
    The bow master came.
"*Hoh hoh hoh hoh hoh.*" This was how he was coming. "*Hoh
hoh hoh,*" with his bow drawn.
    He walked by them one by one. [Faidyufi asked, "Others were
    coming from the watering place?" Muluku, who knew this
    story as well as Madyuta, spoke up: "Yeah."]
Next the one behind him came in their direction,   240
    the one behind him came in their direction. Each man's bow
    was tightly drawn. The others stayed where they were for a
    long time without moving. But they were beginning to feel
    frightened of the fierce people.

"*Hoh.*" Those people rose up from the water.

Now they were frightened. They kept shooting at them . . . they [Ugaki reminded him, "Watching them." Madyuta laughs as Ugaki corrects him: "Kept watching them"] kept watching them from their hiding places. For a long time all of that group of men remained still with their bows drawn.

That was a trick. [Muluku said, "That was a trick, what they did." Excitedly, Muluku tries to tell the story: "Their arrows were aimed at the other men as they walked by. But just after that one of those men who had come up from the water . . . he looked, '*Hoh,*'' and one of Tapoge's group jumped with fright." Madyuta regains control of the story.]

Bok! Someone jumped with fright, and began to shoot wildly, without aiming. All the time this way.   245

[Faidyufi asked, "At that same man, the fierce person?"]
Yes, the fierce person.

[Muluku, still anxious to show off what he knows: "They weren't anything special. But he was a bow master."]

" 'Let's wait a while longer,' didn't we just say that?"

["Tapoge spoke?" I asked.]   250

Tapoge spoke as the other man ran back.

" 'Let's wait a while longer,' didn't we just say that?" he said.

"Why aren't you paying attention to what I say?" he asked.

Tururu. He ran back because a fierce person was still up in the plaza.

["Still in the plaza," I said.] ["Still there," Ugaki said.]   255

Only one more had yet to pass by them. They still stood like this, with drawn bows, because they were still afraid.

But now some fierce people kept going this way, toward the water's edge.

["When they reached the others, they tried to shoot them," Muluku said.]

But unfortunately for them, the moment they reached Tapoge and the others, they couldn't shoot them even though they tried.

["How did that happen?" Ugaki wanted to know.]   260

"*Kah kah,*" *buhruru* some of them scattered to one side. *Tsuhruru,* "*Kah kah kah.*" Shouting, others scattered to the other side. Those by the water's edge *tuk! tuk! tsok! tsok!*

[Faidyufi, excited, spoke up: "Those men really knew how to fight. There were bow masters among them. Tamakafi was one they killed. Listen." "Yes," I said.]

Mbisuk! Those by the bathing place were all done away with.

[Muluku laughed and said, "Just as they'd planned."]   265
Then on the other side, *tuk*. "*Kah kah kah kah kah kah*" as
they shot them all.
   Tuk tuk tuk.
Their arrows were used up. The bow masters' arrows were all
gone. "Every one of our arrows is gone.
   We don't have any arrows left at all," they said to him.
   "We don't have any arrows left at all."   270
"Every one of our arrows has been used up," they said.
   "Our arrows are all used up."
   "I still have a few," he said. (That's right, I'm wrong about that.)
   "All right," he answered. "All right."
   "Let me next," he said to them. "Let me next," Tapoge
spoke.   275
"Let me next," he said to them.
Then Tapoge took up a heavy branch—a war club—and clubbed
them *tuk tuk tuk tuk tuk tuk*.
   He clubbed a good many of them.
   There were only five of them left, five.
                                    ["Five," I said.]   280
   Five.
Those on the other side *tuk tuk tuk tuk* were all gone. They
were done away with.
   "That's enough," he said to them. "This way, those who are left
will go away to tell about us.
   This way, those who are left will go away to tell about us."
That's all.   285

At the onset of the final episode, Tapoge plans the ambush, explaining
strategy to his uncles and essentially giving away the battle strategy of
the fierce people, "his" people. Here too is that bitter exclusive "we."
His description and justification of the entire plan is validated by the
others in lines 220–222; again we might think that these people who
are close because they agree with one another about interpretations and
goals contrast with Januasi and his brothers-in-law, who were never successful at living as a moral community.
   As the story is about to end with the slaughter of the enemy, Muluku
and Faidyufi intrude more and more in the telling of the story; their
agitation anticipates the final murderous blows of Tapoge himself. But
before that happens, Tapoge even more assertively acts like a true warrior by criticizing his uncles for their impatience after they begin shooting prematurely. Although younger than they are, he is at last their
leader. Finally, Tapoge's ability to fully act like a warrior is achieved

when he kills his enemies with a war club, arrogantly permitting five men to live so that "those who are left will go away to tell about us."

The Development of a Warrior Consciousness

In his version of the story of Tapoge, Madyuta seems to focus upon how the warrior attempts to clarify his ambiguous identity. For this reason, my discussion of the narrative has emphasized developmental relations and the contrasts in voices that emerge in Januasi's conversations with others. Most of the narrative consists of a meticulous step-by-step portrayal of the events leading to Tapoge's particular manner of assuming the warrior identity, which occurs in connection with making fixed his obligations to a certain community. These steps or phases in the story conclude with Tapoge asserting loyalty to his uncles at the expense of his father's kin. Tapoge is presented in an ambiguous light because his father is said to have married into a Lake Community group. So part of Tapoge's clarification of identity is a process through which he becomes firmly associated with the Lake Community. Also involved is his maturation, by which I mean his manner of enacting the potential achieved through his puberty training. A third element in his clarification of identity involves achievement of an intensive agency that becomes increasingly more powerful throughout the story, until he becomes not just any bow master but a memorable person, someone whose story will be told to those who are yet to be born. The story concludes in a strongly authoritative mode, suggesting that Tapoge is not simply an especially skilled warrior like his uncles but a man with distinctive moral authority, a leader. And yet, in another warrior biography (the story about Tamakafi, Tapoge's son-in-law) we learn that Tapoge's identity was never fully clarified, to the extent that when he died, he was still considered a foreign *angikogo*.

Evidentiality in "Tapoge the Bow Master"

Both the warrior actions of Tapoge and the incompetent behavior of his father, Januasi, are highly speech-centered. And as we've seen, what is special in this regard is that their conversations with one another and with their relatives are replete with various forms of evidentials (such as *afïtï; nafa; maki; nika; tafa*) and the conventional responses ("All right"; "I see"; "Is that what you say?"; "I can't agree") that indicate validation or disapproval of propositions. In this story, evidentials are constitutive of independence, individuality, and open conflict (Januasi and his brothers-in-law), but in other cases (involving Tapoge and his uncles), they help to form some of the most intense kinds of solidarity. In all cases, claims are being made about shared interpretations of experience. Moral boundaries and personal allegiances are being drawn through these claims.

Motivated Number

A numerical pattern of nine connected events is achieved by the separate contexts in which Tapoge reveals himself through speech in this story. As we've seen in the second part of the story of Wapagepundaka, Kalapalo use this number in extended narrative to indicate a process leading to successful accomplishment of a goal. When a "motivated" number of instances is reached (I often noticed both tellers and listeners counting on their fingers), reinforcement, intensification, completeness are the results (in the case of things done, four times, or during a long story, eight times) and ultimate success and closure (when things are done, five or nine times). That a certain action is repeated, or that people—through activity—are themselves part of a pattern, is a significant matter in any Kalapalo psychological description. In Januasi's case, his need to travel alone and in his own fashion is only agreed to after his fourth insistent request. As for Tapoge, the ninth activity culminates a process of increasingly intensified warrior action, until he actually has the chance to kill *angikogo*.

CHAPTER

8

Kudyu's Story
about Tamakafi

The biography of Tamakafi is that of a bow master who had once
been married to Tapoge's daughter. It is a story whose events took
place many years after Tapoge died, and in it, we learn how that warrior
died and how his death influenced what happened to his former son-in-
law. Taken together, the two stories seem rather like a grim family
history.

While still a young bow master, Tamakafi was asked by his uncle to
guard him during a trip to cut arrow cane. In fact Tamakafi's uncle (a
man named Afiguata) is taking him to this very dangerous place in order
to have him killed by the fierce people, because the hero has been having an affair with the older man's wife. Tamakafi is aware of his uncle's
intentions, as is his mother (who warns him against going by reminding
him of his ominous dreaming). He calls together his friends, who join
him so that they "may all die together" in battle. Along the way, as the
men travel to the place where they will cut arrow cane, various bad
signs appear to them. Dismissing them, Tamakafi persists in traveling
to the arrow cane place, where he is eventually killed along with his
companions.

Listen well now.
His uncle was Afiguata, his uncle,
  his uncle
Tamakafi used to visit his wife.
  Afiguata's wife.   5
He would paddle *po po po* across the lake to visit her.
    That very large lake.
                         ["What's it called?" I asked.]
    Tafununu.
                         ["Ah, Tafununu," I said.]   10
      Tafununu.
Kugufi. That's where his uncle made his house.

Afiguata's settlement.
     At Kugufi.
While his nephew Tamakafi lived at the place called Tefuku.   15
     By the lake.
The other place was called Kugufi.
     He would cross over to the other side.
     He kept going over there to her.
          He went to her over there.   20
     Since he kept doing that, his uncle grew jealous, and so he took
     Tamakafi to the *angikogo* to have him killed.
          To have him killed.
He was throwing up the medicines he used to clean out his
stomach,
pupupu he was using medicines to clean his stomach.
     He was doing that before dawn, while he warmed himself by
     a fire.   25
          It was before dawn, as the day began.
When *pupupu* his uncle came paddling toward him.
     His uncle had put a great pile of arrows in his canoe before he
     started out. He had put arrows there, *bii . . . tik.*
     He could see Tamakafi as he paddled over.
     "There's the kid.   30
          There he is."
     He was coming closer.
     "Why is Uncle coming over here?" Tamakafi said.
          "Why is Uncle coming over here?" he said.
               "What for?"   35
"Kid," his uncle called to him as he pulled to the shore.
"Kid," his uncle said to him.
          "What," he answered.
     "As you can see, it's you I've come to, I have.
          It's you I've come to."   40
     "What do you want me for?"
     "So we can go collect some arrows for me.
          My arrows."
     "I have to think about that. I'd usually say yes, Uncle.
          Usually I'd say yes.   45
I feel terrible, very badly.
     Very badly.
This happens especially at night when I'm entirely surrounded
by peccaries.
     By peccaries.
          By peccaries, *tuk* who were biting me all over.   50

Other times while I sleep," he told him, "some Yamurikumalu
women carry me away.
   And they beat me.
    I've been beaten.
That's just how I am.
   Like that."   55
"No, no. That has nothing to do with you,
   that's nothing."
   "Uncle, really it must not happen.
    I can't do it," he answered.
    "We'll go some other time."   60
   "No, kid," he answered. "Even so, go this time."
He was taking him away, because he had been his wife's lover.
   "No, even so let's go together. Even so let's go together."
"All right, as you say, let's go," Tamakafi answered.
   "All right, as you say, let's go.   65
   You wait here. You wait here.
    I'll go get my arrows, my arrows."
   "All right," he answered.
   So Tamakafi went away.
    Boh his thighs were huge, his calves, and his arms were also
    enormous.   70
Listen.
Tamakafi is his name, Tamakafi.
Then right away he went into his house.
   "Mother," he said.
    "Mother."   75
   "What?" she said to him.
   "Uncle needs to take me somewhere," he said to her, "Uncle
does."
   "Where does he want to go? Where does he want to go?"
   "Far away. To get arrows. To get arrows.   80
    To get arrows."
   "That shouldn't happen," she answered.
   "Let him stay as he is," she said.
   "Think about how badly you've been sleeping at night, how
badly you've been sleeping."
"No, Mother," he answered.   85
   "That's how I'll be. That's how I'll be.
   Those who'll come after him will have something to tell their
children about what's going to happen to me.
    Those who'll come after him."
So his mother wept.

"Don't cry yet, Mother.   90
    Don't cry yet.
    Wait until later if you want to do that.
Otherwise the tears you shed for me will wet my arrows," he told
her.
    He told her.
Then *tiki*. A cousin of his came outside.   95
    Just as he did that, Tamakafi was carrying out his arrows.
    "Well, Bow Master," that man said to Tamakafi.
        "What?" he answered.
    "Are you going somewhere?" he asked. "Are you going
    somewhere?"
    "Yes, Cousin. Yes, Cousin.   100
    You see me doing this because our old man is taking me right
    now to get his arrows. To get his arrows."
    "I'll be there with you. I'll be there with you.
    Otherwise you would miss me if you died apart from me," his
    cousin said.
        That cousin of his was Waga.
                    [I asked, "Waga? That was his name?"]   105
        His name is Waga.
        A cousin of Tamakafi.
                    ["He also was a bow master?" I asked.]
        He also was a bow master.
        Has someone already told you about him?   110
                    ["They haven't," I answered.]
So listen.
"All right," Tamakafi said.
Then *tiki* another one as well.
    "Bow Master, where are you going?" he asked.   115
    "To get some arrows for myself," he answered.
        "Our old man is taking me away now to get some arrows.
        To find some arrow cane."
    "I'll be there with you," he answered.
    Let me think of his name . . . his name was Kafagakati.   120
        A bow master.
                    ["Also a cousin of his?" I asked.]
        Also a cousin of his.
"Where are you going?" again someone else.
    "Our old man is taking me away now."   125
    "Well, let's all join our older brother.
    Otherwise our older brother would be lonely if we weren't all
    dying together. We would be dying apart from him. We would
    die apart from him.

Let's all go together," he said to them.
   "Let's all go together.
   We'll all be there with our older brothers."   130
"As always, we agree with you."
   "Certainly. Let's all go together.
   This way those who'll come after him will really have
   something to tell their children about what's going to happen to
   us, about what's going to happen to us," Tamakafi continued.
      He shivered *pupupupu* while he said that.
      He was trembling with grief.   135
"Let's go, Kid," his uncle said to him.
   "Let's go, Uncle," he answered.
   Pok pok uhpok, they got into the canoe.
   And they all paddled away after that.
      Pu pu pu pu pu.   140
"It looks like my son is going to die," his mother kept saying.
   She'll know when the time comes by the *atanga* flutes, the
   atanga flutes.
      The *atanga* flutes.
Out toward the middle of the lake, out toward the middle of the
lake.
   As they were going that way some *sahundu* fish came toward
   them, some *sahundu*.   145
   Tik Tamakafi shot an arrow directly at it.
   When he did that *mbuh* the fish fled with the arrow in its side,
   popopo and it shook the arrow off as it fled.
   He speared it.
"Leave it, Kid," his uncle said to him. "Throw it away."   150
                              ["The *sahundu*?" I asked.]
   "Let it be as it is," Tamakafi answered. Yes, the *sahundu*.
      "Throw it away," his uncle said. "Let it be as it is."
   "What happened was my arrow *tsuik* sliced right here through
   its head."
      He was lying.   155
      He was angry.
   "All right," his uncle answered.
Popopopo and so they paddled into a creek,
   They paddled into a creek, *popopopo*,
      that meandered around and around.   160
         When they had gone only a very short way on that creek,
         tikii,
   "Let's eat here, Kid."
      "All right," he answered.
      "As you wish."

Kambe with his catch of *sahundu*.

He wanted them to eat there.   165
He wanted them to do that at that place since there was a
campground there.
Tuk! The dead fish exploded.
   "Throw it away," his uncle said.
   "No, no. All that happened was its eyeball exploded.
       Its eyeball."   170
       Tamakafi was VERY angry.
          He was furious.
       So, he ate it.
Then someone else's food as well.
       Everyone's food exploded.   175
   "All right, let's have something to drink."
When they tried to drink,
it turned black. While they tried to do that.
   Yes, listen to that. And then someone else's drink seemed to
   turn to blood.
His uncle spoke up. "Kid," he said,   180
   "let's go back. Let's go back."
   "No, Uncle," he answered.
      "We can't go back now. Let's keep going, that's what you
      wanted to do. So let's go."
         The fierce people were probably coming to kill them, to kill
         them.
Tsuhtsuhzuhzuh then they pushed the canoe farther upstream
through the grass,   185
      they went upstream.
   "Let's go, Kid,
      Let's go."
   "All right," Tamakafi answered.
And so then they went on.   190
      That's all.
So listen.
   I'm asking you to say, "All right."
                                    ["All right," I said.]
Now at the arrow place, at the arrow cane place   195
   bah there was arrow cane all over.
      Those were the arrows he had spoken about.
Tsiuk, tsiuk, tsiuk, tsiuk, tsiuk.
   Finally they began to cut it down.
"I'll go over to the other side," one of them said.   200
   "I'll go over there.
      I'll go way over there," someone else said. "I'll go way over
      there to that side," someone else said. And so they spread out.

Tsiuk, tsiuk. He was cutting it down.

As for that uncle of his, his uncle Afiguwata, he on the other hand was still working where they had begun.

He was hacking it down much more slowly. *Tsiuk, tsiuk bok. Tsiuk bok.*   205

While he was doing that the others worked quickly, *tsiuk, tsiuk, tsiuk,* sharpening the tips of the cane before they set them down *kiuk, kiuk, kiuk, tak,* while he hacked it down *tsiuk tsiuk bok. tsiuk tsiuk tsiuk.*

They were doing that to get ready for the fighting that was to come. That's what they were expecting to happen.

Yes, what they they were expecting to happen.

All the relatives, the cousins were hacking down the arrow cane, *kiuk, kiuk.*

Then tsiuk, tsiuk.   210

Pok, tsiuk, tsiuk . . . they were cutting huge piles of it, many of which they sharpened.

While Tamakafi was doing this . . . say the name . . . she came. She, to grab him. ["Ñafïgï?" I asked.] Yes.

Buh, he threw her down.

Again she grabbed him.

Again he was throwing her down.   215

She grabbed him.

He kept throwing her down when she did that.

["Why did she come to him?" I asked.]

She had taken the form of Tamakafi's dream. He'll die soon, just as he had seen in his dream.

This was what he had been dreading all along.   220

What he'd been dreading all along.

This was what he had been dreading, he had been dreading.

When he was thoroughly exhausted, she left.

Then their uncle, who was far ahead of everyone, *tiki* stopped at a certain place.

He who had taken them all.   225

As he went along, *ti ti tikuu tik!* Suddenly his eyes were drawn to some footprints.

"These can't be the kids yet," he said.

"Not yet.

I'll stay here."

He sat down.   230

He sat down.

He sat there for a while as the sun moved farther and farther over in the sky.

"*Ngaa, ngaa,*" macaws.
    Macaws, "*Ngaa.*"
   Then *uuu*, the macaws flew his way.   235
      The macaws.
      As the macaws came toward him *uuu* he was following them
      with his eyes.
"Those macaws are coming this way," he told himself.
"They're coming this way." *Bik*, an *angikogo* shot up at them.
      "*Ngaa, ngaa.*"   240
   Tciu, ti ti ti, cik.
   The other man saw him miss and watched the arrow fall to the
   ground *mbonk*.
   Crouching way down the one who had shot went to pick up his
   arrow.
      To pick up his arrow *tiki*.
   Afiguata saw him miss and watched the arrow fall to the ground
   mbonk! Like that.   245
      "They must be right over there. Over there.
      I guess we're all done for now, the kids and I. We're all done
      for."
After a while *tititi tiki*, one of the cousins walked up.
      Tititi. Waga walked up.
         Tititi tiki.   250
"Uncle, you're here already?"
   "Where is your older brother? Where's your older brother?"
   "I don't know," Waga answered.
      "Back there still. Back there still."
   "We'll wait a while longer, he'll be here."   255
      "Sit down here."
   "All right." "Wait, your older brother will join you soon."
   He had no intention of telling him about the *angikogo*.
      None.
      He had no intention of telling him about them.   260
   Then shortly after, *tititi tiki* another one walked up to them.
   Boh he threw down a huge bundle *tidik*!
"Kid, I see you're still here, you." "Yes, as you see I'm still here,
Uncle," he answered.
      "I am, still."
   "Where's your older brother? Where's your older brother?"   265
   "Back there still.
      Wait, he'll be here."
         He sat down.
Then *tiki*.

Shortly after *titi*, again someone else walked up. 270
And again following right behind *tiki*.
"Here's your older brother. Here he is.
  Here he is."
Iiitik, someone else came up to them.
"Where's your older brother?" 275
  "He's still back there. He sounded as if he were wrestling
someone."
    This cousin had been working next to Tamakafi.
  "He's still back there. '*Buh, buh, buh,*' he was saying.
  Someone kept grabbing him, that's why he was doing that.
  He was being grabbed by someone. 280
    Yes, someone was grabbing him.
   'Buh buh,' he said.
  Wait, he'll be here soon."
  "His arrows must be heavy for him," he said to him.
    "His arrows are heavy for him." 285
Then after awhile, after a very short while Tamakafi came toward
them as had the others.
  Ti ti, he must have made the ground tremble as he came!
    He carried an enormous bundle of arrows for himself.
      Beautifully sharpened ones he carried.
He had smeared himself with this kind of stuff, with charcoal. 290
  He had smeared it over his face.
Then, *tidik*.
  "Kid, I see you're still here." His uncle spoke.
    "Kid, I see you're still here."
  "Yes," he answered. 295
  "I'm still here as you see.
    I am still."
  "Yes, you are," he answered.
  "Rest yourself here."
"All right, I'll rest awhile," Tamakafi said. "I'll rest awhile." 300
He looked around him at his cousins' arrows.
    They had all been carefully sharpened.
  "Their arrows are all ready," he said.
    His cousin's arrows had already been sharpened.
But his uncle *tsiu, tsiu bok tsiuk* was still working on his own
arrows. That's what he was still doing. 305
    He didn't know the right way to do it.
"I'm thinking about all this, Kid," he said.
  "Let's go, Uncle," Tamakafi said.
    "Let's go," he said.

"No, Kid, no," he answered. "Our people are in bad trouble, Kid. 310
     Bad trouble.
   The club people are right here."
"Where, Uncle?" he asked.
   "Some macaws came right here.
   I was standing right here.   315
        I was standing right here when the macaws came this way.
      As I was looking up at those macaws, *buh* someone shot
      at one.
   I'm certain they're right over there.
      Over there."
"Now they're done for!" Tamakafi said to him.   320
   So they all smeared themselves with charcoal.
      The cousins smeared themselves with charcoal. *Ti ti ti.*
   Next they uncovered their foreheads and smeared their hair
   with white clay, ngiih.
      And they tied on headdresses. Feathers of *pai*, the great
      razorbilled curassow.
So listen to what happened next.   325
Boh, Tamakafi carried a truly enormous bow,
      very tall indeed.
   His cousins' were made just like his.
      That's how those people did things.
         Those people were bow masters.   330
            Bow masters.
"Let's go," the uncle said.
      "Let's go."
   "All right," Tamakafi answered.
To his younger brothers, his cousins: "You must be very careful,"
he said.   335
        "Be sure to watch very carefully.
   As we are now, so we shall remain. As we are now, so we shall
   remain, since it's clear our old man has brought us here for just
   that reason. We agreed he should bring us here."
        "All right," the others said.
   "So it will be. Later those who come after him can tell their
   children about what's going to happen to us, what's going to
   happen to us."
There were some other people like us with them, Adyafi and his
companion.   340
      Two of them.
   Adyafi.
      That was his name, I'm sure.

Kambe in warrior's headdress, at a spear-throwing ceremony. Posto Leonardo Villas
Boas, 1966.

But they were ordinary people.
    I mean they weren't bow masters.   345
Well, listen.
They were ready.
"All right." Now they were going right toward the *angikogo*.
  "Here?" they asked.
  "No, go farther on."   350
  "Here?" they asked.
   "No, go farther on."
"That place over there must be it," Tamakafi's uncle told them.

Tamakafi had passed way ahead of those fools I spoke of
earlier—those ordinary people.
    Those foolish brothers.   355
    The brothers.
Now, he put down his load of arrows after he reached the place.
    His great load of arrows.
    His arrows were piled up high.
    His arrows.   360
Tututu, well, he stamped on the ground.
    Tututu "You Minnow, Minnow, Minnow, Minnow, Minnow," he
called out to them.[1]
    "Now, let's see you show yourself. Bring some arrows to me."
    That foolish man kept listening to everything he said.
And again, this time *tututu* "Now, Agakatu, Agakatu, Agakatu.   365
    Let's see you show yourself. Bring some arrows to me."
    He kept listening to him.
    He never answered with "*Fooh, fooh*."
Again *tututu*, "Now Agaga. Let's see you show yourself. Bring
some arrows to me," he said.
    Nothing at all from that one.   370
    Nothing at all from that one.
Once again *tututu*, but this time something happened.
    "Agakatu, Agakatu, Agakatu, Agakatu," he called to him.
    "Now, let's see you show yourself. My arrows . . ."
    "*Hoh, hoh, hoh*," he answered. *Bok*. Tamakafi readied
himself.   375
    He readied himself.
Tititititititi Tamakafi walked right up to them with his bow
drawn.
      He drew near.
    "Wait, wait, wait." His uncle.
    The one who had taken them.   380
    "Wait, wait, wait until he shoots his arrow."
    One of the strangers already lay fallen.
Then Tamakafi picked up his arrows. *Tik. Tik. Tik.*
    He broke them in half.
    Tsak. Tsak.   385
The sun was over here.
Someone else shot up toward it. *Buuh, nguku.*
    And the arrow rolled over and broke when he did that.
    Buh. Buh. There were many, many *angikogo* shouting,
many of them.   390

Quickly they ran together to form several groups *tutu*.
   They still hadn't come toward Tamakafi and the others.
Finally they did and everyone fought.
      They were really fighting now.
   They were really fighting because now they were all shooting
   at each other. *Kuh kuh kuh kuh,* crying out they finally
   did so.   395
Regarding that other person who was there, Adyafi.
   "Go away.
      Go back there in our canoe and get our people.
         Our people."
   "All right," he answered.   400
      "Let's go," he said to his younger brother.
         Pupupu they paddled away.
   When they had gone only a short way, and they were still close
   by,
   "You," he whispered.
   "Let's climb this tree. Let's climb this tree and watch them
   shoot at him."   405
      "All right," his brother said.
         Titi they climbed up a tree.
That's just what those fools did! They sat far out of the way,
watching Tamakafi.
   They never went to their settlement, no.
      Kuh kuh kuh kuh kuh kuh kuh. Now, he was shooting them
      while they sat there in the tree.   410
         Tamakafi was.
   He hadn't been shot by anyone yet.
   So, *kuh kuh kuh kuh kuh kuh.*
Now, there were some other, younger people. Look:
   Kufidya with Ogokenafa. Ogokenafa was the older brother.   415
   They were also bow masters.
   They were that man Tapoge's sons.
   As for them, they were moving around, setting up a bark net, a
   bark net. They were moving around with it killing fish. They
   never saw Tamakafi.
      Because as they drove the fish into their net,   420
         boh they were shooting at them.
      I remember seeing one a long time ago.
   There aren't any more around here.
      No more.
   Since people decided to give it up.   425

"Listen to our brother," he said to his partner. "Listen to our
brother.

Our brother is in bad trouble. Our brother."

"Let's go see.

  Let's go see."

"Usually I'd say yes, but I'm thinking about something." His
older brother spoke.   430

  "Usually I'd say yes.

But this time we shouldn't go there. We shouldn't go there.

  Don't you remember what happened long ago? I saw our older
  brother throw our old man's head away," he said to his
  brother. "He threw our old man's head away."

    About their father. He was talking about their father.

  That man, that man whom he was talking about . . . Tapoge's
  head had been thrown away. By Tamakafi, Tamakafi had
  done that.   435

"I thought I told you, 'You'd better wait for me here,' didn't I?
You foolish old foreigner," he said to him. [The son is telling his
younger brother what Tamakafi had said to their father, Tapoge.
For Tamakafi, Tapoge was *angikogo*.]

  (He had been killed by some *angikogo*, he had been killed.)

  They had decorated his head by putting oriole feathers in his
  ears.

    As he walked by Tamakafi had seen him. "Wait for me right
    here." But he didn't walk with him. So as he walked on
    alone the fierce people killed him.   440

      His son had heard him say that very clearly.

As they were hurrying along the trail *pupupu* there it was.

As they walked by they saw his head, which someone had set on
a pole.

  There was his head. There was his head.

"I thought I told you, 'You'd better wait for me,' didn't I? You
foolish old stranger." His children had heard him say that.   445

    At that time they were still very young.

"I thought I told you, 'You'd better wait for me,' didn't I?" while
he looked at their father's rotting skull.

  That was why they cursed him instead of going back.

"Let him remain as he is," his children were saying to each
other.

  "Remember when he scattered the remains of Father's
  head,"   450

he told him.

Listen to that.
"He scattered the remains of Father's head."
So listen.
Kuh kuh kuh kuh.   455
The sun was over here,
 when in the middle of it all someone's bow chord snapped *ndik*.
  His bow chord snapped, *ndik*.
 "Bow Master. Tamakafi," Waga spoke.
  "What?"   460
 "Look how badly this snapped.
  It's snapped through."
"Come here into my shadow. Come here into my shadow."
 "All right." He came toward him until he stood in Tamakafi's
shadow.
There he knotted his chord and was restringing his bow,   465
when someone shot him in the thigh. Someone shot him.
 He was shot through with arrows.
  Tik, tik, tik.
   That's what happened to him.
That's what someone did to him.   470
Tamakafi went in that direction. They weren't shooting at him.
On this, that, and every side he shot his arrows, that is how his
arrows went, that's what his arrows were like.
Tak tak that was how they went. He was a bow master.
 A bow master.
He was our ancestor.   475
 He was someone we tell about.
 The bow master.
While that was happening, Waga died.
 When he was shot.
"Too bad," Tamakafi said to himself.   480
"Isn't it sad about us, my younger brothers and me?" That's
what he kept saying to himself.
"Kid," someone said.
 Their uncle spoke.
 "I must be going. I'm going."
 "What? Why should you go now? Why should you go now?   485
 Wait. Don't go until later.
Since you brought me here, someone is bound to be killed.
 Someone will be killed."
 "All right," his uncle said.
Kuh kuh kuh kuh kuh. That was all.   490

["So it really was the uncle who was causing him to be shot?"
I asked.]
That's right.
He was a bow master.
But his uncle was just an ordinary person.
Kuh kuh kuh kuh. That was all.   495
"Kid," he said.
"I'd better go tell the others."
"No. Why should you go?
Why should you go?
Since you brought me here, someone is bound to be killed.   500
Someone will be killed."
"All right," he shamefully agreed.
Kuh kuh kuh atak,
Someone else's bow chord snapped, just as had the one
belonging to the other man.
He also came to Tamakafi, see. He also came close to him, see.
Two people had come to him. Two were shot. That was going
to happen to this one, too.   505
Two were already shot. That was also going to happen to this
other person.
While he was restringing his bow chord, the same thing happened
to him as to the others.
And when he tried to run and get more arrows, someone killed
him.
Afterward the stinking people ate him.   510
They ate him, the *angikogo* did, they ate him.
They were cannibals.
People. They ate people.
So listen well to what they did.
That's all.   515
"Too bad about my brothers, isn't it?" he then said.
"As we are, so we will remain. As we are, so we will remain.
As you see, it was for this reason that our old man brought us here
with him. For this reason. I remember."
Next Kafagikatu's bow chord snapped. There was still one left, see.
Tamakafi was alone when he came up to him.
"Say, Bow Master," he said.   520
"It's terrible. Look how my bow chord snapped apart."
"Is that how you talk about it?
Think carefully about how you used to eat the jelly left from
cooking fish," Tamakafi answered. "That can kill you.

Think of how you ate fish jelly.
  You liked to eat hot food.   525
  Monkey heads.
  It's the food you ate that did it."
    That's what he told him.
"I forgot about that," he told Tamakafi. "You spoke with your
back to people more than once."
"I forgot about that," he told Tamakafi. He was never aware of
that.   530
"If you turn away, an arrow will hit you."
"I forgot about that, that that made a difference, too.
Speaking with our backs to people."
That's all.
  [Kudyu's thirteen-year-old son, Katsïgï, asked from behind
  his seclusion wall: "Why was he saying that about their
                                speaking?"]   535
    Petulantly, his father answered:
    Because it affected how fiercely he fought.
      [Katsïgï, fearfully: "It was dangerous to do that."]
    It certainly was dangerous to do that.   540
Kuh kuh kuh.
"Kid," he said. The uncle spoke up.
  "I've got to go. I've got to go."
  "All right," he said.
  This time he was furious with his uncle. He was furious.
"All right," he said.   545
  "Go away.
I'll stay the way I am," he said. "I'll stay the way I am.
After all, I know you really brought me here with you for this
to happen, Uncle. Didn't you?" he said.
  "For this reason.
  For this reason.   550
What really happened was that you were jealous of me, so
you decided to take me away. I know that's what really
happened.
  You were jealous."
  [Kudyu whispers:] He had been his wife's lover.
    "You were jealous."
[Softly:] "I know why you really decided to take me away," he
said. "You decided to take me away.   555
  So get out of here," he said to him.
"I'll remain the way I am, with your sons.
  So I will remain.

Later I'll become a story for your offspring to tell to their
children."

He kept saying that to him, he was saying that to him.   560
When there was a pause in the fighting *kuh kuh kuh*, his uncle
came to him. His uncle came to him.

"Uncle, leave your arrows here for me."

"Yes, here they are." *Nduk.*

Tamakafi was still using some of his cousins' arrows, and he was
even shooting the *angikogo* with their own arrows.

He had used up all of his own arrows.

There he stayed, shooting the arrows of all those other
people.   565

Well, *kuh kuh kuh, kuh kuh kuh* this was a very large group of
fierce people. There were none of us.

Mbisuk he was the only one on his side.

There were three men in one group, and five in another.

That's how the fierce people were by then.   570

Mbisuk, one group of theirs was gone, since he had killed
them all.

Tamakafi had.

Yes.

So listen.

This is a story.   575

This is "The Killing of Tamakafi."

Tamakafi.

"Well. I've agreed to this."

Pupupu kuh kuh kuh kuh kuh kuh through the shower of arrows
he ran to look for Kapogagi.

His arrows were all used up. His arrows were all used up.   580

Mbiii that was why he went to look for Kapogagi, when just
then *mbiii tak*

That was Tamakafi's own bow chord snapping.

All of a sudden, suddenly.

When that happened he went forward to meet them.

His bow chord, one like this one here, *tik* had broken.   585

He was clubbed over and over again by one man after another
puhk puhk puhk. Mbah.

That's how the fierce people kill us.

"*Huu!*" That was just what they did as they went toward him.

Clubbing him, clubbing him, to club him.

And when they stood beside him to do that he ran away.   590

He ran away.

Through thick branches which he cracked apart with his chest.

Listen to what he was doing next.
He didn't know where he was going.
And he was out of his mind, he was out of his mind.   595
He was very thirsty now.
    He was very thirsty.
"There he goes!"
    They ran after him.
        While he ran away.   600
He ran into some mud, see. Some mud.
    Kulululu tsuhk, tsuhk, tsuhk. He went on until he sank up to
his chest, and he fainted.
The others came to him, the *angikogo* came.
    They were standing all around him.
    "Oh no! Did he get away, did you see where he went?"   605
Mbah they had wounds from his arrows all over their bodies.
        He had shot them all over.
    "Did he get away?" they asked.
After they had stood there for a long time,
    he began to pant, "*He he he.*"   610
        He was panting hard.
The others were just about to leave, the fierce people were
leaving,
when they heard him panting. "There he is. He's panting,"
someone said to the others.
    A fierce person spoke.
"All right, go look." The fierce person spoke.   615
"All right." There were the ones who could fly. *Bu bu bu.*
Three of them rose up in the air until one after another they
landed next to him.
So listen.
    "All right, go tell the others."
    Boh, one of them flew right back.   620
"Did you find anything?" the others asked.
    "He's there."
They all came up to him the way they do.
They all flew up to him *uuu* . . . and *bum* landed right next
to him.
He was out of his mind, and he could no longer see.   625
Next they lifted him up.
    They tried hard to carry him but he was just as heavy as a boulder.
        Very hard to carry.
        Very dangerous to carry.
            Very dangerous to do that.   630

They carried him very carefully because of that.
And then after they had rested awhile from carrying him they
continued to go back.
"Let's wait." They were almost out of breath.
   They were almost out of breath.
Then while they sat there,   635
  they were sitting all around him,
  they touched his arm.
  "Look at that thigh of his!" they told one another.
After awhile they felt stronger.
  "What shall we do with him now?" they said. "What shall we
do with him now?"   640
            [Katsïgï asked, "He couldn't run away?"]
He was still much too exhausted to do that.
      [Katsïgï asked again, "He was losing his strength?"]
That's right. He was weak because of what was happening
to him.
    "Let's wrestle him."   645
  "All right."
  "Because he's like this we'll throw him easily," that man
continued.
One of them grabbed him around his neck from behind. *Tuk*, he
grabbed him around his neck from behind. *Tuk. Boh bum*!
  He threw Tamakafi down.
  Once more he grabbed him around his neck from behind.   650
Buh tuk, buh tuk.
  Tamakafi was dying because they were breaking his body.
  His arms were enormous, has there ever been anything like
those arms?
    They were huge.
      He was Tamakafi.   655
      This is a story about what happened to him.
      A story.
Tuk. For the very last time. *Teh.* One of their beautiful people
approached to do what the others had done.
    A magnificent person who was still a child also wanted
    to try.
    This time he was going to try and kill him.   660
    He was going to try and kill him.
  "Come away with us.
  Come away with us."
It was the women, he wanted to show Tamakafi to them.
  To the women.

He wanted to show him to the women.   665
   To the women.
"No woman is going to see me!" he said to them.
   "The women aren't going to see me," he answered. *Tuk!*
   Tuk! He smashed the young man's chest.
   Tuk. Bom that fierce person fell down.   670
Next Agakatu came up to them. Agakatu.
   "Now, that's not how to deal with this *angikogo*.
   That's not how to deal with this *angikogo*."
He grabbed Tamakafi *buh tuk!*
And when Tamakafi kicked out with his calf the other man
fell over and his back broke. His back broke.   675
Tsik, tsik he walked with a limp forever after, people who saw
him said.
   It was Tamakafi who *tuk* had knocked him down, who had
   knocked him down.
      By stamping on his back.
   The one whose chest had been broken. When he had come
   after Tamakafi. The first one.   680
      He also went about with a limp.
         Then it was over.
         Now listen.
This was what kept happening, just as I said, he was killing him.
   He was killing him.
"Aah, ooh."   685
"Why did you do this to my son?" someone said about that
heavy *angikogo*. "Why?
He came to kill you just like all the rest of us have," he said to
Tamakafi.
   "He came to kill you."
So, he picked up an arrow of his.   690
      ["He never was able to run away?" Katsïgï asked.]
      He was even worse than before.
Tamakafi was so crazed by now he didn't know what was going
on. He didn't.
Sweat poured down his body.
   Sweat poured down his body.
When he was by the water,   695
   he could no longer feel anything. Nothing.
      He didn't realize what was happening to him.
      He was already out of his mind.
      He was suffering from thirst.   700

So *tuk*! right here on his chest again, he was shot with an arrow by
that person I spoke of before.
   He didn't even cry out from the pain.
      He was out of his mind because of what they were doing to
      him, and so he ran on.
   And once again, on his shoulder again.
      He didn't notice.   705
   He was shot above his breast this time *piitsuk*. Once again he
   rose up.
      Once again he rose up.
   He cried out his death's voice as he kept running away. And
   again as he had done before.
   Buh! He fell down.
      He fell down.   710
Then *tuk* one after another they came up to club him.
      Until he was clubbed to death. Until he was clubbed to death.
   "All right, build a fire.
      Build a fire."
         They wanted to eat him.   715
   "Go ahead, build a fire."
"All right everyone, come here."
   "What will happen to his arms? What will happen to his arms?"
   "Let's cut one off so the women can see it. The women."
They cut through him down here on his shoulder *tsiki, tsiki,*
tsiki, tsikigii, and snapped off the bone *ndak*.   720
      There it lay.
   That arm of his was huge!
Listen to what happened next. Now listen.
Now they waited for a while.
   They were going to do something, it's said.   725
   When there were coals in the fire.
   Then the stinking ones put his arm in the fire.
   Next they tried to eat it.
   Taa it was too bitter.
      Bitter.   730
   "Let it be, it wasn't any good at all."
      They refused to eat it.
Some of our people, some of our people who wanted to help
Tamakafi were very close by then, coming toward him. Some of
our people.
      Some of our people.
   This time they were different people. Others.

These people had been back at the settlement while
everything I've told you about had been going on.   735
They knew what had happened to Tamakafi when *taki* those
atanga flutes of his broke away from their cords.
When *taki* his *atanga* flutes broke away from their cords.
"Didn't I say my son is no longer alive?" his mother sobbed.
Holding his flutes in her arms, his mother carried them outside.
Holding them in her arms.   740
He was no longer alive.
When he finally died they fell down. When his flutes fell
down.
"Let's go," they said. "Let's go." The *angikogo* spoke.
"Let's all go."
"*Kakakaka, huu. Kakakaka, huu.*"   745
They went on.
The others were still going upstream, they weren't far away.
"They're still around here," they said. Those who were coming for
Tamakafi spoke.
"Their older brother is around here," they said.
"Here's their older brother!"
But they were hearing those other people, who were traveling
away from there.   750
They were paddling away *popopopo.*
They were going upstream.
When they came toward that place,
the dead man whom they had come to take away still lay
there.   755
Since he was dead.
"Our older brother is no longer alive, that's certain.
He's dead."
"Come on everyone, let's take him back quickly."
They took him up on their shoulders, on their shoulders.   760
Tititi they walked on carrying him for some distance.
His brothers carried him back with the arrows still sticking out of
his body.
His brothers.
He was shot here in his chest.
He was still like that when they were carrying him.   765
The others were coming toward them.
Then after they had gone a short way they looked behind them,
mbii.
The others were coming.

Bom one of them fell down while his companions ran away.
    The others kept running away, *toh*. And so they readied
    themselves again. *Toh.* Another one of that group *tsiki*
    was shooting at them. He missed.   770
"Quick, let's get going."
    They kept walking on.
    They still kept walking.
    They were bringing their brother back.
    While they went on from there.   775
The others were coming.
    However, these were people who hadn't been wounded.
    People who had been left behind by their companions when
    they left.
        When they left.
This time those people quickly carried their relative away.   780
Still with the arrows in him. His own brothers were bringing
him back.
    Well, they saw a fierce person close to them. *Tititi*, he was
    sneaking up on them.
        He sneaked toward us the way they do.
    Someone shot him as he ran away, and he fell down.
        He started running again. *Buk!*   785
    And so he fell again, see.
        He died.
    They had killed two people.
"Quick, let's get going."
    They went on. They went on.   790
    While the others slunk away.
    "Let them be," they said. "Let's get going," they continued.
"Come on, let's take him, let's take him."
    Once again they carried him,
        they again carried him to their canoe, to their canoe.   795
        And they continued their journey in the canoe.
        And they continued their journey in the canoe.
So, they all came back.
    "Is he alive?" they asked.
    "Their older brother is no longer alive, just as you see.   800
    No."
        That's just what they told those people who were there.
        That's just what they told those who were there.
"Just as you thought they would when that man started
everything, we saw the fierce people come. It's all over for him."

So listen.
That's certainly all there is to it.
That's the end of it.   805

In this remarkable story, one of the most vivid of all the many aston-
ishing stories told by Kudyu, there are several developing lines of personal characterization that merit a closer look. One important theme
concerns Tamakafi's anxiety about women (which seems characteristic
of these bow master heroes). His anxiety has to do with the fact that
throughout his puberty seclusion he has been told that contact with
women will weaken him. The fact that he is described at the outset as
being the lover of his uncle's wife, yet also "cleaning out his stomach"
with medicines, alludes to conflicts (not unusual even today among Kalapalo youths) between sexual desires and the wish to marry, on the one
hand, and the intention of developing and preserving through celibacy
manly strengths, on the other. Indeed, Kalapalo recognize that their
medical practices develop these desires and powers simultaneously. As
a consequence of his particularly stringent bow master training, none of
Tamakafi's relations with women have optimistic outcomes; he seems
to have repeatedly strong and complicated conflicts regarding his relations with women. As we learn toward the end of the story, in fact, he
is a widower, a man who had once married an enemy's daughter. Rather
than remarry after her death, Tamakafi has become involved with another man's wife. In addition to human women, the femmes fatales include the terrible monster Ñafïgï, who "takes the form of his dreams"
about "some women" who are Yamurikumalu. These are powerful beings (*itseke*), women with male personalities. Their exaggerated geni-
talia, male musicality, aggressive enticement of women, and hunting
skills allow them to exist independently of men, but they are particularly dangerous to men and seem to have much to do with men's fan-
tasies and anxieties about women.[2] At the arrow cane place Tapoge's
dreaming materializes in the form of the dreaded Ñafïgï, a violently,
ravenously sexual being who captures men in order to copulate with
them until, emaciated and exhausted, they expire.[3] In the story, Ñafïgï
embraces Tamakafi, hoping to abduct him, but he repeatedly wrestles
himself out of her grip. Although he eventually escapes, in doing so he
has lost much of his strength.

During the earlier conversation with his mother (lines 87–98), Tamakafi cautions her not to weep until he is actually dead, lest her tears
moisten (and thereby soften) his arrows. Here, he seems to be resisting
his mother's instinct to preserve and nurture his life, the very opposite
of his own bitter desire to go to war and be killed. Toward the end, we
learn that long before Tamakafi was unable to prevent his wife and

father-in-law from being killed in an ambush by fierce people. A final, negative reference to women is heard in Tamakafi's last words, which come as he is dying. "The women aren't going to see me," that is, he will not allow himself to be ridiculed by the enemy women at his moment of defeat. From the story of Wapagepundaka, we know something about this female ridicule; women are described spreading their anuses, telling the captive he would "come out" from there. During the cannibal feast, these most virile of men became the substance of women's bodies. And so it was the practice for women to insult the victims before they were killed. But in the end, these enemy women are the reason for Tamakafi's physical mutilation, since they are presented with his arm as a trophy.

Alongside Tamakafi's unsettled feelings about women, a second line of personal characterization involves his increasingly more and more openly acknowledged estrangement from his uncle. Although we know from the beginning the two are alienated from each other by sexual jealousy, they are also relatives who should resist open expressions of anger. An important narrative development, then, involves the way Tamakafi talks to his uncle. His early polite disagreement eventually turns to disgusted, sarcastic defiance. At the same time, the suppressed anger and jealousy of the uncle gradually change to fear and a wish to escape (and to escape responsibility for) the scene of death.

Looking more closely at the responses of Tamakafi to his uncle in terms of the narrative progression, we find, expectedly, an increasingly explicit resistance to his uncle and an increasingly obvious use of evidentiality (these are italicized in the examples). Consider (a), the first conversation between Tamakafi and his uncle:

(a) "Kid," his uncle called to him as he pulled to the shore,
       "Kid," his uncle said to him.
           "What," he answered.
        einangoaka uge.   40
       "As you can see, it's you I've come to, I have.
          It's you I've come to."
        titomima.
       "What do you want me for?"
       "So we can go collect some arrows for me.
          My arrows."
        um. eh he kingi awa.
       "I have to think about that. I'd usually say yes, Uncle.
          eh he kingi awa.   45
          Usually I'd say yes.
          [lines omitted]

afïtï, afïtï, talokitotsalegei.
"No, no. That has nothing to do with you,
   talokito.
   that's nothing."
afïtï ekugu aketsange awa.
"Uncle, really it must not happen.
   afïtï wela nïgifeke.
   I can't do it," he answered.
"We'll go some other time."   60

At first (as in [a]) Tamakafi firmly but calmly opposes his uncle's plan, thinking it imprudent. He is reserved and only marginally polite. When he first sees his uncle approach, his response is: "What is Uncle coming over here for?" and after his uncle greets him, rather than returning the greeting he asks in a negative way, *tïtomima*, "What do you want me for?" coupling the rhetorical question form with the *ma* doubt evidential. Yet he is still polite, as indicated by his use of the formulaic expression *eh he kingi* ("Usually I would agree") in lines 44–45, when Tamakafi has to object (for the first time) to his uncle's request to collect arrow cane. As a rule, the reasons for such a disagreement follow this expression, and indeed we have such reasons for Tamakafi's disagreement with his uncle in the next lines (up to line 56), in which Tamakafi correctly interprets his dreaming as a warning. More urgent disagreement, though still polite and perhaps conveying a pleading tone, uses the "urgency" form *ketsange*, the negative *la* suffix, and the negative emphasizing phrase *afïtï ekugu* (in lines 58–59), when Tamakafi responds to his uncle's dismissal of his dreaming. Line 60, "We'll go some other time," suggests Tamakafi is still accepting his uncle's request as legitimate rather than deceptive. In this conversation, incidentally, the uncle must ask four times—a completed set—before Tamakafi agrees, or, more accurately, before he gives in to the wishes of this older relative, whom he seemingly cannot refuse after such a repeated request. But this very insistence causes him to realize what his uncle intends for him.

After Tamakafi is joined by his bow master cousins (who together constitute another completed set of four), the men travel across the large, shallow lake, Tafununu, shooting fish from their canoes with bow and arrow, then stopping for a meal. Various bad signs begin to occur. The fish isn't shot directly and food takes on the appearance of blood. Tamakafi's uncle begins to worry, and suggests that they leave the fish and prepared food alone. Tamakafi begins to respond angrily and ironically:

(b) "Leave it, Kid," his uncle said to him. "Throw it away."   150
               ["The *sahundu*?" I asked.]

"Let it be as it is," Tamakafi answered. Yes, the *sahundu*.
   "Throw it away," his uncle said. "Let it be as it is."
"What happened was my arrow *tsuik* sliced right here through
it's head."
       He was lying.   155
       He was angry.
"All right," his uncle answered.

Here, Tamakafi deliberately misreads an ominous sign as if it were
a positive one, mildly contradicting his uncle's correct understanding
of what it means. At the arrow cane place this happens again, more
strongly (as Kudyu makes very clear by talking explicitly about Tamakafi's "fury"):

(c) *Tuk*! the dead fish exploded.
     "Throw it away," his uncle said.
     "No, no. All that happened was its eyeball exploded.
     Its eyeball."   170
         Tamakafi was VERY angry.
             He was furious.
         So, he ate it.

Now the contradiction becomes a little stronger; Tamakafi uses the
more explicit "You're wrong, you're wrong" before lying about what the
sign means. In line 307, there is a suggestion that his uncle is starting
to doubt his own judgment, when he uses the introspective evidential
expletive *um* ("I'm thinking . . .") but Tamakafi cuts him off, urging him
to continue on. Later, the uncle openly suggests they leave (this request
is repeated three more times as they discover the fierce people are close
by, and later as the cousins begin to be killed, one by one). Tamakafi's
responses to these suggestions of his uncle are heard in more defiant
emotional modes: he speaks bitterly and ironically, and finally with disgust and open fury. In (d) the uncle's first suggestion about returning is
made after the food turns bloody (beginning with line 180):

(d) His uncle spoke up. "Kid," he said,   180
     "Let's go back. Let's go back."
     "No, Uncle," he answered.
         "We can't go back now. Let's keep going, that's what you
         wanted to do. So let's go."
             The fierce people are probably coming to slaughter
             you, to kill you."

Here is where Tamakafi's bitter irony is first heard, as he tells his frightened uncle not to leave because he (the uncle) has come there in order
to ze protected from the fierce people. A second instance of this voice

occurs in (e) after the fighting has begun, when in lines 485–488 Tamakafi sarcastically uses both the surprise (*ki*) and doubt (*ma*) evidentials. Also, in line 487, Tamakafi responds to his uncle's second and more urgent request to leave with the strong combination of the evidentials *nafa* (which contradicts an immediately preceding assertion by referring to the speaker's firsthand experience) and *wāke* (which indicates that there is no other possible explanation other than the one being uttered). Here, he is contradicting his uncle even more powerfully and authoritatively, even contemptuously.

(e) "Kid," he said.
    Their uncle spoke.
    utelaketsange. utelï.
    "I must be going. I'm going."
    ah, tïkima etengalï. ah, tïkima etengalï.   485
    "What? Why should you go now? Why should you go now?
      Wait. Don't go until later.
    egey eluiña nafa wāke wïngïtïfïgï wāke efeke.
    Since you brought me here, someone is bound to be killed.
      Someone will be killed."
    eh he, idyogu kilïfa.
    "All right," his uncle said.

After he repeats this statement in lines 496–502 (f), his cowardly uncle feels shamed. This is the second place in the story where Kudyu openly describes a person's emotion. In each case, Kudyu is trying to clarify the particular conversation that has just occurred, so as to emphasize the quality of the relationship between Tamakafi and his uncle. He is not just referring to one or the other character's feeling.

(f) "Kid," he said.
    utelaketsange keñifatanifa.
    "I'd better go tell the others."
    afïtï, tïkima etengalï.
    "No. Why should you go?
      tïkima etengalï.
      Why should you go?
    egey eluiña nafa wāke wïngïtïfïgï wāke efeke.   500
    Since you brought me here, someone is bound to be killed.
    Someone will be killed."
    eh he ifutisu kingalï.
    "All right," he shamefully agreed.

Finally, after all the cousins have been killed, for the fourth time the uncle begs Tamakafi for permission to leave, and so Tamakafi agrees:

(g) "Kid," he said. The uncle spoke up.
uteluaketsange. uteluaketsange.
"I've got to go. I've got to go."
eh he nïgifeke.
"All right," he said.   545
    This time he was furious with his uncle. He was furious.
eh he nïgifeke.
"All right," he said.
    "Go away.
    "I'll stay the way I am," he said. "I'll stay the way I am."
igetomi aka wāke wïngïtïfïgï wāke awa nïgifeke.
After all, I know you really brought me here with you for this to
happen, Uncle. Didn't you?" he said.
    "For this reason.
        For this reason.   550
*afanganofoi wāke wanïgïpile wāke wikukineta atïfïgï wāke
efeke.*
What really happened was that you were jealous of me, so you
decided to take me away. I know that's what really happened.
    You were jealous."
[lines omitted]
    wikukineta atïfïgï wāke efeke wāke, nïgifeke.   555
    wikukineta atïfïgï.
    "I know why you really decided to take me away," he said.
    "You decided to take me away.
So get out of here," he said to him.

In (g), Tamakafi violently declares (beginning line 548) that he is will-
ingly going to his death and that he has known all along of his uncle's
true reason for bringing him to the arrow cane place. Using the evidentials *wāke* (incontestable truth) and *aka* (seeking confirmation of a firsthand experience) Tamakafi suggests the uncle can and must also validate this declaration. Combined with his declaration in line 559 that
"I'll become a story for your offspring to tell to their children," this is a
most profound and defiant condemnation of his uncle and an assertion
of utter conviction about his own moral authority. The declaration in
line 559 is actually the last of a series of four virtually identical statements that accompany a fatalistic, even suicidal expression spoken in a
profoundly depressed mode: *lafa kutsanini* (like that + 2nd person/
inclusive + exist + punctual potential mood + plural), literally, "So
we shall remain," or, more colloquially, "Let us die as we are now." By
this expression, he says: "Whatever happens to (me/us), so be it." When
Tamakafi first says this to his mother (lines 87–91) she bursts into tears,
realizing he intends to die. His second declaration (line 133) is made to

his cousins before they leave; Kudyu says Tamakafi "trembled with grief" as he said this. The third utterance (lines 337–339) is made to his cousins as they prepare for battle; they ratify this declaration, making a kind of suicidal pact. The fourth instance occurs in line 517, as he sees that all his friends have been killed. The fifth and last use of this fatalistic expression occurs in line 548, as Tamakafi speaks to his uncle. He receives no reply. This is the last real conversation Tamakafi has, because soon after he begins to die and only speaks once again to declare that he will not allow himself to be taken to be mocked by the enemy women. Tamakafi's tragic end thus was configured by his earlier dreaming but only accomplished through his own purposeful, suicidal action.

So far, I have focused on Tamakafi's talk with his uncle and his failure to perfect himself by staying away from women. From the way others talk to and about him, though, we see that he is also remembered for his arrogance and disdain. Recall the conversation he has with his friend Kafagikatu, who is about to be killed:

(h)   "Say, Bow Master," he said.
            "It's terrible. Look how my bow chord snapped apart."   520
      "Is that how you talk about it?
      Think carefully about how you used to eat the jelly left from
      cooking fish," Tamakafi answered. "That can kill you.
      Think of how you ate fish jelly.
            You liked to eat hot food.   525
            Monkey heads.
            It's the food you ate that did it."
                  That's what he told him.
      "I forgot about that," he told Tamakafi. "You spoke with your
      back to people more than once."
      "I forgot about that," he told Tamakafi. He was never aware
      of that.   530
      "If you turn away, an arrow will hit you."
      "I forgot about that, that made a difference, too. Speaking with
      our backs to people."

Even more fatal to Tamakafi was how he behaved toward the mutilated remains of his former father-in-law, Tapoge. Tapoge's sons happen to be fishing nearby, but when they realize Tamakafi is in trouble, they seem to relish the thought that he is about to die. Echoes of many of the same expressions (wāke, the incontrovertible evidential, and the curse, laitsa, used by Tapoge earlier on) are found in this segment:

(i)   "Usually I'd say yes, but I'm thinking about something." His
      older brother spoke.   430
            "Usually I'd say yes.

But this time we shouldn't go there. We shouldn't go there.
tingilanika wāke kupiñanofeke wāke ukwoto itïgïpe
agipïgï wāke, nïgifeke. ukwoto itïgïpe agipïgï.
Don't you remember what happened long ago? I saw our older
brother throw our old man's head away," he said to his brother.
"He threw our old man's head away."
About their father. He was talking about their father.
[lines omitted)]
    ulepefiñe fegei tute laitsa.
That was why they cursed him instead of going back.
laitsani idyimope kigatofo.
"Let him remain as he is," his children were saying to each
other.
"Remember when he scattered the remains of Father's head,"
he told him.   450

Most of the elements contributing to Tamakafi's killing emerge from
his own character, these being inconsistencies of feeling that are the
result both of incompatible personal values and social strains (such as
the difficulties between male kin of different generations who are victims of sexual jealousy). In Wapagepundaka and Tapoge, social strains
also contribute to the difficulties a man has with his warrior role, but
these strains are resolved differently in each case. In all the stories, the
stresses between father and son, uncle and nephew—that is, men belonging to different families or communities but who live together—
incite ideological attitudes and the elaborate symbolic structures (including evidentiality, but also nonverbal activities such as brutal acts
of extermination and activities of hunting and sharing meat described
in Wapagepundaka) through which those attitudes are given public
meaning.

By describing the hypocrisy underlying certain practices of warfare
and showing how these practices often led to fanatical forms of self-
destruction, the storytellers dispute in plausible ways any glorification
of the terrible image of the warrior and offer in place of this image a
peaceful man, empathic rather than antipathic, tolerant rather than vin-
dictive, constructive and productive rather than destructive and venge-
ful. It is the warrior-hero himself who sometimes attempted to change
from the first to the second. Although he did not always succeed, by
trying to extend the locus of cooperation, mutual interest, and social
harmony beyond the immediate setting of his family and parental (especially paternal) community, the warrior demonstrated the practical
utility of peace.

PART
3

9

Kudyu's Story of
the Wanderers

There is no founding narrative of Upper Xingu society, nor should we expect any. Despite a strong conviction of shared values and practices, as well as certain mutual interests, people of the Alto Xingu see these as having been adopted piecemeal, and in some cases (most critically, peaceful behavior and maintaining a diet free of animal flesh) incompletely. Moreover, the idea of "society," conceived in the abstract and independently of the actual ongoing relationships between people, is foreign to them. Kalapalo stories about ancestors associated particularly with present-day communities are very specific in describing relationships between individuals, the formation of social ties between families encountering each other almost by chance as they settle in the region. The stories are concerned with the problematic nature of these newly formed relationships and typically juxtapose one group's sense of community or family solidarity against another's perception of those same people. Additionally, we often hear the contemporary narrator's own opinions about the people in question. These are typically expressed through the subtle use of particles (like *su/sï*) that carry pejorative implications, or (in the case of positive feelings) more open expression of admiration for individual efforts. Shifts in the narrator's point of view correspond strongly with shifts in a character's identity, especially when people in stories openly label themselves and choose (or reject) to ally themselves morally with others.

The community biographies, as I will call these stories about ancestors, are particularly important to the Kalapalo because they constitute a kind of narrative bridge leading from actual experience at the end of the twentieth century to the much beloved myths of the dawn people (*angifolo*) who lived "in the Beginning," the very distant past that is a different kind of time/space. The fact that narration is so important generally to Kalapalo makes the content of these community biographies perhaps especially resonant with current life. The Kalapalo are very much aware of the "early days" (*ingila*) as a domain of experience that is in some ways quite different from that of more recent affairs (*ande*, or "here/now").

The dawn people were able to "approach" powerful beings (as Ugaki put it) in ways present-day Kalapalo cannot, unless they are shamans. Thus stories about *angifolo* may be called "mythological" as a useful way of distinguishing stories in which there is reference to special kinds of relationships between various categories of entities: powerful beings, animals, humans, pets. Complementing and in large measure helping to develop this thematic difference are various tropes we do not see in the present Kalapalo stories, including metaphors of feeling in which *angifolo* are given names of animals; quoted speech of tricksters, in which evidentiality is virtually absent; references to the experiencing of time and of traveling that set up contrasts between different kinds of places and experiences of hyperanimate power (as with dreaming). It is important to remember, though, that the Kalapalo do not make any explicit distinction between "myths" and other narratives. All are called *akiña*, "narratives."

The content of stories about the more recent past is also important for their descriptions of the most ancient settlements. They validate people's occupation and use of the land, as well as present-day use of resources in certain territories settled by ancestors, to which people hope to return year after year, even though they no longer permanently reside in those places.

Community biographies are also used to counter accusations of attacks on outsiders that have plagued the Kalapalo. When I once asked Enumï about something I had read of Kalapalo having killed the Fawcett party, he vigorously denied this as a lie and told me about the outsiders who had come to kill people in the Alto Xingu, exterminating entire communities (the story of Saganafa). These stories correspond to some degree to what Brumble calls "self-vindications" (1988: 38–39), although the Kalapalo examples are not autobiographical but rather focused upon the entire community that has been accused of wrongdoing.

There is often a narrative integrity based upon identification of places that links older stories like Afuseti (and even "myths") with more recent narratives about people still alive during the early decades of this century, some of whom were actually remembered in firsthand accounts like the story Kambe told me of the "Ingelisi." Many more stories are based on reminiscences of older people's parents and grandparents (as is Tsangaku's narrative of the Dyaguma). The sense of time depth is far more shallow for community biographies than in the case of warrior biographies, which seem to memorialize rather more distant ancestors.

Contained in many of these historical narratives then is a foundation of knowledge for evaluating one's contemporaries from various perspectives that tend to keep people at some political and psychological
distance from each other. Sagama, telling his wife's son-in-law about
extinct communities (Dyagamï, Anagafïtï) the two older people once
belonged to, offers the younger man a different, broader understanding
of how they all came to live together in the Kalapalo settlement of Aifa.
The long sad story of disease and witchcraft accusations, told over several weeks, became integrated into Tupagatugu's knowledge about the
more recent events he and other younger people were more familiar
with (such as the settlement of Aifa) through their own active partici-
pation. The accusations (had there been any survivors) would have laid
the foundation for accusing men who had descended from the earlier
witches.

From these narratives we learn there comes a time when residents of
a settlement begin to experience themselves as a community—when
people experience continuous validation of their feelings, actions, and
utterances to the extent they come to experience a lessening of that
anxious tension which accompanies constant negotiation, dispute, and
argument that are the consequence of new encounters. Musical ritual is
closely associated with this more relaxed social environment. It is not
that social differences temporarily vanish in the musical moment, but
that musical performance allows people to communicate across the for-
midable divisions of gender, age, and especially household affiliation
they create among and between themselves. What is most successfully
expressed in the environment of music paradoxically emphasizes formally opposed categories of being by bridging the chasms that separate
them. Although most Kalapalo musical events are verbally messageless,
participants are fused into a unity of performative discourse. Elsewhere
I have described how participants in ritual organize themselves into
work and dance groups that transcend household divisions and networks of relatives, so that one's sense of participating in group efforts as
a community member—identifying oneself with a place that one has
helped to build and maintain through ritual effort—becomes experienced very differently from situations whose meanings are built upon
relationships with other individuals through descent and marriage. In
an earlier work, I wrote about how this reordering of the settlement's
day-to-day life during ritual contributes to an understanding of socially
oriented motivation and action. During ritual life, economic activity
requires a set of productive relations different from those of nonritual
economic life. The productive forces are more complex in ritual contexts; more efficient technology is used, resulting in greater produc-
tivity, a need for more, and more greatly intensified, labor than normally

occurs in the kinship network and household contexts. The organization, coordination, and scheduling of labor become more complex, to such an extent that it becomes necessary for new roles and relationships to emerge. In this context we see *anetaū* (hereditary leaders) at work, organizing people in their labor, supervising the distribution of food and other products of that labor, and formally in attendance in myriad other ways during the entire ceremonial season. In some of the present stories, we see men doing similar things: teaching others how to make musical instruments, organizing dances, and inviting guests to the ceremony. The performance of musical ritual thus becomes an important index of a community's autonomy and identity vis-à-vis others. The *anetaū*, so important today, are presented as the "core persons" within that community, its raison d'être.

According to the Kalapalo, there is a special "happiness" which emerges during ritual performance, said to result from the lessening of anxiety among many individuals with their specific grievances. That happiness (which is not as much personal but collective) is called in Kalapalo *ailita* and located most impressively for Kalapalo men and women in their collective musical performances.[1] The ritual season is thus the season of collective joy, while other times of the year private claims and preoccupations lessen people's awareness of their shared interests and values. This awareness is a function of the redefinition of the connections between self-identity, moral representations, and the extension of a field of ethical judgments. Here it is pertinent to mention Victor Turner's notion of *comunitas*—special, complex feelings of social unity engendered by a ritual experience constructed through symbols of liminality. In his many explorations of the subject, Turner discussed the dissolution of normal social boundaries and the unification of persons principally in terms of their affectual consequences. He left open the question of what happens as a consequence of such changes in feeling. In the case of self-identity, Turner claims that participants in a liminal process have effectively effaced the "normal" components of their culturally constructed personae, to have redefined their ties to one another so as to appeal to their common humanity, experienced through the enactment of meaning particular to the liminal symbols of the culture in question. For the Kalapalo, "common humanity" is not a universal concept but one that is pertinent to their ideas of *kuge*, that is, community membership. This is not quite the same as being human, though it means adopting the most fundamental moral representations; this unity can be extended to Alto Xingu people and the rare foreigner who might reside among them. But it is as crucial for such outsiders to want to participate in their ritual behavior as it is for them to follow Kalapalo dietary practices and ideas about *ifutisu* behavior.

What happens when a crisis befalls such a community? When they are forced by enemies to move away from their homeland? When the sheer necessities of existence are jeopardized, and a new environment encountered, one that cannot be taken for granted, whose natural features must be carefully studied and evaluated, when (in part through this very process of study and evaluation) people come to question whether the community can even survive?

These are the kinds of questions that seem to motivate stories the Kalapalo tell about migrations into the Alto Xingu and of contacts made with other peoples. These narratives are thus in many ways parallel, in their thematic treatment of emotional processes, to the warrior biographies. And like those stories, we ethnographers should be suspicious about our convictions that these small groups of people were all significantly different from one another prior to their entrance into the region. Whereas one might expect an emphasis placed on linguistic, cultural, and personal differences, in fact just the opposite is the case. These strangers are presented as if they were just, or almost just, like the narrator's own people, the Kalapalo. In descriptions of the actual migrations, the searching for a suitable place to settle down, the ambiguities of identity and moral-ethical boundaries are played upon, just as in the warrior biographies. So community biographies and warrior biographies are all permutations of the same, more general, but untold narrative of how Alto Xingu society came into existence: piecemeal, unintended, unplanned, but gradually and more determinedly with an emergent ideology shared by its participants.

Kudyu, the Kuikuro man living among the Kalapalo, told me a story about his distant ancestors, the people who lived by a creek called Iña. This story is perhaps the closest to any I heard of the first Carib settlements in the Alto Xingu area. However, there are other such stories (described, for example, by Bruna Francetto and Gertrude Dole) which suggest that several small early settlements were established about the same time by people coming into the area somewhat ignorant of one another, all fleeing *angikogo*.

In this story, there is much to learn about the process of creating a new settlement: how a new site is selected, cleared, planted, and only later actually settled by the people who have farmed the land. In this process, bitter manioc plays a crucial role, for this staple root crop can remain in the ground for several years, growing larger season by season. When manioc is harvested, it can be easily dried and stored, thus serving (as it does in Kudyu's story) as food for people who are waiting for a new field to mature. Of equal importance to this ecological material is Kudyu's description of why the people initially decided to move to a new place: problems with manioc blight, which they attributed to sorcery.

Kudyu with two of his five children, 1982.

Unlike warrior biographies, in this story we are made aware of enemies from within, the consideration of witchcraft and internal dissensions that are very different from the difficulties faced by communities represented in warrior biographies.

In the second part of Kudyu's story, we learn how the newly founded community is discovered by some others, people who have wandered in the forest fleeing enemies. Clearly underscored in this part of the narrative is the suspicion this entails, the delicate maneuvering that overcomes fear of outsiders, and (most important) the way music is performed in order to generate that spirit of happiness conducive to the generation (and perpetuation) of community.

Validation, as always, is an important matter, developed through the quoted speech of the participants. If we compare this story with the warrior biographies discussed earlier, the repeatedly validating speech of people sharing plans and feelings about particular situations (especially involving newly encountered places and individuals) is most striking. Rather than the harsh, argumentative speech so common in stories about warriors, these community biographies seem to emphasize the importance of shared enacted values.

Arnold Krupat observes that writers such as Devereux, Lee, and Kluckhohn in the period following the Second World War characterized American Indian ideas of self so as to unify the individual and social. "It was Devereux's opinion [Krupat writes] that for Native Americans, 'maximum individuation and maximum socialization go hand in hand,' while Lee concluded that Lakota cultures demonstrate 'autonomy and community in transaction'" (1987: 5). These writers paid tribute to the characteristic emphasis on personal decision making but within a context in which the person was "identified" through social life or interpersonal relations rather than as an autonomous individual. This may be true, but it is perhaps too much an impression and in need of specific demonstration. With regard to Kalapalo thinking about social life and individual decisions and choices, a way is offered through the notions of validation and verification.

In earlier chapters, I described how validating and verifying features of Kalapalo conversational speech (including but not limited to "positive" evidentiality and the use of inclusive "we" pronouns rather than exclusive "we" pronouns) can create a social context characterized by certain qualities of interaction between persons that progressively build in intensity and complexity over time. In the present story of the Iña people certain formulas people use with one another validate goals and plans whereby they can be achieved progressively; this process of repeated validation constructs a social environment with its particular atmosphere of community, that is, collective effort to achieve collective goals. The story opens with a classic Kalapalo conversation, a dialogue between a young person proposing an activity and another who validates it. In this case they are father and son. This is followed by the father's presentation of their plan to the other members of his family.

Most of the first part of the story involves continuation of this pattern of step-by-step detailed presentation and ratification of plans, followed by enactments. Those who do not participate in this pattern of action are portrayed by Kudyu as members of a different, perhaps even somewhat hostile faction in the original settlement. Even members of a family must engage one another in this repeated expression of solidarity; they are not "naturally" predisposed to help one another but must constantly and actively do so. (Remember that in the warrior stories, there are many instances, already described in earlier chapters, of family members who do not ratify one another's goals but rather attempt to thwart them.) The process involves repeated concrete speech-centered activities, all linked together by their being located within certain settings, places whose environmental qualities are carefully remembered. The story includes open declaration and demonstration of shared values (including statements to the effect that the persons involved shall live peacefully with one another, and virtual proclamations of dietary practices that exclude certain game animals). Shared goals are also important, involving both cooperation among people to create the conditions for food production and sharing; agreements to marry in which both parties actively support the relationship; as well as mutual assistance in the creation of a ceremonial gathering in which new ritual knowledge is introduced and shared. Just as the environmental conditions suited so well to agriculture and fishing make the places in question important, so too does their use as ceremonial centers, places where musical celebration of community occurs. Although the word *ifutisu* never appears in this story, it may be taken as a narrative of what can happen—ultimately, the virtual establishment of the Carib speakers' presence as a distinct ingredient in the Alto Xingu—when people enact virtually everything that word suggests to present-day Kalapalo.

So listen.
   They were the Iña ancestors, it is said. It is said that they were
   the ancestors of Iña community.
   Though not true ancestors.
   These were people who lived somewhat earlier than those who
   ultimately became known as the ancestors.
   When at last they began to settle down.
Like, for example, this group of people here who made our
settlement at Kwapïgï.

That was a place someone discovered.
The Kwapïgï owner came there to make a clearing for Kwapïgï,
Dyukagi came to search for it.
    Searching hard for it.
He was like the person I'm talking about now.
This other person was like Dyukagi.
Think, if you will, Dyukagi was the person who made it,
who was making a different place that he worked to clear,
    to clear Kwapïgï.
That other place was something like that.
    That other place was something like that.
        Something like that other place.
Dyukagi came to clear Kwapïgï.
    That other place was something like that.
    I'm telling you about someone else who searched for another place.
    Not like the people from the VERY beginning.
                              ["I understand," I told him.]
        Yes.
People found that place, my people.
So listen.
"I'm thinking about something," someone declared.
    He had four children, boys.
    And three girls.
    This one [that is, the youngest] had no husband.
    Her sisters had husbands.
    Two of them had husbands.
    This one had no husband.
        That one.
    She was still immature.
    Finally she menstruated.
        She menstruated.
        His daughter.
    As for the boys, there were four of them.
        Four of them.
    This one here was unmarried,
        was unmarried.
            That's all.
    But she was still unmarried.
Alone with their father and their mother, that's all.
They lived that way because unexpectedly something happened to
the food they were growing.
    A sorcerer.

I don't know why those people were harmed,
   those people,
      so badly.
   So in order to end that state of affairs, they did something,
   they moved away.
     They moved away.
"Father," he said.
   "Father."
"What?" he answered.
"Tomorrow I'll go.
Tomorrow I'm planning to travel around."
He was a bow master, their older brother.
   A bow master.
He was a person who traveled widely.
  I'm talking about their older brother.
   Their older brother.
However, I don't have any idea what his name was.
     Yes, the son's name.
Fortunately, I do know the father's name.
     Yes, I know it.
He was Aumika.
    Aumika.
"All right," he answered.
   "All right," he answered.
   "Go if you wish."
At the beginning of the next day while it was still dark, the son
packed his things.
   That's probably what he was doing.
   He came directly there, by way of Iña Creek, where he had
cleared some space for his canoe to pass through,
    to Kunumai.
     To that place.
      To Kunumai.
      A canoe passage.
To where he had earlier turned back.
That was how he would continue to travel.
   His traveling.
On that thing he had made.
   On that thing he had made.
    Popopopopopo, he paddled through the forest.
He had been at the mouth of the creek.
   Tik he had come out onto the river.
    Onto the river.

"What's this place here?" he asked himself.
"What's this place here?" he asked himself.
"I'll go take a look.
    I'll look."
Then *tuu* he went up the outlet through the flooded forest,
through the flooded forest, through the flooded forest, until . . .
aandiki,
        right into an oxbow lake.
                                    ["In the canoe?" I asked.]
        Yes, in the canoe.
There, unexpectedly, he heard a locust calling [indicating there
was dry land ahead].
        A locust.
The locust started to call him, the locust.
"Well, what kind of place can this be?" he asked himself.
"I'll just take a look.
    I'll go see.
        I'll go see."
    He beached his canoe.
The entry place was very small,
very beautiful, farther along the way such as from here over to
our meeting place [i.e., ceremonial house, called *kwakutu*] he
found himself.
"Well! Here's where my settlement will be.
    Here's where my settlement will be.
Here's where Father and I should have our settlement.
    I'll come here.
        I'll come here."
    At last he went away.

The site for his new settlement, a piece of forested high ground alongside an oxbow lake, where the fishing should be excellent, is also close
to an outlet to the river that flows through the lower forest during times
of high water. Kudyu is describing an ideal place for a settlement.

The sun was over here.
    The sun was over here.
    He landed his canoe.
        He landed his canoe.
I'm thinking how he might have arrived.
"Here comes their older brother.
    Here comes their older brother," as he pulled to shore.
The people did say that to each other as he kept coming.

That's what they said as he landed his canoe.
    He landed his canoe.
Then in the plaza he distributed his catch.
That's all.
The others who were sitting outside saw him, his followers who
were sitting outside their houses.
That's all.
After that, then at dusk [whispers],
    "Father," he called to him.
    "Come here to me, let's sit together here.
        Let's sit together here."
    "All right," he answered.
    Pok, he went outside.
    "Father," he said to him.
        "Father."
    "What?"
    "I've just come upon a splendid place for us to live, Father," he
said to him.
        "I've found it.
We should go there.
    We should go there."
    "All right," he answered.
    "Can that be so?"
    "Yes," he said.
    "I've seen it for myself.
        I've seen it myself.
As you know, we need something like that, so that's why I've
been traveling around,
        why I travel," he said to him.
        "As you know that's why I've been traveling around. [His shy
        little son—about five years old—put some food in front of me,
        and his father said to him: "That's right, give it to her. Bring
        us some peppers, some pepper sauce for the fish."]
    That's all.
As you know, since we need something like that, that's the reason
I've been traveling around,
        I've traveled around.
    This is it, Father," he said to him.
        "This is it.
Let's go there."
    "All right, let's go as you say."
    "We have to go right away."
    "Today!"
    "We've been living here for such a long time," he said to him.

"Unfortunately, that's so.
    We have to go as you say.
        We should go."

In this section, the emotional quality of the move is described in considerable detail: the accusations of manioc sorcery; the young man who
repeatedly looks for a better place to live while exploring the surrounding country by traveling through the forest along outlets which he
knows must flow from hidden lakes, riverine embayments that line the
larger rivers. Then there is the discovery of a good place and, implicitly,
through the description, why it is so good; the sense of needing to move
away from a place; the constant and specific validation of his plans by
his father.

"Well, my children," he addressed them.
    "Listen to what your older brother has been saying.
        Listen now.
    We should go as he says.
        We will go to some faraway place.
            We will go far from here."
        Their father spoke.
        Their father spoke.
    "All right," they answered.
So after that,
        it was rumored about.
    People said they were going away once and for all.
    "Those people have found a place to live.
        That man has found a place to live."
        Others told one another.
    "Let them go far away.
            Let them go far away."
        They even said that.
    Those who sat around the graves were talking.
        Those who sat around the graves were talking.

In other words, men who sit together discussing community affairs. At
the present time, men gather in the middle of the settlement, before the
kwakutu, in front of which the graves are located. Kudyu is describing
what is apparently a fairly large community with several factions.

    "Let them go far away."
        "Let them go far away."
    "We should do it," they said.
    That is, considering themselves to be different now, they threw
        out the remains of their food.
        Threw it away.

They slept, they slept five days,
    five.
They were going to see that place.
The next thing they were going to do was go see it.
    The next thing they were going to do was go see it.
All of them went.
They slept there three days.
      Until then.
        Yes.
Then they came back.
"At last we have a good place" after they "went beneath" it.
[that is, the group slept (and dreamed) well beneath the trees of
that place].
"You're right, it's just as you say, my son."
    "Yes, I can see you were right about this place."
  "We'll move here, as you said. To this place."
"We'll move here."

The father now utters a sort of prayer or blessing, speaking rapidly and
with a low, breathy voice to represent a "song spell" (*kefege*). This
prayer concerns the new manioc, a wish for it to be healthy and to provide enough food for the settlers.

    "Let's hope for success in this excellent place here, so that we
will have success in what we do, and we will live better than we
ever had before.
What this community does will be successful, for the sake of
what sustains us," he prayed.
    "May what sustains us be the best it can be.
  Yes," he declared.
    "What sustains us."
      He was talking about the food they were going to plant.
      About the food they were going to plant.
    "All right," he answered.
    "Let's all go as you say."
They arrived home right away.
      It was late in the day when they finally arrived.
      That place was far from where they had started out.
      Far away.
      That place was far from there.
            ["What is the name of the lake?" I asked.]
        The lake?
               ["Yes," I answered.]

That was called "Many Turtles."

["What?"]

Its name is "Many Turtles."

["I see."]

Its name.

["Many Turtles?"]

Yes, "Many Turtles."
It was named after that really large turtle.
Yes.
There, I remember . . . I don't know why that was so.
Kusetange, Kusetange, that was the really big turtle.
It was where many turtles lived.

["I understand."]

All right.
That's exactly where it was.
Like that.
That's all.
That's an oxbow lake, an oxbow lake.
There were *sahundu* fish there.
There were *tañe* fish living there.
I used to go there once in awhile.
I used to go there.
Once in awhile with some success, that's how I used to go.
There were lots of other things to catch there, too, look.
I'd eat those creatures that live in groups.
["I see, those creatures that live in groups," I answered,
puzzled. The name of the animal was taboo to him, and I
wasn't sure what he meant.]
Say it, "so-and-so," Daughter.
[Aloko answered the taboo name: "Howler monkey." "Howler
monkey," I repeated.]
That's right. That's what I was eating.
Many of them used to live around there, all the time.
That's how they lived.
Once in awhile I would go there just by myself.
Yes.
The real Kusetange.
Listen well now.
"I think you're right after all."
"Old woman," he said to her.
"Old woman.
We've found our settlement," he said to her.
"You should see the fish there!" he said to her.

"That lake is filled with fish.
So many fish. That lake must be the place where they spawn."
   The *safundu*.
"Let's try staying there for a while," he said to her.
"All right," she answered.
   "That will be fine."
      "Fine."
   That's all his wife said to him.
   "As long as we don't argue, we'll remain on this side.
      As long as we don't argue."
The early people were able to live together by speaking well
with one another.
   That's how they were.
      That's how they were.
When their crops were entirely used up,
      their crops were all used up,
   "I think we should all go," he said to them.
      So they packed up all their dried balls of manioc mash in
      order to do that.
      The manioc meal was packed up.
      I'm thinking they did that, everything was packed up so they
      could live off it before a new field was made.
   They all went away.
      The next thing would be to clear a field.
         To clear a field.
Then they cleared their fields there,
      they cleared them.
   And they finished doing that.
   It was finished.
   They finished doing that.
   It was finished.
"That's all, children," he said to them.
      "That's enough."
   "All right," they answered.
      "All right."
When everything that needed to be done at first could be done
there,
   they all came back to their houses.
   "Is it ready?" the others asked.
   "It's ready, for sure."
      "All right," they answered.
   And so at that place the clearing now existed.
It was ready.

"Father," he said to him.

"What?"

"I should go tomorrow to our clearing to burn it," he said to
him.

"To burn it."

"All right," he answered.

"That's what you should do to it.

That's what you should do to it.

You go, then," he answered.

"Go burn it.

Go burn it."

"All right."

Again, the formal beginnings of the new settlement, involving preparing
a new manioc field, are presented as goals by the son and validated by
the father.

At the start of the next day he came right back to that very place.

He was by himself when he did that.

He was by himself when he did that.

Do listen now.

This is what we say next.

What we say next.

He burned that place at last,

It was burned.

It spread all over the clearing.

Next they came there to do the planting.

And they went at it.

To plant manioc, to plant corn, that's what they put in that
place.

And it was soon to be finished at last.

It was going to be finished at last.

Next they set the corn in place.

And they set the manioc in place.

It was finished, so they all came back home.

There was nothing more to do so they all came back home.
at last.

To their settlement.

However, after that they could do nothing but wait there while it
rained.

They remained in their settlement still, at Iña Creek.

At Iña, at Iña, at Iña for so long, until finally during this
fourth month when the manioc had finally given out they
went away.

That was a place that lasted a LONG time!
    For a long time.
They didn't have to move somewhere else right away.
That's what those people were like. [Kudyu became distracted
by one of the children playing with fire: "Something's going to
happen when that goes *piiiï* . . . !" he warned him.]
So they did come back home at last.
    They come back home at last.
        That took a long time!
            Long.
"Well, this is where we'll be living, children.
    We'll be living here."
The corn was ripened.
They wcre to create their settlement in the middle of a cornfield.
    Among the corn, Ugufi. Ugufi, they lived among the corn.
    They lived among the corn.
After a short time the manioc was harvested.
    The manioc was harvested.
That was all.
    So one of their dry seasons passed,
    while they stayed among the manioc.
        They did make another clearing.
    They made another clearing, larger than the earlier one.
        A very large one this time.
            Very large.
    The manioc began to grow in that field,
        the manioc did grow.
Then after another one of their dry seasons, they made another
clearing,
    they made another clearing.
That's all.
    After another one of their dry seasons they made a clearing.
        At this new [fifth] dry season, as it was beginning, the fifth
        one, after the dry season had begun, some *angikogo* came.
        To them.
                              [I asked, "*Angikogo?*"]
            Angikogo.
    Those *angikogo* were our people.
        People like us.
    [Puzzled, I continued, "Wouldn't you say *kuge*, rather than
    angikogo?"]
No, they weren't exactly like *angikogo*, those people I'm talking
about.

They were people like us.
    Not like our killers. [He decides to instruct me, interrupting
    his story.]
Let me explain the difference to you. On the one hand are
angikogo who are like us. They aren't the sort who kill us.
Those others I'm talking about are that kind of people.
                                    ["I see," I replied.]
But there are other *angikogo*, yet other *angikogo* who are the ones
who kill people, they on the other hand are the only real *angikogo*,
the only ones who kill us.
                        ["I see," I answered, and Kudyu resumed his story.]
Listen well now.
    So listen.
    That's what those other people were like.
It was from the *angikogo* that they kept fleeing, no other reason.
    Away from some place far from the one I've been talking
    about.
        Away from some place far from there.
One youth.
    A youth.
                                    ["A youth," I said.]
    Yes, a youth. He was an untouched boy.
        An untouched boy.
And his father was no longer alive.
Having been killed by *angikogo*.
Only the wife remained.
    She was by now a very old woman.
        She had grown old.
        She was an old woman.
The boy had almost become a person like this one here, like
him.
Like this person, like our son. [His teenage son Katsïgï, who was
in puberty seclusion.]
    He grew up while he was still in the forest.
    They were terribly thirsty all the time.
        Thirsty.
                                    ["Thirsty?" I asked]
        Thirsty.
They lived deep in the forest.
    They were fleeing from the others.
        They were running away.
    To avoid being killed by the *angikogo*.
    That is just how they were.

They still slept in the forest.
   The next day, they still slept in the forest.
     The next day, they still slept in the forest.
On this fourth day, he found some water.
      It was a creek.
       A creek.
They spent two days there.
      Two.
    The *angikogo* slept.
           The *angikogo* slept.
               [I said, "The people slept."]
    The people I've been talking about slept.
     The *angikogo*.
But finally on this one [points to his third finger], on the new day,
   they found an abandoned path.
From where at last they heard *tok tok tok*.
   "Oh," that startled him.
   That same person I'm telling you about.
It was the Iña community themselves chopping down trees.
   That's what they were doing.
   That's just exactly what they were doing.
            ["He heard them?" I asked.]
       He heard them.
"Oh!" he said.
   "I should get closer so I can listen.
    So I can listen."
   Tsïgï tsïgï, tsïgï tsïgï [he walked through the fallen leaves of
   the forest]
   until he came close to the sound.
Tok tok while the others were still at it he had come near to the
bank of the river.
   Far away, the river curved.
   He was very close.
    He wasn't very far.
     Not very far.
"Did you see anything?" his mother asked.
   "Yes," he answered.
   "I'm not sure but there might be some game for me around
here," he said to her.
    "Around here.
  My game may not be far from here."
"We should walk further on and look.
   We should go and look."

As she was saying that *tsïtsïtsï* they pushed through the trees.
Again they came close to that place.
   Those people walked among the forest trees.
Tsïgï tsïgï tsïgï toward the others.
Mbisuk they came out onto the riverbank.
   The river was very close.
"Let's go over there!
   Let's go over there.
Let's go, there's no more forest!"
   They arrived.
"Do you see anything?" she asked him. "We'll soon be very close."
   "We'll soon be very close."
      "Very close."
   "All right," she said.
But before they reached there *tiki*, when the sun was low on the horizon,
      they came to the path of the one who doesn't see very well, to
      the path of that animal. [Since Kudyu's affine bears the tapir's
      name, it is prohibited to him, so he uses descriptive terms or
      the Portuguese word.]
      Name it now.

                                        [No one answered.]
      Name that creature who can't see well.
                        [Kudyu's wife, Isani, said, "The tapir?"]
   That's it, that's it.
   On the path that one made.
                                        ["The tapir," I said.]
   That's right.
"Look! That creature lives here," he said to her.
   "That creature lives here.
      Here."
"Something should be done," he said to her.
"Old woman," he said to her. "What?"
"Your poor son will need some help, some help, your son will
need help.
   When he's caught something.
      It's been caught.
   Yes, after he has caught an *anta*."
   That's just how those people were.
"Very well," she answered.
So let's see. That was all, the sun had set.
   She saw its footprints.

"That's right, look at this.
Look at this.
Now I see that it drank water."
It drank some water.
"Now I see that it drank some water."
"Something should be done," he said to her.
"Wait for me here," he said to her.
He did it, the youth.
"Stay here," he said to her.
He was still a young boy.
"Stay here.
Stay here."
He was still like this person here, think of it. The son of the old
woman.
He was still a very young boy.
Still a youth.
That was what he was like.
He was capturing it by hand.
Capturing it by hand.
[Astonished that someone could do this, I asked again, "The
tapir?"]
Yes, that one.
Then when it was still around dusk for them, while only traces of
the day remained,
pudududu that creature arrived there at last.
It did arrive.
Until it was next to the man, who was up in front of it.
When it was right next to the man who was up in front of it,
buh, finally.
Buh, piaaa, finally he threw it down.
Piaaa, right in this place, around its throat he grabbed it *pupupu,*
and he threw it down after that.
He threw it.
Pudududu, the animal trotted forward toward him once more.
Buh, and again he did the same.
Piaa, bububu, he threw it down again.
"Here we come!"
Budududududu, bïh.
And again as before, that man.
Biah! Only a bit farther on *pupupupu* he threw it down again,
while it ran on *tutututu,* that man, think of it,
he had a very firm hold on it this time.
Buuk! Gïdïk! He squeezed it around its throat.

Biaa, harder!
   He kept trying to throw it down, he kept trying to throw it
   down,
      he almost threw it,
   while his mother came closer, *buh* in order to help him, *buh*,
   buh buk, it thrashed around
      until finally it was all over.
   They tied it up once and for all after he did that.
Tolok! "Let's club it!"
   He took hold of it here.
He did that, the boy who was up ahead did that to it.
      The boy who was up ahead did that to it.
   Puï, *puï*, finally he was successful,
finally it was all over when he did that.
      [Still uncertain I was understanding all this, I asked, "He
      didn't kill it with an arrow?"]
He didn't.
   It was seized.
      It was seized.
That's how those people lived.
   Those people were *angikogo*.
      Angikogo.
It was over. The tapir finally died after all that.
   It died.
   "I'll do it," *kidik*, *kidik*, *kidik*, yes, he butchered it then and
   there.
   He took out its guts.
Next he cut it all up *tsiuk*.
   He cut it up then and there.
   He cut up the flesh.
   Its head was for his mother.
            His mother.
         I mean the old woman.
      Its head.
"This part of it will be for me, my son."
That's just what she said to him.
   "This part."
Then they ate it up, until they were finished.
Then when they could eat no more they went on.
   They slept.
   Beside the creek.
   They were VERY CLOSE, think of it.
      Probably as near as from here to there, think of it.

About as far away as the river is from here.

A creek like this.

They had come to a creek.

They were next to the water.

There were many of those people.

Many of them.

The same number (of the others) had been killed by *angikogo*.

Just as many of them.

Lots of them.

That's all.

Do listen.

"I've been thinking," I'm told he said to her.

"We'll be staying here."

Yes, while it was still night, while it was still very early and dark,

tok tok tok, I mean those same people.

Caused by the Iña people.

Caused by the Iña people.

"I think you're right," his mother said to him.

"Very well."

"Think of it!

Think of it, those people are the ones I've been talking about.

Those are the people we've been hearing, after all."

"What kind of people do you think those people are?"

He spoke about them that way, I'm told.

The leader spoke.

"My child, go look, you should go see who it is we're hearing.

Who we're hearing."

So at last he came toward that place to see who it was.

To see who it was.

There he was. Wood that had been cut up was there.

He saw manioc growing there.

Next, he crept up *uuuuu* to the house.

"I don't care what happens to me," he said.

"I don't care what happens to me.

If someone kills me, so be it.

If someone kills me, so be it."

Titititititiiii, tikii. He walked up to the house and went inside.

I'd like you to think of a person in seclusion.

A maiden who was secluded.

A maiden.

A maiden.

When she saw him, "Ah!" she was frightened of him.
    She was frightened.
"You're wrong," he told her.
    "You're wrong.
Actually I've come to be with you," he said to her.
    "You.
    We really aren't killers," he said to her.
        "You're wrong," he repeated to her.
        "You're not what I think?"
He touched her gently.
    He touched her.
As he stroked her hair he said, "It would be wrong for someone
to shoot me.
    It would be too bad if someone were to shoot me.
Because I haven't come to kill you but for some other reason.
Please keep listening to what I say.
    Please keep listening.
Where are your people?" he asked her.
"They're in the manioc fields.
    They're in the manioc fields."
"I see," he answered.
"There are a whole lot of us.
    Many."
She was afraid of him.
    "Many."
"Where are your brothers?"
"They are still far from here," he answered.
"It was Mother, though, who sent me to you," he said to her.
    "To you."
He was lying.
    He was lying.
"I was sent to you,
    to you," he said to her.
"All right," she answered.
"Please keep listening to what happened to us," he said to her.
    "We have come so far!" he said to her.
    "We've had to flee from far away,
        to this place," he said to her.
"We're the only ones left.
    The only ones.
When we built our shelters,
angikogo attacked us.

When we made our fields,
angikogo hunted us down.
We slept, we slept five days, *angikogo* attacked us.
We would sleep twice, *angikogo* attacked us.
We slept three times, *angikogo* attacked us.
That's what we people were like, like that.
The only way we could escape was to flee from there.
So we fled."
That's what he said to her.
"We fled."
"I see," she said to him.
"Now I want you to have something to drink," she said to him.
"I want you to have something to drink."
"All right," he answered. *Kukukuku*, he quenched his thirst
once and for all.
She was going to become his wife.
His wife.
She was going to become his wife.
Next he drank some of it.
He drank some of it.
"I'm thinking that perhaps you people are like us," he told her.
[He wants to know if they eat the same food.]
"Like us," he told her.
"What do you mean?" she asked him.
"As you're about to see, I've killed one of those creatures," he
said to her.
What's-its-name, the one who has a smooth hide.
A smooth hide.
["A smooth hide?" I asked.]
Yes, say it next.
["Tapir," I said.]
That's it.
"I have really killed one of them."
"You have, have you?" she answered.
"You have, have you?
But that's wrong," she said to him.
"That's wrong." [It would be wrong, however, to impute to
the young woman feelings of sympathy for the hunted
animals.]
"No, we people won't involve ourselves in that sort of thing.
We're involved with other things."
"Very well," he answered.

In other words, with this response, he is letting her know it is all right that she won't eat his game. His validation of her people's diet is thus a crucial moment in the story.

"Since our own food, you'll see, is very different.
    Our own food.
    Our own food."
"All right," he said.
    "All right."
    "You'll see that we people eat monkey," she said to him.
        "Monkey."
            "All right."
His people were also very good at shooting monkey for food.
    Just as they were very good at shooting the "smooth hide."
    They were very good at shooting the *anta*.
    That's how those people lived.
                        ["Tapir," I said in Kalapalo.]
    They were very good at shooting that creature.
"All right," he said to her.
"Tomorrow we'll all come see you, without fail.
    Tomorrow."
    "Very well."
He said to her, "We'll come here directly by canoe,
    by canoe."
    "Now wait here.
    Wait here for now.
    Now I'll go see my father.
        My father.
    I'll go see my father right away.
    He'll want to see you.
        Want to see you."
"All right," he answered.
"Go if you wish," he said.
    "You go.
    You mustn't show fear.
        Don't be afraid."
Tutututu she ran until she came to the manioc fields.
    Tītītītī.
"Father!
    Father."
    "You shouldn't be here. Go away!
        Go away."

"You're wrong, Father," she told him.
  "Come quickly and hear what I have to tell you."
"Go away, you're supposed to be secluded.
  What do you think you're doing here?
    What are you doing here?"
"You're wrong," she said to him.
  "You're wrong.
Please listen to what I say," she said to him.
"Another person's here.
Someone's here.
I only want you to say that it's all right.
I only want you to go ask him who he is.
  I only want to you go right away with the brothers and see
  him."
"Who could such a person be?" he asked her.
"Who could such a person be who came here, who came to the
Iña people, to this place?"
  He agreed to what she said about the man.
"The brothers should go see him," she persisted.
  Just so her father would go speak to him.
  So her father would go speak to him.
  So her father would go speak to him.
"No, Father," she said to him.
  "No.
Please go see him.
  Please go see him.
'What happened was we fled in your direction as the fierce
people slaughtered us.' That's what he kept telling me.
  'Right to this very place after that happened.
    To this place.'"
"My son, go see the person your sister discovered."
Ka ka ka. The brother shouted like that over and over, ka ka ka,
  in order to make the visitor be a little frightened of him.
  Her husband.
So that he would be a little frightened of him.
"Ho ho ho!"
  "There's no reason to make him frightened of us," she told her
  brother.
    "To make him afraid."
"Why do you say that?" her father asked her.
"I can't agree," he told her.
  "'I assure you I've come to be with you.

To be with you.'" [The woman is quoting her suitor in order to
convince her father of his peaceful intentions.]
    "All right," he answered.
    "I agree with you. You two should live together."
    Thinking that she was to be his wife, that the stranger would
be with the woman who was successfully seated. [That is,
she was still in seclusion where in order to prevent her from
becoming lazy as an adult woman, she was made to spend
much of her time sitting rather than reclining in her
hammock.]
        So her father agreed, yes, she could marry him.
"All right," he said.
        "All right."
"We will live just like you do," the man told him.
    "Just this way.
    Just this way.
    We people will.
Here is where we people will finally live.
There are going to be lots of us," he said to him.
        "Going to be many of us."
"But where are your people?"
"They're far from here, beginning to gather.
    At the water.
        They're at the water.
I alone came to see you all."
    That's what he told him.
        "To see you all."
    He did tell him that.
That's how those people were.
Those are my people.
    Those are my people.
So this is what they said to one another.
So, "All right," he said.
Since there was nothing more for him to do there, he came back.
    "Very well," the father said.
"You go then, as you wish," he said.
"Please go!
    Go now."
He didn't want the *angikogo*'s people to be afraid of them.
    No.
"You'll see that you don't have to be afraid of us," he said.
        "You won't be afraid of us."

That's what he said.
"We shouldn't be afraid."
"Very well," the older man answered.
"Very well."
Well, that must have ended that.
Then he went away after all that.
So he went away.
"Did you find something?" the young man's mother asked him.
"What did you find?"
"I've found some people.
I've found them, Mother.
I've definitely found my wife.
I've definitely found my wife.
Teh! She is so beautiful.
She is beautiful."
"But how can we possibly go to them?
We people are good, not killers."
That's just what they had told him, nothing more.
They had told him.
They had told him.
"There are these many men," he said to her.
"Four of them.
As for the women, there are three of them.
They are all alone.
Let's go to them right now." So they went to them without talking
about it anymore.
Kïdïk kïdïk kïdïk, they pulled down their hammocks right away.
Just one little one that had belonged to a child who had died
from thirst,
that was what he owned, only one little one.
Also there was still one like this one here, which I can barely
sleep on [he is letting his wife know he needs a new one],
that's what the old woman used.
Deep in the forest the old woman had made them.
While they were suffering from thirst.
That's how those people lived.
That's what had happened to them.
They were our people.
Then, they came toward them again.
Finally, even a lot more of them came to join the others.
Many people.
That's what those people were like.
Many of them.

Iii at last they came to where he had gone earlier.
　　So many of them.
But before they actually arrived, the others brought manioc to
them.
　　For them to eat with their meat.
　　　Howler monkeys were being carried.
　　　Tapirs were brought.
　　　Monkeys were carried there.
　　　Birds that had been shot.
　　　That other beast that had been shot.
　　But they themselves only ate monkey.
　　That's what the people ate.
　　What those people, the Iña people ate.
　　Only monkey.
　　One thing.

　　　　　　　　　　　　　　　　　["But not tapir?" I asked.]

Not that. None of it.
　　One thing.
　　That's what those people were like.
　　　They were that way.
The manioc that was there was finally used up, so they brought
more to them.
　　Some of this older, processed stuff was brought to them to
　　drink.
　　　Some of this kind.
And then when there was nothing more they could do there, they
went away with those people who had been discovered.
One dry season passed.
　　A second dry season passed.
　　Another dry season passed.
　　And when the rains came,
　　　they cleared a field,
　　and then what else but the fourth dry season came, the fourth
　　one,
　　and then yet another one. As this fifth dry season was
　　beginning, something happened.
He wanted to speak to them.
　　To the children [that is, the younger male members of the
　　settlement].
　　　The children.
　　"Is there any large bamboo around here?" he asked them.
　　　Large bamboo.
　　　"What do you want that for?"

"For *takwaga*," he said to them.
"For *takwaga*."
"What's that *takwaga*?" they asked him.
"*Takwaga* is an object.
Takwaga.
That's what it's called.
That's its name.
With that we perform our music.
Our music."
"We've seen some over that way," they answered.
"There's some around here."
Large bamboo.
Large bamboo.
"Tomorrow we'll go cut some.
We'll go cut some."
They went right away.
Pupupupupupu, they paddled to Kunumai.
On the other side of the mouth of Kunumai Creek.
That's just where *sangakafi*, the large bamboo, lives.
There they cut some of it, *tchiuk*.
They cut it all up.
Each of the sons was cutting his own share of it.
They finished.
Late in the afternoon when the sun was over here they arrived.
"As he said, we've found some *sangakafi*.
We found some."
Next they each trimmed them to shape.
Next they hollowed it out.
That was finished.
There and then they became his followers.
Think of it. They are still in the plaza.
Afterward those same things were made.
The same things were made.
Were made.
All of them were made, in each and every house.
They were being made in the plaza.
And even in the houses.
That's just what those people did.
That's what they did.
Now changing to something that I talked about earlier—the
brother.
The brother.
I mean the brother of the Iña owner.

His brother. [Kudyu is referring to another man who had
stayed behind in the original community.]
"Look! Tomorrow I'll go see your father, children," he said.
"Tomorrow.
I'll have to spend the night there.
I'll spend the night."
"All right," they answered.
"Please go right away.
Go away."
Then very early, even though it was still dark, he got up to leave.
Tititititititi he walked until he came to that place.
"*Kaah, kaah,*" he called out.
"*Kaah!*" "Oh! Who is that calling out?
Someone with a message is coming here!"
He was coming to see his relatives.
He was coming to see his relatives.
"All right, I'll be the one to go," he said.
Their youngest born.
Their youngest born.
Pupupupupu he paddled to where the other man had called out.
To bring him over in the canoe.
He drew close to where he was.
He drew along the shore of the grasslands lake.
"I wonder why Father has come here this time?" he said.
"Why has Father come here this time?
What for?
That can't be anyone but Father," he said.
"Father, why are you here?" "I've come to see all of you, my son,"
he answered.
"I've come to see you all."
[Guardedly:] "You have, have you?
You have, have you?"
"We poor people are also still alive, my children and I," the
visitor answered politely.
"We're still there."
"Where is Father, then?" the older man asked about his brother.
"He's still back there, too.
He's still there.
Father."
"All right, let's go," *pok* he got into the canoe.
Pupupupu they paddled away.
And when they had gone just a short way,
"Father," the young man addressed his visitor.

"What?"

"You must not be frightened of my follower," he said to him.
    "Don't be frightened."

"But who is your follower, my child?" he answered.
        "But who is your follower?"

"I have a different kind of follower, but he is a person like us,"
he answered [in other words, no longer considered *angikogo*].
        "A person like us."
    "Where is he?"

    "You should come with me to see him.
    Teh! He has proven himself to be a good person.
The man has always shown himself to be so.
    That's the way he is."

"Is that right?"

"That's what he's like,
    that's what he's like,"
        he did say to him, I'm told.

"Very well," his father answered.
    "Very well."

They came to the place.

As they drew closer, they could hear the others playing their
instruments.

"Listen, listen to that!
    That's him!
    He's a very good person," he told him.
        "Good."

"This is what we've been trying to learn to do with our older
brother," he said.
    "With our older brother."

"Very well."

That man was still playing as they came closer.

"I see! But what is that he's done to himself?
    But what is that he's done to himself?
    That's like *genipapa*, only those people use *urucu*," he told him.

The strangers have brought the domesticated red dye plant *Bixa orellana* to the region whose inhabitants had relied on the semiwild *geni-
papa* tree of the *cerrado* for black body paint. This is a casual reference
to an extremely valuable contribution of the immigrants.

He spoke to the older brother.

"Yes," he answered. "Yes.
Those people were able to find me while they were far away," he
said to him.

"They were able to find me.
They were able to find me.
Those people.
They were able to find my settlement.
They were just fleeing from *angikogo* who were slaughtering them.
They were fleeing.
Until they came right here, to where I live.
Here."
That's how those people were, really.
That's how they were.
But now they were doing something very different, they were finally able to celebrate.
After all that their celebration was taking place.
They all celebrated.
Doing the *takwaga*.
Soon all those same people played, one right after another.
They all celebrated.
They all celebrated.
While they did this new thing, the Iña people came there.
More of our people.
Our people came, to that same place.
To perform *takwaga*.
Some of them from that settlement made another place at Fafukugi called—say it–

[Isani said, "Agafagu."]

Agafagu, think of it, it was HUGE.
At that particular place, even more new songs were performed, new songs,
that's how they were.
Like that.
They were living there, living,
in a settlement of their own at last.
Their own settlement.
Which came from a settlement of *angikogo* ancestors.
The settlement of our people's ancestors.
That was very large.
Very large.
It was very large, and a creek ran out from there, it flowed far away.
I remember some of us saw that when we visited the place
where those people had made their settlement. Yes, that's right,
and their fields.

A creek ran by the settlement they had made.
That's how they lived.
   Teh! It was a beautiful place!
There, there were always fish! In huge numbers!
   That's the way those people lived.
   Please say "yes."

["Yes," I said.]

That's all.
So the others as I said, all prepared to leave.
They planned to sleep there five days.
   When this one came around, they did all go
      to that same place.
         To that same place.
      They moved.
   Just to play the *takwaga*.
      Those people were like us.
      Those people were like our people, those *angikogo*.
   That's what they were like.
      That's what they were like.
   Yes, now I've just told you this about those people.
      What is told of those people.
         This is it, then.
"Mm, hm, hm. I wanted to have this very thing. Truly a story."
Say that right away, Aloko.

                  [His daughter Aloko replies with an old
                  listener's thank you to the storyteller:
                  "Mm, hm, hm. I wanted to have this very thing.
                  Truly a story."[2]]

Iña was a creek.

The Role of Validation

Appearing in virtually every conversation that Kudyu represents, validation is clearly central to this story, which ends with the appearance of Agafagu, one of the original settlements of the Carib-speaking people in the Upper Xingu region. Agafagu, as Kudyu describes it, seems to be a regional or settlement cluster name, with the ceremonial center located at the original settlement beside Kusetange.

The main steps leading to the formation of the new settlement at Kusetange by the people who have left Iña Creek because their manioc has died of blight are all presented in validating conversations. Thus the initial search by the oldest son, the suggestion to the father to move to that good place, the presentation of the site to the mother, the making of the fields are all validated activities. Similarly, among the refugees in the forest, the mother validates her son as he plans to hunt the tapir, when he suggests that he approach the strange settlement, and later when he proposes that she and he join the group he has discovered.

When, as sometimes happens in this story, there are conversations in which one of the speakers expresses caution, the interlocutor either quickly persuades the other of his good intentions or (as with the young man speaking to his future wife) quickly agrees to behave in a certain way, following a different custom. The adoption of new practices by potentially antagonistic people—virtual strangers to one another—is a particularly curious dimension of this story, so much so that we must accept their behavior as fundamental to the storyteller's representation of how a new community comes into being when older fragments engage one another. Rather than repeat all the conversations I will simply refer to those in which these kinds of engagements occur. In the first instance, the boy must persuade the maiden in seclusion that he has come in peace. He first tells her so, persuading her not to be frightened of him. He engages her sympathy by telling her how his people had fled from repeated massacres. Then, after she gives him something to drink and he wishes to reciprocate with the game he has killed, he must renounce this food and adopt her own people's practices in order to demonstrate his good will.

The young woman leaves her seclusion chamber to find her father in his field. She persists in trying to get her father to listen to her, until he agrees to send her brother to meet the stranger who is courting her. It is clearly the girl, not the father or the brother, who makes the decision to marry this particular person, but she needs their agreement to do so in order for the couple to live in this settlement.

After the stranger has joined the settlement, he teaches the other men how to make musical instruments that will be used in a ceremonial gathering. This occasions a return to the original settlement, from which the daughter's father had come (described at the beginning of the story). The people are invited to visit the new settlement, apparently for the first time. The ceremonial gathering is thus a kind of musical celebration that brings together several local communities into a new sense of social unity. In strong contrast to Wapagepundaka's people, these more recent ancestors successfully reinforced their unity through the actual performances of the *takwaga*.

CHAPTER

10

Ausuki Tells of the Trumai People

One of the smaller and most fragile communities of the Upper Xingu region is the Trumai. The earliest Trumai communities that we know of (reported by the German explorer Karl von den Steinen during his mid-nineteenth-century trip to the region) were two: one located far to the south in the region of the early Carib settlements, the other found in the northern region to the east of the Rio Culuene. The Trumai suffered considerably during their residence in the north, being attacked by the Suya and continuously intimidated by their neighbors the Kamaiura. Disease substantially reduced their numbers, as did attacks on their senior men, who were accused of sorcery by various people in neighboring communities.[1]

By the time of my first visit to the region, the Trumai had become isolated socially by their inability to adequately participate in the Alto Xingu ceremonies. They were eventually persuaded by the Villas-Boas brothers to move to the far northerly region of the Parque do Xingu but there suffered yet further attacks by their *angikogo* neighbors, who persisted in thinking of them as sorcerers. The Trumai in fact never seemed to be able to fully integrate themselves into Alto Xingu society. Some writers claim they were the last group to enter the region and make the attempt.[2]

The story of the Trumai ancestors is presented here as it was told to me by the young leader Ausuki, who learned it from his distinguished teacher Kambe. Although Kambe was a rival of Ausuki's grandfather and namesake Ahpĩū (at the time of my last visit, Ahpĩū was called Ulutsi by some, Mïdaa by others), he gave this story to Ulutsi's grandson knowing that Ausuki was going to become one of the younger Kalapalo leaders. Despite the personal rivalries of the two older men, they were bound as hereditary leaders to share their knowledge with one another's families.

Ausuki's story dwells upon group identity, solidarity, and loyalty and what we may call modes of relationship from which such themes are constituted. The opening lines ("Listen. To what the Trumai ancestors used to do to people . . .") suggest we are to take the perspective of Kalapalo about these strange intruders.

We can imagine that the story was first told by some important protagonists in the story—the Carib-speaking Oti children raised among the Trumai—after they returned to their natal settlement. The Oti formed an early cluster of settlements and are considered the immediate ancestors of the Kuikuro and Wagifïti people (Francetto 1986). So the story of the Trumai, which is clearly a Kalapalo story, came only indirectly from the Trumai. Yet much of the story of the Trumai migration, up to the capture of the Oti children, must have been learned by those children from the Trumai themselves. Their own experiences among the Trumai were probably added to the Trumai narrative of their migration to form a single story.[3] To say it is a Kalapalo (or even a Kuikuro) story is consequently an oversimplification. And yet, a certain intolerance emerges about the Trumai; their nasty customs and their mysterious ability to approach powerful beings underscore the suspicion with which these very different and relative newcomers to the Alto Xingu were held by the Kalapalo and their neighbors.

From the very beginning of the story, the narrator emphasizes how important it was that the Trumai were able to share food among everyone in the group. This theme is repeated more than once, particularly in connection with how important it was for there to be strong young men in the group who could provide such food—namely, bow masters. Bow masters figure in the story in other important ways: they are valued as guards and scouts, and insults to them are treated as insults to the group as a whole (as represented by the manner in which a leader and a shaman were called upon when a bow master left the community, his wife having rejected him). As in other stories, the Trumai bow master has problems with women; here, he is described as a man unloved by his wife. But notice that this is a typical way of describing bow masters and lends nothing to his distinctiveness as an individual person; rather, it seemingly assists in delineating his role within the community. In this story, the bow master (while sharing the important feature of sexual difficulties with his wife) is not a seriously deviant individual but rather the opposite: a representation of community values and virtues.

Just as the bow master's actions register all his group's aspirations, so portrayals of the ambiguous place of captives in the group seem to articulate group fears of the collapse of ceremonial celebration: *ailita*. The Oti captives are treated as inauthentic because they do not validate the group; they are avengers of their parents (killers within), they are people who are incapable of showing loyalty to the group (violators of

Ahpĩū and Ausuki distribute cooked fish during a ceremonial gathering, Aifa, 1980.

significant norms), and they yearn to return to their parents' group, to which they really feel loyalty. In fact, this theme dominates the concluding events of the Trumai ancestor story, which we could expect from the very opening lines quoted earlier.

There is no real description of the selection of a permanent settlement by the Trumai, because the story is told from a perspective of participants in events who left them at a certain point in their history. More important to the Kalapalo who tell this story are events that occur in the Trumai settlement which question the validity of the community feeling of unity at the very moment of making music. It is then that the "inherently disloyal" captives are made to leave. The Trumai claim that the sister has observed the secret ritual objects that only men are permitted to see. Faced with rumors that they are threatening her with execution, the brother-sister pair are forcibly and decisively expelled through their own decision to flee to their own group, the Oti. This decision is motivated by their realization that they have no relatives to support them in the community and therefore that they cannot participate in the collective experience of *ailita*. Like witches (both collectively defined as such and expelled by threats of execution), they become enemies through a brutally decisive act of group rejection.

Ausuki refers constantly to places in this story. We had often talked about my recent travels to some of the very sites where Trumai had lived, far up the Rio Culuene near the Tanguro tributary, where the Kalapalo who allied themselves with Ahpĩũ's younger brother Afinitse were building a new settlement. Of particular interest to Ausuki were the places I had visited. With these experiences of his listener-responder in mind, Ausuki deepened my enjoyment of his story by reminding me of what he wanted me to remember about the setting: the mysterious scrub forest that Kalapalo did not penetrate too deeply, the vast sandbanks in the middle of the river where turtles laid their eggs at the end of the dry season, the deep waters of the embayments along the Rio Tanguro that were filled with fish—in the past, monstrous fish that were large enough to fill a fisherman's canoe.

> Listen [he said to me].
> To what the Trumai ancestors used to do to people,
>   the ancestors of the Trumai.
> They came,
>   from where they had lived around the Araguaia River.
>   They wanted to make camp along the Culuene River, that's why
>   they came up this way.
> "Children, let's go far away from here," their leader said to them.
>   "To someplace far from here."
>   "Let's do that!"
> They did that, probably they came this way even though they
>   doubted they would have anything much to eat.

Since it is the end of the dry season, the *cerrado* trees would not yet have borne fruit; nor were there any significant bodies of water that would offer fish to the travelers. Interestingly, it did not occur to Ausuki (a noneater of game, like all Alto Xingu people) that they might have hunted animals.

> *Bah haa,* as they came they saw flocks of hummingbirds
> swarming around the flowers of the *akaga* trees.
> "Let's kill some right now, children.
>> Let's kill some."
> They shot them, *tak, tak, tak, tak, tak, tak,*
>> until they had shot a pile of them.
>>> A pile of them.
> Then, "You should do something about that. Share them among
> yourselves."
>> As they shared them among one another *pok, pok, pok,*
>>> thcy almost didn't make it, but in the end every one of their
>>> women had some.
> "Yes, we did do well to come this way.
>> The *angikogo* aren't going to kill us after all.
>>> They're not going to kill us.
>>>> No."
> If there had been people left over, they would have turned back
> on that account.
> They would have turned back because they would have felt
> frightened.
> But because of what had happened, they came this way.
> "Let's go," they said.
>> *Tititititititititiiii* they walked and walked until
>>> they stood beside the Tanguro River.
>>> That was very far from here, where they were,
>>>> beside the Tanguro River.
>> *Tikii.* "Let's think about what this place is.
>>> What's this place?"
>>> "This has to be the Tanguro.
>>>> The Tanguro."
> "All right," they said.
>> "Let's make our canoes here.
>>> Let's make our canoes."
>> Each man cut out a canoe for himself.
> "Let's go!" The canoes were all there together.
> They were right there, so they could be used to go on the river.
>> So they could be used to go on the river.
> They were doing that, because two canoes had already come up
> this way.
> But there were many more canoes than that.

There was a whole crowd of those contemptible Trumai people
who were doing all that. [Here the narrator's opinion is obvious,
building upon a shared dislike of the Trumai.]
But those who were in the lead were the scouts.
Bow masters.

>In case some *angikogo* shot at them.

>>Some *angikogo*.

>So the people all waited there together, and when the sun had
>almost set the two scouts returned.
>They had gone on ahead *pupupupu* and at dusk they returned
>to their camp.

>>To their camp.

"Is it all right?" the scouts were asked.

>"Yes," they answered.

>>"Yes," they answered.

>>"Tomorrow we'll all go together."

The next day they came together, *pupupupu* paddling toward the
place from where the scouts had returned.

>"Right here was where we turned back.

>>Right here.

>Right here was where we turned back."

"We'll stay here."
So they all slept there.

>They spent the night in that place.

Then, the next day, and the day after, some other people came
ahead.

>>Some others came ahead.

>Two more canoes.

Pupupupupu they returned when the sun was at its height.
To where the others waited.
So, they arrived.

>*Mah*, they had shot the "old man."

>>They had shot some *tañe*.

Each man had shot some *tañe*.
"Those were tiny, weren't they?"

>About the *tañe*. [The Kalapalo consider this one of the largest
>fish in the region.]

>"How small they are!"

They expected much larger *tañe*.
"These are such small *tañe*, even though they're very old."
Actually they were quite large.
Back there in the Araguaia they were even larger.
That's why they asked each other about the fish.

Sagama carries a *tañe* past manioc starch drying behind his house.

Those others back there in the Araguaia were very large.
Because they were like that the people asked each other about
the fish in the Tanguro.
Next they came this way, and they went on until they came to the
place from where the scouts had turned back,
        to the place from where the scouts had turned back.
"We turned back from this place here."
(It was probably very close to where you and the others all were.
        You must have been very close.
    Where you all were.)
"All right, let's go."
The next day, they were ready.
Popopopopo, they paddled into the shallow lake that you were
telling us about.
        That shallow lake.
    There, someone began to pound a mortar.
        An old woman began to pound a mortar.

She was an ancient person, *teh* with sparkling white hair.
　She.
"It looks as if someone's here," he said, one of the Trumai spoke.
　"I'll go look at her.
　　I'll go look at her."
"All right, go ahead," his partner said.
　His partner.
So the man dove into the water *tum*. He went on to that same
place, where she had begun to pound her mortar, *tum tum*.
　There he watched her closely as she pounded something in her
　mortar.
　That was all happening underwater.
"I'm trying to figure out what that is that you're doing?"
　"Oh, I'm just pounding my mortar.
　I'm pounding my mortar."
　"I see."
　She was a truly powerful being.
　　A truly powerful being.
　He had gone to a truly powerful being.
"I'll go now!"
"Go then."
　Just as he was leaving her,
　　he was bitten by an alligator.
　　By a monstrous alligator.
　Kuo he was bitten right here, on his waist.
　Koh, koh, while he was being bitten he lay quietly.
　　How could he rise to the surface?
The sun was here now.
　He was still in the jaws of the beast, he was still in the jaws of
　the beast,
　　so that other man who was waiting for him came to him.
　　　He dove into the water.
　Tom. "What's the matter with you?" he asked.
　"Just look at how this beast has bitten me."
　"You're right!
　I'll wait here awhile longer.
　It will have to be tired by this evening."
He waited for him, he waited for him, he waited for him, he
waited for him, he waited for him,
　until, when there was but the faintest light to the west,
　　then it was over.
　The alligator became tired of holding him in its jaws,
　　and so it opened its jaws and released him.

He'd been held in its mouth,
    the alligator wasn't about to release him right away.
Now that he was released, the man was in bad shape.
    Tik, tsuk it was awful after the creature withdrew its teeth.
    Water filled his stomach.
       His stomach was full of it.
    It had gone inside his stomach.
"What happened to you?"
    "Just look.
    Look at me. Only an alligator could have bitten me like that."
He jumped quickly into the canoe.
    Boh! They were ready. "Let's get out of here!"
    And they returned.
There was hardly any sunlight left,
    when *popopopo* they hurriedly paddled back to their camping place.
    "Let's get out of here."
    "They've come back again, they've come back to us again!"
    "But we're in trouble here. He was bitten,
       an alligator took him in its mouth."
    "Very well," they answered.
Then the next day they came farther up this way.
    All of them came together.
The son of an old woman had been rejected by someone.
    An old woman's son.
    His wife couldn't stand him.
       His wife.
       She rejected him.
    This old woman's son was a bow master.
       An expert shot.
    And his wife couldn't stand him!
So there were consequences, there at that same place.
There, concerning that other person.
    "I was bitten right here by an alligator."
    "We'll stay here one more night."
    They had made their camp there.
So the next day they continued up this way.
    "Show them, take them there!"
    "All right," the man answered.
       "All right."
They all kept coming up this way.
    Two canoes.
When the sun was still very low in the east,
    the two canoes came to the mouth of the Tanguro.

"Who knows where this will take us?" they asked.

Pupupupu as they paddled into the mouth of the Tanguro *ndiki*,
   they came out onto the Culuene, that place where you and
   the others were some time ago.
   Tiki, right at the Culuene.
      Right at the Culuene.

"Do we know what this is called?" they asked each other.

"This is the Culuene."

"All right, we'll go downstream," they said.

Across from where they were was a sandbank,
   opposite the bank along which they moved.

"We can sleep over there."
   They got out at that same place.

Turtle's babies were there, eggs were there.
   They looked around for them, the Trumai people searched for
   eggs in the sand.

How small they were!
   "They're tiny!" they said.

"They aren't like the others we've found before, are they?"

"I don't know. It looks like they're all this size," his partner said.

Boh ah! They expected to find big ones, this size.

Like the eggs they had known from the Araguaia.
   They hoped these eggs would be like those others.

"How tiny they are! They are not like the others, are they?" one
of them said.

"It looks like they're different, they're all like this.

I'm surprised they look so different, they're all like this," his
partner answered.

Then they came farther up this way, in our direction.
   Some droppings lay on the sand.
      Droppings.

"Look!" one of them said.
   "Here's something that looks like droppings.
      Droppings."

They were hard and dried out.

"Show me."
   Puh, the other man scooped some up in the palm of his hand.
   Feces.

"This looks like droppings," as he examined it.

He began to crumble some of it between his fingers, *ku ku ku*.
   Right away, he began to crumble up those droppings.

"This does look like droppings,
   this does look to me like droppings."

"Bring it to me," said his partner.

The other man wrapped it up in some leaves,
   he wrapped it up.
And he carried it over to his partner.
   So he could see for himself.
"Now let's go farther on to shoot some food for ourselves.
   Our food."
"All right," the other man answered.
They were shooting their food,
   they aimed their bows,
     they threw away what they had shot.
Boh hoh hoh because of the enormous size of what they had
shot in the past.
They didn't expect anything less than those very long fish.
Actually, it's said those others grew very large, you see, like a
little *afi* fish.
   How those others grew, it's said.
Boh like those enormous *wagiti* fish which live in the Araguaia!
   They realized all of them were like that first little one he had
   shot when *tuk* he shot another one.
Next, as they came this way, *tsoki*, he shot another one.
"Let's go back up there!"
   And so they turned back.
A powerful being still lay in the shallows,
   at the mouth of the Tanguro.
And so they went on.
The sun was over here.
"It looks like this is the river at last," he said.
   "Here it is."
"Let's do something with this." They handed round the turtle eggs.
"What tiny things they are. They're very small, aren't they?"
they said.
After all that was over,
since he still had that stuff from the sandbank, you see, he showed
them the droppings.
"Doesn't it look like droppings to you? Droppings?"
"I'm not sure, but it does look to me like human droppings."
"You should show it to the others," the scout continued.
The man brought it to the other people, and the people at the
camp crumbled up what he brought them.
Each and every one of them had a chance to smell it.
   They were smelling it.
"This looks like droppings he's brought us, doesn't it?" they told
each other.

They crumbled up what they held in their hands.
    What they held in their hands.
The next day, "All right, let's go!" as they came up this way.
    Right to the Tanguro.
        To the mouth of the Tanguro, you see, to where you
        yourself stayed.
    But their place was farther back in the other direction, up the
    Ugikufuku.
        Up the Ugikufuku.
            That's where they had a settlement.
"We'll settle up that way."
    Mbah, there was so many monsters there! [very large catfish]
"Come on, everyone," he said, and they killed those monsters.
    Then they ate them all.
    There at that very place they made their settlement.
While they lived there, someone turned away an old woman's son.
        The son of an old woman.
    "Say, you," he addressed someone.
        That was their leader he was addressing.
    "Uncle," he said to him.
        "I must go far away from here.
        I'm being turned away by my wife.
        I'm going far away, because I hope the club people kill me.
        I want someone to shoot me."
    "Go then, go then."
        The leader agreed.
And so he paddled away in his canoe.
    He paddled away in his canoe with *mbah* a great pile of arrows.
Popopo, he went on, determined.
    As for his wife who had rejected him, the people were furious
    with her.
        Very, very much so.
"We should take that foolish woman out to the middle of the sand.
        To the middle of the sand.
    Since she was foolish enough to refuse him, her genitals must
    rot away.
        Her genitals must rot away."
"Very well."
In the very middle of the sand,
    tugu tugu tugu buried up to her waist.
    That way her genitals would rot, since she was buried up to her
    waist.
        They wanted her genitals to rot.

They wanted them to rot because she had refused to make
love to him.

"Didn't we say she refused to make love to her husband so he
would leave her?"

Since she had acted differently from him, they took her out to
the middle of the sand, in order to rot her genitals.

Yes.

So think of that.

They were Trumai.

Pupupupupu the man kept paddling on as I described.

Around one bend, around another bend, toward Kutsu.

But at that same place, where the river bend led to Igupe,
the tail of something stuck out of the water.

A monster.

That was Tisakuegï.

Yes, Tisakuegï.

That was a monster whose tail stuck out of the water, a fish.

One of those beings who swallow us.

"I see something! There's something here!

There's some kind of monster here.

I'll try to shoot it quickly."

That was a river guardian.

"Here's one of those river guardians," he said to himself.

This was at the mouth of the Iguku.

He spoke to himself while it rested there.

"Oh, here it is," he said.

"The river guardian.

Here.

I'll try to shoot it."

He drew close to the shore so he could do that to the creature.

When he reached the shore he ran alongside it.

Tutututu he must have run until he was right above it.

An *aku* tree was bent over the river.

An *aku* was doing that, a tree.

Right there.

Onto it, *tititi* onto it *titititi*.

Now as he sat right above the creature, he shot directly into
its back.

Kikiki the creature shook off the arrow the man had shot.

So he shot another arrow of his.

And finally after he did that the creature died.

When that happened, the man came down from the tree and
tutututu jumped quickly into his canoe.

He paddled hard and took hold of his arrow.
"Here it is!" and he clubbed it after he hauled it up.
But when next he tried to set it down along the bottom of his
canoe,
    he wasn't able to fit it in.
So in order to squeeze it in hard, he had to use his knee to push
it down.
And finally, after he had done that,
    the head of that creature was up at the very tip of the bow,
while its tail reached all the way to the stern,
    the stern of the canoe.
It was huge, big like this.
    A monster as big as the door of the house.
      That was Tisakuegï.
"I'll have to go back now.
I'll have to go back now!"
That's what he did.
    As he paddled there he sang about it.
      He sang about it.
Unfortunately I don't know that song at all.
This is only what Kambe told me, so I don't know that song.
But anyway, he came back singing all the while.
    He paddled right back, hurriedly fixing his singing in his mind.
So anyway, just as he came around Kutsu Meander, someone heard
him.
    "Old woman," someone else said.
      "That has to be your son singing out there.
        That singer out there can only be your son."
    "Can it be that my son didn't die after all?"
    That's just what she said to him.
"Start smoking right away."
Their shaman got ready.
He was Ingeu, Ingeu.
I'm talking about their shaman, Ingeu.
    He was Ingeu.
"Something's happened," she informed him.
    "Smoke your tobacco now, smoke your tobacco now."
      To Ingeu.
"All right," he answered.
He smoked until he went into a trance.
    He sucked his breath in. "Something's happened, you person.
    Listen carefully to what your nephew tells you.
    Something's happened," he said to her.

"But he's too far away for me to hear clearly.
Your son said to you he would let the river carry him off where
it would,
     that's what your son said."
"Very well," she answered him.
  Because of what she was trying to do, she called on another
shaman of theirs from some other settlement.

Ausuki has become very involved in his story to the extent that he is
using current practice as a model for what the Trumai woman might
have done. He appears to assume that the woman, having received less
than satisfaction, would call on a more powerful shaman from another
community. Obviously this could not have happened among the group
of Trumai travelers. So he corrects himself in the next line.

(She couldn't have said that.)
"Now I'm hearing something else.
     Something else.
Go ahead, smoke again."
     And so, once again,
          Another person.
Tsitsitsitsi, he inhaled until he fell unconscious.
     "He seems to be coming closer.
He's not too far away, he's almost at the river bend.
His canoe is riding very low in the water.
     Oh, how he is panting!
Can you hear your nephew?"
"Something's happened. Can't you reach him?" she asked.
"That's not it. Your son has killed a river guardian."
His mother tried to learn more about it.
He himself was so far away Ingeu couldn't hear him clearly.
     "What actually happened was your son killed a river guardian.
          Your son did.
You should go meet your son, that's what you should do."
     His mother came toward him.
          Wasn't it true they cut their canoes from *jatoba* bark?
               His mother's canoe was one of those, cut from that kind
               of bark.
               His mother's canoe.
     "How small that must have been," say it.
          The body of the canoe.
So anyway, because she had that kind of canoe, his mother, the old
woman, brought out her canoe.
     She had almost reached the mouth of the stream, when there
     he came.

He came as she approached the mouth of the stream.
"Mother!" he said to her. He told his mother what had
happened to him.
"This is a monster I've just killed.
   A monster I've killed."
"Very well," she answered.
   She said that because that was how he asked her to bring it
   back for him.
      She said that because that was how he asked her to bring it
      back for him.
Then and there she turned back to get some people to help
carry it.
   Next *tak tak tak* she hacked it into pieces.
   Next she passed it around, and all the people ate what she had
   given them.
      Portions were passed around to everyone, *pu pu pu pu pu*.
         Even each and every one of their children.
            Toki some of that monster was put before each of their
            children.
         Even every single child of theirs got some, until there was
         nothing left.
Now his wife was still buried up to her chest in the sand.
   That foolish woman was put there like that so her genitals
   would rot.
      So her genitals would rot.
   "You should go get his wife."
      So they went to get her.
         That was done.
   Then they brought her back.
Because of what had almost happened to her, she desired her
husband now.
   She desired her husband.
   And so they lived well together.
   She let her husband have his way with her.
      She no longer rejected him.
      Her genitals had almost rotted away.
So they lived there.
   They lived there a long long time.
   But eventually the flesh of the monster gave out and they knew
   it was time to continue on.
"I've been thinking," their leader said.
   "We should move our camp.
      Let's move our camp.
         We should move our camp.

Have ten of our canoes move along one side of the river.
Have another ten of our canoes go along on the other side of the
river.
    That's how we'll travel."
"All right," they answered.
    They agreed to separate into two groups.
The next day the canoes departed.
    They were surrounded on all sides by their warriors. On each
    side were five of those men.
"We should go now." Agamanadya was paddling.
    He was still a young, unmarried man.
        An unmarried man.
            Agamanadya was that kind of person.
    A bow master, one who knew how to shoot.
    There was another one, you see, Ugukutsu.
        He was another one of those people who knew how to shoot.
        One of their shooters.
The two groups of canoes came together upstream.
They moved slowly, killing monsters.
        Killing monsters all the time.
    Alongside a sandbar.
        Alongside a sandbar.
    Called Ana.
        Alongside the sandbar.
There were some others who had been pushing their way upstream.
        People who were coming from an oxbow lake.
        People like us, this time.
    Members of the Oti community.
        Members of the Oti community.
They paddled along—"There are some people over there!
        Over there."
    "All right," the other answered.
    So, they came toward those people.
"Come over here, come over here, come over here," one said.
The two men made a fire because they planned to do something to
the other people.
    They made a fire.
    And when it was lit they heaped some sand around it.
    Quietly, while the sand was heating they took out some resin.
        Quietly.
        A portion of their resin caches.
The others landed their canoe. "Land over here, you people."
    They came to the shore.

Why did they do that? I don't know what their reason was for coming over to those people.

So they finished landing.

Then, right after they left their canoes, the others captured them.

There at that same place they threw burning lumps of hot sand all over them.

Ouch!

And now with the resin, *tuk* they killed those people with that stuff, until they were all dead.

They died.

When the Trumai were certain they were dead,

"Let's do it!"

And they captured the children.

Two, a tiny girl, this small.

A little boy, too, that's how he was.

"Let's go back now!"

They went back.

To their own settlement, once more.

To their own settlement.

Beside Agikufuku Lake.

To the Tanguro area.

That's where they went.

There's an oxbow lake there.

Near the Tanguro River.

Is it beside the Tanguro?

It's near the mouth of the river.

That's where the oxbow lake is, the oxbow lake.

That's where they lived.

They were still living there, those contemptible people.

So that's just where the Oti children were raised.

Where they grew up.

So at last,

When those who were being raised had grown up,

"It's time for us to tie up this boy's foreskin."

To tie up his foreskin.

"We should do it, let's get ready to tie up his foreskin.

Let's get ready to tie up his foreskin."

"All right."

So they tied up his foreskin.

They made him lie with his face staring up at the roof.

Facing up.

He was lying face up with the penis-tier beneath him.

Facing up.

Reminiscent of practices following a boy's ear piercing, the penis-tying ritual was apparently given up by the Trumai during their temporary "integration" into Alto Xingu society. At least, it was not practiced by the time Quain visited them in 1934.

> He dreamed very beautifully in that position.
> He slept soundly then.
>> His head was covered by a basket.
> "How was he? How did you sleep?"
>> His adopted father, the man who had captured him spoke.
> "With his head completely covered by a basket. [This was a dreaming sign that indicated he would be invisible to enemies, thus a person worth training as a bow master.]
>> By a basket."
> "That's perfect!
>> That's perfect, just what I hoped for!"
>>> "Yes, a bow master."
>>> "Very well," the father said.
> Because of what had happened to him, as he grew up
>> he could kill wild beasts.
> He was called Madyawagi.
> His sister also grew up there.
>> His sister too, his sister.
> I said her name, didn't I? Kamisu.
> Kamisu was his sister.
> Madyawagi's sister.
> She was his sister, his sister.
> Well, he continued to live there after that, they both remained there.
>> His sister had grown up together with him.
>> His sister had grown up.

At this point we took a break. This was a good place to do so since what follows takes on a very different point of view. We are now seeing events from the perspective of the Oti captives. The preceding reference to the sister's experiencing of time—her maturation into a full-grown woman—and the following reference to the man having fully grown are typical means of segmenting narratives in Kalapalo in order to make significant shifts in topic.

> Listen.
> They lived there together.
> He was an adult, living there after all that had happened to him before.
>> He had finished growing.
> He had finished growing.

While he still lived there, someone became angry with him.
Because he was feeling that way about him, he said something
about the Oti man.
    Ugukutsu was speaking.
Afterward a friend of his told him about it.
    A friend of his told him.
        In their plaza.
"Let's go relieve ourselves," he said to him.
        "Relieve ourselves."
"All right," the other answered.
    "Let's go relieve ourselves."
The two men walked out onto the entrance path.
        There,
"Look," he said to him.
"Our brother has been speaking very badly about you to us all,"
he said to him.
    "Our brother has been speaking."
"Very well," he answered.
    "Very well."
"Something happened. You know about yourself, don't you?
You're not really Trumai at all.
    Not Trumai.
You're Oti, you know.
    Oti."
And so he remembered, and so he remembered.
"It was that same awful person Ugukutsu who set your father on
fire with lumps of heated sand,
    with lumps of heated sand.
He was burned with resin, that is the truth about how your real
father died."
Now he remembered what had happened.
    Now he remembered his father.
"As far as I was concerned I thought I was Trumai.
    Trumai.
I'll have to leave as you say," he said to the other man.
    "I'll have to leave."
But he stayed there for the time being.
    While the other person kept on doing what he had been doing
before.
Ugukutsu spoke.
    "Tomorrow I'll try to shoot some *kusu* birds.
    Tomorrow."
The two signaled directly to each other while he was saying that.
The two friends signaled to each other.

"As for me," he said,
  "I think I'll do that also," because he had said that.
  "Tomorrow I'll go shooting,
    tomorrow."
  (Yes, he was lying.
  He was going in order to kill him.)
  He was going in order to shoot Ugukutsu dead.
  Madyawagi was going.
"I'm thinking about it," he said to the others.
  He went, very early while it was still dark he went in order to
  do what I just told you.
    He went away.
Then when it was daylight this man was following him.
  He followed him.
As he paddled along he went shooting *kusu*.
  Tuk, he shot *kusu*. That's all.
Then he himself, the man I spoke of earlier, he also shot *kusu*.
    I mean the one following behind did that.
  But now as he came closer, he came more carefully.
  Carefully, because he was just about to kill him.
    Ugukutsu sat eating some passion fruit.
  He was eating passion fruit,
    seated in the branch of a tree.
"There he is! There he is!"
Quietly he came to shore and got out of his canoe.
  He was still sitting right in the tree eating that fruit, while the
  other man was doing all that.
  Tuk! And so at last, he shot him as he had been planning to do
  all along, and when he did that, the other man fell down from
  the tree where he had been eating the fruit,
    he fell down.
  He died right after that happened to him, he died.
"I'll go now," he said.
  Next he tied the body to the man's canoe.
  He tied the body to the man's canoe.
  And he sank the whole thing underwater.
  He pushed it away.
    Underwater.
"I'll go now," and he went away.
  The man's children were worried about him.
  It was already getting dark, and they were worried.
  They suspected something had happened to him, that's why
  they were worried.

"Where could he have gone?" someone asked.
"Something terrible must have happened to him."
"It's too bad I went in the other direction, isn't it?
The other way," he said.
Even as he spoke, he knew the other man was already dead.
Next he slept.
Then his sister saw something being done.
His sister saw the *kagutu* being played.
It was that man . . . that man . . . Agamanadye.
He was the one.
The *kagutu*'s mouth was uncovered.

The reference is to the beginning of the *kagutu* flute ceremony, which women are prohibited from seeing. This suggests the Trumai have already learned some Alto Xingu ceremonies or perhaps have a flute ceremony of their own.

[Here, Ausuki hummed a *kagutu* tune.]
Because that was how it was, when they started to do something with the *kagutu*, Kamisu saw it.
"We should kill her," that's what the Trumai people said.
So they opened the house, intending to kill her.
With their arrows.
While that was going on her brother spoke.
"Those worthless Trumai, those worthless Trumai.
Don't think I'd ever let some strangers kill my dear one.
Those worthless Trumai.
They'd better be careful."
So he picked up his arrows.
Mbuk! And they ran away.
They ran away.
Then, as the two stood together,
"Let's get out of here," he said to her, to his sister.
"Let's get out of here now.
As you've guessed, our people aren't anything like these here.
As you've guessed, our people aren't Trumai.
It's true, our people are Oti.
Let's get out of here!"
And so without waiting any longer they came farther up this way.
They came.
They came after all that happened to them, to their settlement,
to that place far from here called Oti.
That's all.
Without waiting any longer, these people came after that.

And that ended everything that had happened to them before. That's all.

After ending this extraordinary story, Ausuki looked proudly at his grandfather, as if seeking confirmation that he had told his narrative particularly well. The old man was smiling. His grandson had needed no prompting, knew how to tell his story well, and demonstrated how detailed and precise was his knowledge not only about the Trumai migration but about the signs and symbols of Kalapalo thought. I mention all this, because Ausuki was a young man when he told me this story, no more than twenty-five years old. While his expertise was certainly a consequence of having been taught by the two old leaders of Aifa, he was not unusual among people his age in having an appreciation of the deeper meanings of cultural forms. He had the capacity for and appreciation of "learned commentary" because so much of what he had learned had inner significance for him. This was why, when he told me the story of the Trumai, he evoked a reality that corresponded closely to his own experiences of life, so much so that (as his grandfather sometimes did) he occasionally experienced the images that he was creating through his narrative as if they existed in the here and now, as if they were more than evocations of a distant past.

11

Ugaki Tells of Afuseti, a Woman Stolen by *Angikogo*

Once the Alto Xingu communities recognized that they had come to share common values, they began to develop ways of dealing with outsiders that were peaceful rather than aggressive. This was sometimes even the case in situations where outsiders posed threats to them. In certain stories about events that took place long after the end of cannibalistic blood feuding, the warrior remains an important though more peaceful figure. But a more ominous practice is developing: the killing of known people, usually people living within a community, because of witchcraft accusations. The fear and anger directed formerly against enemies living elsewhere is now turned inward. Another important context for local tensions is sexual at base; rivalries between men over women who would flee their husbands to live with lovers in other settlements now appear as a theme in stories about more recent communities. In this and the following chapter, I present two stories that speak of these matters at some length.

Each of these stories happened to be told to me by a woman, which raises the question of whether they demonstrate a distinctive Kalapalo woman's narrative voice. To answer this decisively would require analysis of far more women's stories than I have presently completed, but with regard to these two alone, I would say that each illustrates what was, to me, something distinctive about each woman, just as the men's stories varied in keeping with their individual personalities. Yet it is clear that women's activities are never neglected (as they might be passed over by a man, though not a particularly fine storyteller), so that even the preparation of food for men who are about to embark on a trip is mentioned. Also, each story seriously examines the important place of women in establishing contacts with strangers, making clear that their part in these matters was not always in their best interests.

While the Kalapalo were living at Kwapïgï, a woman named Afuseti disappeared on her way to draw water. At first, her disappearance was attributed to an unknown lover; a man must have enticed her away from her family. Only after searching in nearby settlements did her relatives realize that she had been abducted. Her brothers and husband eventually traced her to her captor's settlement, which they found several days' walk to the east of the Rio Culuene. There, Afuseti was discovered to have had several children. An agreement was made with her captor—the father of her children—to allow her to remain.

The story called "Afuseti" is something of a detective story, describing how the woman's brothers searched for her, following a trail of clues, but it is also concerned with the consequences of their discovery of Afuseti. The solution was to preserve peace and have Afuseti remain behind with her captor, but only after her new husband had given considerable payment to the brothers for her. The story is not one of mutually beneficial and agreed-upon alliance (no one ever bothers to return to Afuseti's new home) but rather just the opposite: an abduction, followed by payment that is accepted but which has little value for the parents.

Ugaki, the woman who told me this story, used the pair of labels "wife" and "husband" (when talking about Afuseti and her abductor) ironically and was clearly unhappy with the final outcome of the story. Unlike Kambe, who also told me about Afuseti, Ugaki seemed to feel it necessary to justify the men's decision to me: "How else could she have left him, she had been there for so long?" As if to say (as she often did), "If it had been me . . ."

Ugaki begins her story by imagining how the captor might have looked a young girl over before her maturity, much as Wapagepundaka was said to have done. The narrative is put together from this kind of speculation as well as firsthand knowledge gathered from various sources: Afuseti herself; the girl's relatives in Kwapïgï; fishermen and bow masters from other communities; Afuseti's original husband and brothers, who travel in search of her. Judging from the names of the settlements mentioned in the story (Kwapïgï; Kuikugu; Dyagamï; Afuafïtï; and Agafanugu, people who preceded the Anagafïtï group),[1] these events must have happened after the incidents described in Ausuki's Trumai story, perhaps toward the end of the first half of the last century, when the Kalapalo were still living at their settlement Kwapïgï.

Perhaps [she began] it was after something happened to him that
he came to find a wife for himself,
    to find a wife for himself.
He only did that because his own woman was turning away
from him,
    she was turning away from him.

That was why he came long ago to this other person, to find a
wife for himself.
> To find a Kwapïgï woman for himself,
>> a Kwapïgï woman.

And so he must have come after that happened to him and the
woman, coming this way by means of, coming this way by means
of the Uginga River.
>> The Uginga River.
>> Along that river.

He came, toward Kwapïgï,
>> toward Kwapïgï.

And so that's where he seems to have stayed, because he was
looking for a wife for himself.
He waited outside the settlement after that, watching them.
He was watching a woman.
> A woman.

Teh! He was watching a beautiful woman.
> A beauty.

"I've decided. This one will be my wife," he said.
> "She will be my wife.
> My wife, my wife."

And so eventually he went away, he went away after that.
A year of his passed, another year of his passed, and he came back
again.
> To check up on her.
> I imagine he wanted to be certain about her.

Now that it was so much later when he did that again, she was
ready.
She had finally grown up.
> She had finally grown up.
> She had finally grown up.

This motif appears in the Wapagepundaka story as well. The man se-
cretly watches the young girl until she is mature enough to marry. But
Wapagepundaka approaches the girl and her mother appropriately, as a
suitor.

> He came there.
> After she had completely grown up.
> After someone had already cut her bangs and she had grown up
> completely.
>> She already had a husband, he was the one who had cut her
>> bangs [one of the events of the marriage formalities].

She already had a husband,
   she already had a husband.
So, after that she would go at last to the manioc fields.
   She would go with her mother to the manioc fields.
   Well, one time she arrived home from the manioc fields.
   The last thing she had to do was go to the water's edge, to draw
   water.
   And so she went, the daughter went.
   She wore her necklace when she went there, her shell-disk
   necklace.
She was at the water's edge.
   But HE was there, waiting for her.
      Waiting for her.
         That's what he had been doing.
She went in.
   While he stayed at the water's edge watching her.
   He ran up to her after that.
   He took hold of her, after that.
   "*Aah haah*!" she screamed when he did that,
      she screamed,
      she screamed.
   She bit him but it didn't stop him from doing that.
   She never agreed to go with him,
      she never agreed to go with him.
   He held her very tightly after she did that,
      he held her very tightly.
   And then he pulled her arms behind her, *mbisuk*.
   So he finally carried her off that way,
      he left, running all the way back with her that way, he carried
      her off.
   Earlier, he had taken some manioc starch to the riverbank.
   He had taken a manioc griddle that someone had left outside,
      he had taken a small manioc griddle.
   He had stolen one of those things.
   And an old discarded manioc press.
   He had stolen one of those things.
   He had left them at the riverbank.
      At the place where he had started out.
Then her mother arrived home,
      her mother arrived home.
   "Where could Older Sister have gone?" she asked right away.
   "Getting water," the others answered.
      "All right," she said.

Someone else went at last,
    a person who lived in another house came outside and went to
    where that man had arrived.
    She found it, she found it.
       Afuseti's water bottle.
    She must have taken off her necklace, and *mbokï*, her necklace,
       tïkï she put her necklace around the neck of the water bottle.
       Mbokï.
    "Whose bottle is this?" the person who lived in the other house
    asked herself.
       "Whose bottle is this?"
       "Those must be that woman's things, Afuseti's things."
    "Surely this is HER necklace, that must be her necklace there."
       Then her parents wept.
    "What could have happened to her?"
    No one knew anything about it.
Finally her husband arrived home from the manioc fields.
       He arrived home.
    "Your wife is no longer here. It looks to us as if she was stolen,"
    the people in his house said.
       "Your wife is no longer here. It looks to us as if she was
       stolen."
    "I see," he replied when they told him that.
    "Someone from around here stole her," they decided.
    "I see," he said.
    "Let her stay stolen," he simply said [that is, he didn't show
    anger, thinking she had run off with another man].
       Her husband spoke.
After all that they slept.
Then the next day,
    that man put her into a canoe with all the other stuff.
    She was still crying!
    After that they came back by means of Italo.
    They headed for a distant place that way.
    Upstream,
    upstream.
Finally, when the sun was still very low on the horizon,
    at that very place they came into the mouth of the Uginga.
       They came into the mouth of the Uginga.
    Across the way were some bow masters, some bow masters.
       Members of Agafanugu community.
           Across the way.
              Across the way.

They had been fishing downstream.
    Fishing.
They paddled alongside the *igigisi* bushes that lined the shore.
Although he tried to sneak past them, they managed to see her.
    Hoping that they hadn't gotten a good look at him, he quickly
paddled away.
        Her husband paddled away.
    He entered the tributary.
    He entered the mouth of the Uginga.
    He went away after that.
Then the others came quickly toward that place, *uum
tïkï* they raced over there.
    Right away, one of them asked, "Who could that person be?"
    "Who knows? Probably that was one of our brothers."
        That's how the other one answered his younger brother.
    "Probably that was one of our brothers."
    He didn't know who it was.
And so they returned home, while the others kept going on as
before.
But later on these bow masters learned about what had happened
from some other people.
    They were told about it.
    "That woman's daughter has been stolen.
    Her Afuseti."
    Other people told them.
    Yes.
    Some of the Kwapïgï people were talking about it.
    "Her Afuseti has been stolen, her daughter has been taken away,
no one knows where," they told them.
    "Her parents haven't been able to find her," they told the others.
    That was a year later.

Here, creating a new time frame, Ugaki shifts back to the events connected more directly with Afuseti's abduction. The simultaneity of events in two different contexts—the parents' search for their daughter and the daughter's own ordeal—is thus made clear.

    The others had come to the canoe landing,
        they had come to the canoe landing.
    Then, even after they had landed the canoe, she didn't eat
anything at all,
        nothing.
    He was carrying her on his back after they landed.
        Finally he walked among some trees.

There she was finally able to mark a tree with some paint
from her forehead.
   She did that.
"This will make Older Brothers notice since they'll probably
come looking for me.
   This will make Older Brothers notice."
   She had left her sign.
     That was all.

Kambe told me that the abductor made temporary hammocks with
some palm branches, so later the brothers also took these as a sign of
where the two had gone.

He continued to carry her far away after that, toward the forest.
   I think he must have made their bread as he traveled.
     He made their bread.
       Her husband made their bread.
"There's nothing else to eat so take this." But she didn't eat any
of it,
   none.
   She kept crying.
The next day, they still slept.
   She didn't drink a thing.
   She didn't eat any bread.
The following day they came out of the forest.
   Onto the grasslands.

Just as in the Trumai story, the narrator begins to talk of the protagonist
using -*su*. Our attention has been drawn away from him for a time as
we concentrate on the details of the search. Now that her brothers are
coming closer to the abductor, we are reminded of his sinister character,
which must have been foremost in their minds as they traveled through
unfamiliar territory.

Onto that worthless man's grasslands.
   Now, they were arriving,
     they were arriving at his settlement.
       Yes, at his settlement.
Eventually, she stopped crying.
But now her parents were looking for her.
   In other settlements.
   Her father went to look in one of those places,
     Kuikugu.
Nothing.
Then he went to Dyagamï, to Afuafïtï, nothing.
Nothing!

Then he came way over that other way, they say.
To Agafanugu.
He went to Agafanugu, to the bow masters' own community.
He must have asked them about her there.
"Perhaps your sister came here for a while, my children," he
asked them.
"Your daughter never came here," they answered.
The bow masters realized they had seen the very person he was
talking about.
"That couldn't have been his daughter we saw, could it?
That person we saw?"
"Yes, that might have been your daughter who went up the
creek.
That must have been *angikogo* we saw, stealing your daughter,"
they continued to tell him.
"That was probably *angikogo* we saw, stealing your daughter.
I saw with my own eyes how he snuck away when he saw one
of us,
as we were moving toward him,"
he said to her father.
And so he concluded,
"Just as I thought, your sister was stolen by *angikogo*.
Just as I thought, it was *angikogo* who stole your sister."
That's what he decided happened.
After all that, her brothers made their arrows,
that's what her brothers did.
There were five brothers.
The sixth person was someone different, her husband.
Her husband.
That was all.
They made their arrows.
The next day, the day after, until they finished.
While they were doing that their wives were toasting manioc
and preparing their drinks.
"It's time we begin searching for our sister."
They went by canoe from where they were over to our landing
place at Akagape.
That's where they slept.
And so they came to where she had camped before.
The same place.
So they saw something.
"Look! Our sister's left a sign here.
She's left a sign."
That's what they said, I'm told.

"Our sister's left a sign here!"
Well, they followed her after they saw her sign.
   They still slept.
   The next day they slept again.
   And again, they slept another night on the trail.
   And the next day, that was all.
   The next day was the last.
     They slept three nights on the trail.
They walked out of the forest.
   This time they walked onto the grasslands.
     Onto the grasslands.
   They came out of the forest.
Now, in the distance they could see some trees that had been planted, as they came out of the forest.
   In the distance.
   "There are the trees of our sister's settlement."
Then they went toward that place,
   and it soon grew dark for them, it was dusk.
   "Let's stay right here.
     Let's stay right here.
   When it's dark we'll go look for our sister.
     When it's dark."
   "All right."
And so they all stayed there.
   The sun had set.
   They stayed there until it became dark.
When that happened,
   "Let's go, let's go.
     Let's go see our sister."
   Through the *piqui* trees they went, to find their sister.
   This was the season when the *piqui* fruit were beginning to fall.
   They walked through the falling *piqui* fruit.

When Kambe told me this story, he said this was the first time his people had seen groves of *piqui* fruit. *Piqui* fruit and its processing techniques, he said, were learned from these *angikogo*.

   The husband was starting to talk outside the house.
     The husband was starting to talk outside the house.
   In the plaza.
     In the plaza.
   But while he was beginning to do that, his son was crying.
     His son was crying.
   "Oh, be still," she said to him, I'm told.
     To her son.

"Be still. If your uncles lived here all the time, I wouldn't mind
if you kept me from sleeping."
    That's what she said to her son.
Her brothers heard her.
    Her brothers did.
    "Oh! Here's our sister.
    Here she is," they said.
    "Look! Our sister's here, just as we thought she'd be."
Then she finally got up from her hammock and went over to
where her *piqui* fruit was cooking.
    To take the fruit out of the pot.
    It was night when she did that,
        the sun had set.
Her older brother called out to her,
    "Little one, little girl, little girl."
    "What?"
    "Come outside."
    Her older brother spoke.
    The first-born spoke.
All the brothers stood clustered together.
"Just as you thought we would, we've followed you to this place
and found you."
    "All right," she answered.
    "That's good that you finally came looking for me.
Because it certainly wasn't one of our people who stole me from
you, I can assure you.
It certainly wasn't one of our people who stole me from you, I
can assure you.
That man made himself your nephew's father as well, believe
me," she said to them. [This is a way of talking about her rape.]
    About him.
    About her husband.
    Her husband, who had been speaking outside.
"Now, before you do anything else, send your child to get his
father."
    "Go get Daddy right away."
    She had quite a few children, in fact.
        A lot of them. [This is quite unlikely if Ugaki was correct in
        saying the event occurred only two years after her abduction.]
        "Go get Daddy."
        (This child was like that boy over there, he was the size of
        that grandson of ours.)
    "'My uncles are here.' That's what you must say to Daddy."

"All right," he answered.
And so, out in the plaza:
  "Daddy, Daddy.
  My uncles are here.
    My uncles."
  "Be still about your uncles.
  Right now it's these people I'm trying to speak with.
  Right now, it's these people I'm going to speak with."
  "Daddy! My uncles are here.
    They've come to see Mommy."
So he stopped what he had just been doing, he stopped his speech
making.
  And when he stopped,
    he came to his child.
  "My uncles are here."
  This time he acknowledged what his son had told him.
He came at last after that
  to join his wife.
  "Your brothers-in-law are here.
    Here."
  "Do you agree with that?" he acknowledged what she said
to him.
    "Do you agree with that?" [This is a nonvalidating response.]
At last he went out to them after that.
    Out behind the house.
  And when he did that he saw them all standing there, clustered
together.
  "My relatives, I see it is you!
    I see it is you, my relatives," he said to them.
  "Yes, as you see it is us.
  We did this because we were looking for your children's mother,
and we hoped she would be here."
  "You think that's good?
    You think that's good?"

Again, a nonvalidating response. Although he has greeted Afuseti's
brothers politely, he is worried they are going to take her away by force.
He's anxious, obviously, about how they feel.

  Because he was frightened of them.
    He was frightened.
  Look, as I said there were five brothers.
  And there was a sixth person.
  Her husband, by himself. That is, he had no brothers.

"Very well.
It was very wrong that I just did it without thinking of your
sister's payment." That's just what he told them!
    "It was very wrong of me to do it without thinking of your
    sister's payment," he said to them.
"Bring your brothers inside."

Here he has validated their visit. In turn, the brothers agree to enter the
house peacefully. The psychological style of this entry, though, is still
not fully conducive to a friendly settlement of the problem. There are
still some matters regarding payment and whether Afuseti wishes to
remain with her husband that still need resolution.

They came forward after that, they came inside because they
saw he was afraid when he said that.
    Then they went over to the side of the house.
He went to tell the others.
    "My relatives are here!"
    That man came to those same worthless *angikogo*.
    "My relatives are here!"
So those worthless *angikogo* all grabbed their arrows.
    How heartless they were, shooting at the house.
        With their arrows.
    "Stop, stop, stop!" he said to them when they did that.
        His followers stopped.
    "Stop."
        His followers stopped.
    "Be careful I don't kill you, too.
    Because I also know how to shoot."
    His followers quieted down.
    And they all went away. [Because of how he is able to influence
    the others, the husband convinces his guests they are safe in his
    settlement.]
After that she told her brothers what had happened to her.
"Believe me, Older Brothers. That person who stole me from
    you was not at all like one of us," she told them.
    "Your nephews' father was someone very different from that, to
    take me from you to this place."
    That's what she told them.
While they were drinking something.
    "You should fix something for your brothers to drink."
        She made some when he said that.
        That's what he said to her.
    Just that. [Now he is trying to be nice to them.]
That's all.

At last they all went to sleep.

The next day they rose at dawn.

"You should take your brothers-in-law to bathe."

"All right," he answered.

He took them all there, to bathe.

"We should go and immerse our bodies," he said.

"All right," they answered when he said that to them.

Taking visitors to bathe is a formal gesture of hospitality. In this way, and with his formal speech ("immerse" rather than "bathe") he is showing special respect for the brothers-in-law. Although they agree to go bathe, they are still aware of being visitors in a community of *angikogo*.

So, they took their arrows along when they went there.

Each one had them.

So, those same people who went to the bathing place washed themselves there.

When they had finished they came up in the direction of the house.

But before they reached there, some macaws flew toward them.

As they were leaving the bathing place.

Six macaws flew toward them.

Macaws.

Yes, and they perched on a tall dead tree standing by itself.

This was where those macaws roosted.

The roost of those macaws.

So the macaws flew toward them as they walked to the house, *pupupupu*.

And they sat on the tree,

they sat on the tree.

All the men wanted to shoot them.

Those parrots that had come there.

"Well, His Uncles," he said.

"His Uncles." ["His Uncles" is a politely affectionate way of talking to brothers-in-law with reference to their relationship to his own son.]

"Go ahead and shoot them, for I've never had much luck killing them before." [More polite speech here, in which the speaker modestly suggests that he is a bad hunter, which will make them all look good after they shoot the birds.]

"All right," one of them answered.

"All right."

The older brother, their first-born, answered.

Their first-born.

"All right," he answered.

"Shoot what your cousin left when he hunted that time in the past.

Shoot them."

Their sister spoke. [Here, the wife speaks of her current husband as if he were a relative with the right to marry her.]

Well, their older brother got ready when she said that.

He took a single arrow and prepared to shoot.

Next he set his bow just barely outside the doorway.

And he shot a macaw after he did that.

Pupupupu, it died as it flew away.

"All right, you do it, my relative," he said.

To the next oldest.

"All right," that one answered.

He set his bow.

Then he aimed at it and again, the same thing happened,

again, the same thing happened.

It died like the other one when he shot at it,

it fell to the ground.

It fell to the ground.

Next, this one, the third brother.

"My relative, go ahead and shoot one of those left over from when I hunted in the past."

"All right."

And again, the same thing happened!

The last-born, their younger brother.

He too!

And that other person shot it, even her former husband did that.

The macaws were all dead, there were none left.

There were no more macaws left alive.

After all those men had done that, the *angikogo* were afraid of them.

They were afraid of them all.

Because those same men who had shot the macaws were all bow masters.

Bow masters.

That's all.

Then they all came inside.

Next they pulled out the tails of the birds they had shot.

To give to their brother-in-law.

For their brother-in-law. [By doing so, they affirm their respect for him as host.]

When they had finished,

they prepared to leave.

They prepared to leave.

"I'm thinking, my relative," the older brother said.
  "My relative.
I really need to take my children's mother back from here.
  Take my children's mother."
"You need to do that, do you?" that's all that he said to him.
[Afuseti's husband doesn't want her to leave, but he disagrees in
a mild way.]
"Something must be done, my child," I'm told he said to the
oldest brother [that is, his oldest son]
    as they walked to the latrine area.
  "My child. Get that thing of mine for your uncles,
    I want you to give that to your uncles."
  About something he owned.
      About something he owned.
"Take this thing here to them."
He was telling him to present a *magawka*, that's a bag made
from beaten bark, a kind of sack, he was telling him to present
them with a *magawka*.
Something that had been beaten.
So, his son took it over to them.
  He put it down before them.
Next he hurried over to them with a feather headdress,
    a feather headdress.
      He brought over an *agafi*.
        A shell belt.
Pok, this time a toucan feather ornament.
      A toucan feather ornament.
To another man as well, and also to another man.
He did own a great many things!
Next he handed them all *pokï* to the older brother.
  "Take these things of mine, my relative."
  "You want me to, do you?" [Here again, we hear the polite form
of mild disagreement. To accept would mean that he permitted
his sister to remain behind.]
Pokï, pokï, so he put everything down before the older brother.
And in front of each and every one of them.
He gave these things out to each man.
  He gave out everything he had.
Even to her former husband.
  To her former husband.
Macaw tails braided together.
The tails of birds that were braided together.
  Harpy eagle tails.
That's all.

"Now look, brothers," the oldest of them said.
　"Now look, brothers," he said to them.
　"What shall become of our sister now?
　I don't know if we should leave our sister behind to live here,"
　　he said to them.
　"Our nephew's father gave all this to us."
　　That's what he said to them, I'm told.
　"How can we make our sister live with us?
　Our nephew's father has given all this to us.
　　Out of love for our sister,"
　　　he continued.
　"Continue to live here," I'm told he said to their sister.
　　"Continue to live here.
　Look how your children's father has given us all these things in
　payment for you."
　　"All right."
　　She agreed with him after he pointed that out to her.
　"I shall remain this way here, like this.
　How can I go away and leave your nephews here?"
　　She was talking about leaving her children.
　　　There were so many of them.
After that was over,
then they slept again, and they slept again.
　　There at that same place.
　The next day they prepared to leave.
　Their sister wept because she was going to miss them.
　　Yes.
　　Their sister wept because of that.
　They all went hunting.
　They all went hunting.
　　Yes, they all went hunting.
　While they were doing that by themselves,
　"Watch your nephews' fathers carefully.
　Do that when they all leave, merciless as they are.
　　Watch them!
　　　Watch them!
　They want to take me away from here forever.
　　From this place.
　Tomorrow you must watch carefully when your nephews'
　fathers get ready to leave,"
　　she said that right away.
　　"All right."
Then, his followers left.

They all went away after that.

All of them had gone hunting at that time.

They had gone hunting.

The *angikogo* had gone hunting.

They all went away after that.

When the sun had moved over here, however, those others were
ready to leave.

They packed up.

The husband packed up.

"All right, if you must leave, then go, Their Uncles." The
brothers agreed with what he wanted to do.

"Do this, if you must."

"Very well, we should all be going.

We're all going away now."

They were going away from that place.

Indeed, they all flew away from there.

They flew away after they finished getting ready.

Those *angikogo* were fliers, Elena.

They could fly.

[A listener offered some details: "His name was Pañeta.

Pañeta was one of those who stank."]

And so they went away after that.

"Too bad.

To realize that we searched for our sister for so long only to have
this happen." That was the last thing they said.

Then,

after all that they came right back home.

They came back.

"Let's go."

They had *piqui* soup to drink.

Their sister had made them some manioc bread.

While she was doing that they waited another day.

And finally on the following day they came right back.

Then they all came back home.

The brothers came back.

They took their canoes back from that other place where they had
left them behind.

From Uginga.

Afterward they took their canoes.

And they came back that way.

And they arrived home that way.

They all arrived home.

To join their mother.

"Well, have you found your sister?" she asked.

"Have you found your sister?"

"Yes. Yes.

Just as we thought, it wasn't anyone like us who stole our sister, not one of our own people."

Then they gave the payment that had been given them to their father.

They gave their mother the payment.

A shell collar, another shell collar,
    so many things!

That was everything that man had paid for her, merciless as he was.

"The person who stole your daughter was not one of us, Mother, I assure you.

And your daughter has so many children.

That's why we think your grandchildren's father paid for your daughter this time.

    This time."

And the oldest son gave those things to him.

    To his father.

    The toucan feather ornaments.

    The macaw and harpy eagle headdresses.

    There were so many of them!

"As you said, we shall let your sister live among *angikogo*, my sons.

Let your sister live permanently among *angikogo*,"
    he decided in the end.

How could she return?

She had been there so long, she had been there so long.

As the title suggests, Afuseti is the focal character, in the sense that she is the person who motivates everyone else of importance (all men) in the story: her abductor, husband, and brothers. First, Ugaki describes her as a beautiful young woman who captivates a fierce person; second, resisting all the way, she is abducted by him (this segment of the story reveals the most about her); third, her family looks for her, finally learning where she has gone; fourth, her brothers successfully search for her; fifth, they agree to her marriage by receiving large amounts of wealth from her abductor, because he wishes her to remain behind with all their children. The large number of children seems to be what motivates him to offer to pay for her. Despite the title, the story is really about the relationship between the men concerned with Afuseti; it is Afuseti's peculiar position as a woman illegitimately married to a fierce person, and not her personal disposition, that makes her memorable. This "male motivator" role is frequently the case with women in stories.

In this story, the bow masters begin to take on the character of sharpshooters, although they are still capable of fighting. They are also portrayed as suspicious of being inside a settlement of fierce people, anticipating an ambush. What is interesting about this story, though, is how their fighting skills are used in the service of creating an alliance between people who are extremely distant from each other—geographically as well as culturally. There is no further contact between the two groups, though. The brothers leave Afuseti forever, their alliance being only a temporary, "face-saving" one.

Ugaki's story is also interesting for the way relations with neighboring settlements are portrayed. These too are not necessarily informal but tentative insofar as men are suspicious that their women have been seduced to leave for other communities. And men whose communities are the targets of such suspicions need to be careful in their dealings with the aggrieved husbands; thus the rather formal etiquette between visitors and local men that is portrayed here.

CHAPTER

12

Tsangaku Tells of the Dyaguma

One afternoon in late January 1979, during the height of the rainy season when food was particularly scarce, Tsangaku, one of Kambe's two elderly surviving wives, began to tell me stories of her father's settlement, Kanugidyafïtï. Men had repeatedly gone out to fish and had returned with nothing, commenting upon how close the flood-waters had come to the settlement. The young men in Tsangaku's household went out mainly for the form of demonstrating their affinal duties but without any hope of actually finding something to eat. We were all living off manioc soup and bread, yellow squash, corn, and the very occasional piece of bird or monkey someone lucky with his bow had managed to kill. There were twenty-seven people in the household, so all we ever managed to receive was a tiny portion. The children were always given the biggest shares.

For several days, the children had stood around a leaf-cutter ants' nest behind the house, waiting for the queens to swarm. Each held a thick straw, hoping to impale the insects as they walked out of the nest. When the children excitedly called to us women to see the ants, we all ran out to join them, all of us snatching at the insects before they flew away. Wrapped in freshly made manioc bread, their wings roasted off in the coals of the fire, the ants made a meal I shall never forget.

We were hungry, and we were constantly bitten by swarms of tiny gnats. It was something of an ordeal to go for water, since we would invariably come back with horrid-looking welts on our bodies that itched maddeningly. Above all was the unceasing rains, the difficulty of doing any work outdoors, the increasing feeling of claustrophobia from staying inside a smoke-filled house whose mud floors began to give off a choking fungus from the damp. Everyone was coughing, fortunately not from colds, but from this oppressive miasma. So when Tsangaku began this story from her place beside a new hammock she was weaving, many of the women and children of her household gathered around to listen. Tsangaku was at the time the most important female hereditary leader (*anetu*), a woman with many living adult children and grand-children. While speaking to us of the Dyaguma, she was as frequently interrupted by visitors to the house (whom she was expected to formally greet) as by the crying children around her. Like most older women, her attention always seemed to be half drawn to the far corners of the house where grandchildren were playing. Seated close to us was Tsangaku's youngest daughter, Kakangafu, holding her infant son while her cranky daughter tried to get her attention throughout the storytelling. And quietly seated behind Tsangaku was her even more elderly co-wife Kofoño.

Like her mother, Kakangafu was *anetu* and asked many questions as the story came to details of marriages and offspring, which linked participants in the narrative to living members of the Aifa community. These links suggest the events of her story occurred relatively recently, around the turn of the century. The genealogical details are of course yet another way that people, especially women, remember the past. Although they can be clearly recalled independently of a narrative (as Tsangaku and others had done for me in earlier years), they are considerably enriched when they are included in a story; that is where they certainly seem to belong.

Aside from the actual discovery of the Dyaguma, perhaps the most dramatic element of the story is the clubbing to death of the Dyaguma man who has married into the Kalapalo community. Here we see the consequences of the turning inward of fears, the movement of aggression away from distant enemies toward people living within local communities. At this point, the witch is easily executed because his own people are far away; he has few people to support him. Nonetheless, the event is typical of witchcraft executions: men with few or no brothers who also are without powerful allies (fathers-in-law or brothers-in-law who are leaders) tend to be accused and eventually killed over witchcraft accusations.[1] And it is here that the two older women became very upset, since the story reminded them of a recent incident in which someone else was executed. The killing was performed on the initiative of men belonging to a faction differentiated over many years from that of Kambe and his sons.

Kakangafu's frequent questioning of her mother is typical of people listening to stories told by their closest relatives. Rather than having to be restrained and wait until the main segment breaks, in such a context the story is frequently interrupted as people ask for details not immediately offered by the narrator. This occurs especially when genealogical matters are being described, and since women seem particularly concerned with these matters, they seem to interrupt the stories more often than do men. But I think this is a matter of context and not "female" versus "male" speech habits.

Tsangaku gathering charred bark for firewood at the edge of her new manioc field.

So listen [she finally began].
I remember listening to my father telling about the Dyaguma.
The Dyaguma finally came to us from the Tanguro. I remember
my father telling me about them. My father was telling me. I
remember my father telling me.
Do you understand?

[."Yes," I said.]
The Dyaguma probably came while the Kalapalo people were
going to find a lake, to Fifi.
   [."Ah, to Fifi," I said, not really knowing where this was.]
   They went to Fifi.
      They went there to fish.
         Everyone went.
   Afterward they were going to make a ritual.
Afterward they were going to make a ritual. That's all.
"*Etutueh*." They planned on making a big ceremony afterward.
That's all.

They went, and for that reason they placed a net across Fifi.
They placed a net across Fifi, across Fifi.
"They must have been there during that whole time," he told us.
About the Dyaguma. At Tanguro, Tanguro.
"They must have been there," he told us.
So the fish net was shut. It was shut.
   They were killing fish. They finished grilling what they had
   killed.
Then when the sun was here, the next day, early in the morning
they came back here.
   Tititi. They all arrived home. They arrived when the sun was
   here.
      The people arrived. The Kalapalo community.
And the Dyaguma followed behind. To their campground. To the
campground. To the campground.
And there they found bread that had been thrown away. Fish that
had been thrown away, fish that wasn't any good.
   Bread that had been thrown away.
      With the bread that had been thrown away and some leftover
      cold drink. That's what they had, *kuku,* the Dyaguma ate it
      all up.
      Kui, kui, kui they drank, they had bread and fish.
   There were this many, five.
      Five Dyaguma. "What are their names?" say it.
                              ["What are their names?" I asked.]
   Now their names: Tagupage.
                              ["Tagupage," I repeated.]
Yes. And um, um, wait . . . Tagupage, um, Tunggege.
                              ["Who?" I asked.]
Tunggege.
   Let's see, Agataki.
                              ["Agataki."]
   Yes, Pikuga.
                              ["Pikuga."]
   Yes. Let's see, did I say Tagupage? I said Tagupage.
                              ["Yes," I said.]
   Yes.
Let's see . . . there were so many names
                              ["So many names?" I asked.]
Lots of Dyaguma. [Kakangafu, who was sitting with her hungry
children, asked, "Mother, is there any fish?"] There isn't any. Wait
for your younger brother [that is, her husband]. [Kakangafu turned
to her young daughter, saying, "There isn't anything to eat."]

So, they came back, they came back to Kalapalo.
  Someone named Ondo was still back there, Ondo. One of us.
                                   [Kakangafu said, "One of the people."]
  A person, Ondo, Kalapalo.
  His younger brother was Kuama. Kuama was his brother.
                         ["Kuama was his brother," I said.]
   His brother.
  Someone had made his knee hurt through sorcery.
   His knee.
  At that time he wasn't able to travel very fast.
  He was bewitched, Ondo was.
That's why his younger brother was carrying him at that time.
  His younger brother was carrying him.
               ["His younger brother was carrying him," I said.]
   He was being carried by Kuama.
Some of the Dyaguma, *titititi*, were com . . . were walking along
the path, along the path.
  They were walking along the path. So . . . Who's that crying?
  [Like all the Kalapalo grandmothers, she could hear a child cry
  over any noise in the immediate vicinity and kept alert in case
  of any trouble among them.]
Near a settlement of our ancestors, a clearing of theirs.
Then, "Kid," I'm told he said. "I'm dying of thirst. Of thirst."
  He wanted him to bring him water.
  "Wait, I'll go get some for you.
   I'll go get some for you." So he walked away to get some
   water. He went to get some water.
While he was doing that, *tititi* . . . Dyaguma!
  Yes, Dyaguma. He walked right into them!
  "Ah ha ha!" they cried out in surprise.
  "Who could these be?" I'm told he said.
   "Who could these be?"
  They had their bows drawn . . . set with arrows.
  "Be careful, careful, careful, careful," he said.
  "Be careful, careful, careful."
   "All right," they answered.
   "Give me an arrow.
   Give me an arrow."
    "All right."
  They gave him one arrow.
  "Who ARE you?" he said. "What is your name?" he asked.
  "Dyaguma uga, Dyaguma uga."
  "I'm Dyaguma," he told him.
   "I'm Dyaguma," he answered.

"All right."
So, the younger brother:
"Kid, come here quickly.
There are some what's-their-names. Here are some 'Indians.'"
Listen, Daughter. The name for "Indian."

[Kakangafu said, "*Angikogo*."]

That's it.

[I repeated, "*Angikogo*."]

That's it.

Tsangaku could not use this word, because it was the name of one of her sons-in-law. Because the Kalapalo often use proper nouns for names, it was odd-sounding but not unusual that a person would bear such a name.

"Here they are, Kid."

"All right," he answered.
The younger brother was about to be shot, they were aiming at him.
"No no no no, give me your arrow." "All right."
They relaxed their bows.
"*Fuu fuu*." They blew on the arrows to make them safe.
"Who are you? Who?"
Dyaguma. "*Dyaguma uga*," he answered. "*Dyaguma uga*," he
answered.
"I'm Dyaguma," he told him.
Yes.
He told him.
I remember Tadyuwi telling me this.
My father.
While I was secluded he was telling me this.
Yes.
The arrival of the Dyaguma, right to Kalapalo.
Children of theirs to Kwapïgï.
Mm.
And far away at your own settlement you'll play this.
Far away, at your settlement you'll do that with this.
This tape, will that happen?

["That's what I plan to do," I told her.]

Then, "We should start back," *titi*.
"Let's go, Kid," he said. "Let's go," he said. "Let's go."
Titititi as they walked back. "Let them kill us if that's what
they want to do. Let them," he said.
"So we'll be killed, Kid," he said.
"So we'll be killed." "All right," I'm told he answered.
"All right," he said.

They entered the regrown forest.
The path went through the regrown forest.
That was all, then,
    the Dyaguma kept running ahead of them.
"Don't do that, that, that," he said. "All right."
"Give me your arrow."
One of their arrows. That was all.
Then farther on, they were approaching, *tititi.*
    Far from there, I don't know where they were but they had
    entered the Kalapalo path. [To her fidgeting grandson: "What's
    the matter with you?"]
    By now they had entered the Kalapalo path.
    They did that as it went through the forest.
There the Dyaguma ran ahead of them.
    They ran ahead.
      They ran ahead.
      "*Hooh, hoh hoh hoh,*" they did say.
"Be careful, careful, careful, careful," the others answered.
"Be careful."
    "Give me your arrow." "All right."
So the Kalapalo men went ahead of them, back this way, they were
approaching.
    "Dyaguma, Dyaguma," they called out.
    Then,
      that's all.
They were very close. The sun, here . . . when it was right here all
the other people arrived.
    The sun moved across the sky, moving, moving, moving.
Right here
some were preparing to bring them back.
"Those brothers are still not here," they said. "Where are those
brothers?"
"We should go find them right now." "All right."
    So they approached those brothers.
      Looking for them.
        Yes.
Well, a turtle image was on the ground.
                              ["A turtle?" I asked.]
Its image.
                              ["An image," I repeated.]
Yes. [I think if Kudyu had been speaking, he would have gone
into a lengthy explanation of what this meant, but Tsangaku
passed over it.]
    On the ground.

They came . . . they began to come.
    They were all together. The same as they had been before.
    They kept together. They came, he was carrying his older
brother on his back.
    The Dyaguma were with them.
Then, that's all.
Then, *tititi* they came to where some other people could see them.
They joined the others. They joined the others.
    They joined other Kalapalo people who could see them.

Tsangaku was interrupted by a hungry child seeking food. All she could
give it was a piece of manioc bread and a small cold lump of baked
squash, which she took from the ancient storage basket she kept hanging above her fire. This was apparently a portion she had kept for her
own meal, but she could not bring herself to eat in anticipation of the
children's hunger.

Listen to the names.
    Kagia, another one um, Agataki. And Egekogi.
                                   ["Egekogi," I repeated.]
Yes. He himself, and Tugoko.
                                       ["Tugoko."]
    Yes. Let me think. That's all, look. Only one of those who came
with them was a bow master.
So listen.
Then the fierce . . . "Here are the so-and-so's." About the
"Indians."
                                  ["*Angikogo*," I said.]
Yes. "They're here."
    "Where? They are coming here now with us."
      There were two of our people, two. Two of our people.
        So they could see them running up.
    "Look. Look."
    "Look."
    There were only two strangers.
            [A child who had just come up to us asked, "Who?"]
    Dyaguma.
Dyaguma . . . Aguma . . . Aguma was what the people first
called them.
But later they changed to a different way,
        to "Dyaguma" finally.
      And they had kept arrows of theirs.
        Some of their arrows. They kept their arrows.
    [Kakangafu asked, "They hadn't seen arrows made of cane?"]
      They hadn't. The Kalapalo people.

[Kakangafu asked, "Who were our people?"]
    What? The brothers, who were doing all that, the traveling
    brothers. Then, that's all.
So . . . so "*Ah ha haaa*," they said. "*Hïï*" threateningly. "Be
careful, careful, careful," the Kalapalo answered.
    "Give me your arrow." "All right," they said.
    So to the settlement.
    "Go tell the rest," they said.
        "Go tell, go tell the rest." "Go tell the rest." "All right."
    So, they turned around.
        "*Kah*, so-and-so." "Indians."
So, directly where the Kwapïgï people were.
    Where those who had already arrived home were.
So I'm told they were on the Kwapïgï path.
So they were on the Kwapïgï path.
There were these many houses, ten.
    At Kwapïgï.
        By "Arrow."

Tsangaku continues more energetically. She is talking about her father's
settlement, of which she was quite proud that he was the hereditary
leader.

Some of the people were moving to Kalapalo.
    There were so many houses in that house circle, there was no
    more room!
        They wanted to live there.
    At Kalapalo.
    But now Kwapïgï was merging with them.
So those others who came by themselves told about what had
happened.
    At Kalapalo.
Ah, Dyagu . . . "So and so, there are some of them here," they said
about the "Indians."
    They came.
    "All right now."
Have them go over to the other side, over to the other side.
    Have them go where all our people are gathered."
        "All right."
    Those men crossed over in their canoes.
    They waited for the Dyaguma.
        Dyaguma.
        The Dyaguma were arriving.
"This is one of their arrows," they said. "One of their arrows."

How beautiful it was.
They were playing around with it.
   Playing around.
     Yes. Playing around.
   [Kakangafu asked, "One of the arrows they had taken away
   from them?"]
An arrow they had taken away from them.
    One of the Dyaguma arrows brought by those other men.
      Those who had gone to get the brothers.
At last they approached their settlement.
  Those people were still arriving, I mean.
  [Needing to remind me to respond,
  she then said: "Say 'Yes' Elena."

                                   "Yes," I said.]
   Those people were still arriving, the one who was being
   carried was arriving.
Most likely, as they came toward the settlement, fish were being
grilled.
   Because the next day they were going to perform in the
   ceremony.
    The ceremony was being completed.
Then, "Let's go."
   They came into the plaza.
    As they did so, they saw how beautiful my people were in
    their decorations.
They must have just erected a grave enclosure,
because they were all lined up behind the grave.
With solemn faces,
   lined up one by one. That's all.
   The Kalapalo people.
    Our people.
There were SO MANY of our people.
So then seats were brought out. Yes, seats.
  Seats like this one here.

                             ["I see, seats," I said.]
   There were so many of this kind.
   These many, five.
So, "Please drink this."
   "Please drink this," they said.
   They gave them something to drink.
   They didn't. They only placed it on their laps.
So, fish were brought.
   They ate it. They saved the bones that were left over from
   their fish.

["Oh, they finished," Kakangafu said.]
They finished . . . yes, that's right . . . when it is given . . .
that was how the Suya killed people, the Suya.

["Oh?" I said.]
Yes. When Mïgitsitsï give us fish,

["Not that!" Kakangafu said to her mother.]
beware of stomach pain.
That is the way Suya kill people, Suya kill people.
Don't let the Mïgitsitsï give you fish, because if you throw your
bones away they will do something with them.

["I see," I said.]
Be careful to prevent them also from doing that.

["Oh."]
Yes. Be careful, we die.

["Oh."]

I couldn't find the enthusiasm to strongly sympathize with her problems with accepting food from others. Her daughter Kakangafu hardly
ate anything that came from other houses and was very conservative in
her diet. However, neither Tsangaku's oldest daughter nor her sons
seemed to have problems accepting food. As leader, Kambe was often
given presents of food from other houses which he shared with his own
family. Those who wouldn't eat passed it on to me and to other less
fastidious people in their household.

Be careful when people give us food, be careful in other
houses.
Then after it was all done they stayed there.
Their arrows had been taken away from them, their arrows.
[Kakangafu handed her infant to her daughter, saying, "Your
younger brother's tiring me out, take him."]
Their arrows were broken up.
They were broken up *popopopopopo* until they were done
away with.
Next, Grandfather did something, Grandfather. Name him now,
the person who was a bow master did something.
["Tafudyani," Kakangafu told me. "Tafudyani?" I asked.]
Yes, he was the person who did something.
He decided to paint himself with charcoal and tied toucan
feather ornaments around himself.
He had toucan feather ornaments here, look, around his chest
like this.
That's all.

"My children," he said. "I'm surprised that you're sitting where
'Father'—name him—

[Kakangafu answered, "*Angikogo.*"]

are," he said to them.

"That's our grandmother we're remembering," he declared
[about the ceremonial gathering, to commemorate a death that
occurred the previous year].

"*Kah, kah, kah, kah.*" Aiming, one by one he pointed his
arrow at them.

Right in their faces.

Yes, and they wept.

So he relaxed his bow.

Then, "I'm lying to you.

I'm lying. I'm lying to you."

Then he removed his arrow from his bow.

He was the bow master.

That's all.

For a long time, for a long time, one by one they went into a
house, they went.

With Kagia, beautiful. Oh, with Kagia.

Beautiful.

Then, that was all. They stayed there.

They slept for a very long time.

For a long time one by one they were taken inside for a long time.

For a long time. Yes.

For a long time they lived there.

[To her granddaughter: "Look, here's your fish."]

[Kakangafu asked her, "They lived with our people?"]

That's right, each one was taken care of by one of our people.

That was all, then they slept for a long time and left,

they went away, they went away,

when the sun was here they went away.

They went away.

Another time they approached with fish to give out.

Dyaguma were friends of the Kalapalo.

Dyaguma.

Friends of the Kalapalo.

Friends. That's right.

They gave them shell belts and shell collars. What beautiful
shell collars the Dyaguma had, shell collars.

Yes. This kind [she held up her necklace to me, a man's belt].
Shell belts.

["The yellow ones?" I asked.]

No. Shell belts.

["Oh, I understand," I said.]

The Dyaguma had this kind.

Payment for women, for women. Oh, the Dyaguma.

Oh my, the Kalapalo, the Kalapalo went there all the time,
to the Dyaguma.

They had become REAL friends.

["Say 'they went there to get married,' " Kakangafu prompted.]

Yes.

["What?" I asked.]

To find spouses.

["To find spouses?" This was an expression I didn't really
understand.]

Mm. They married them, the Kalapalo.

["I see," I said.]

So they went there to find husbands.

So a wife went to Kagia, a wife.

Kanga, a Kalapalo woman.

The wife of the Dyaguma.

["I see. Did you say her name was 'Fish'?" I asked.]

Fish. [laughs] Kanga. Fish.

["That was the woman's name?" I asked.]

The woman's name, Kanga.

["Kanga," I repeated.]

Yes.

The mother . . . her youngest granddaughter was Ahpĩũ's mother.
Their elder's mother.

["Ahpĩũ's mother?" I repeated.]

Yes, Ahpĩũ's mother. [Tsangaku whispers, because it is also the
name of a woman who had died just a few years before:]
Fukangaigu.

["Fukangaigu," I repeated.]

Yes. She was a co-wife of Tagupage.

["Who?" I asked.]

Tagupage's wife.

["Yes," I said.]

[Kakangafu asked, "The Dyaguma's wife?"]

Yes. That was her older sister Kanga.

Then they approached . . . oops . . . She became Kagia's wife, Kagia.

Tagupage had two wives, one of Okodyo's grandmothers, Mageata.

Her younger sister Agifua [tightly] also became his wife.

[Kakangafu, apparently picking up a disapproving tone in her
mother's voice: "Was that a good thing for them to do?"]

It was. [Now Tsangaku begins to really warm to her story.]
So then when at last Kagia came,
   he became one of our grandfathers.
How beautiful he was, the most handsome of all.
   When all the men painted themselves believe me,
   he was MORE beautiful than any of them.
                              ["The Dyaguma man?" I asked.]
   Yes, the Dyaguma was who I've been talking about.
The Lahatua were going to club him.
      That's so. He was a married man, his wives were there.
      He was married.
      Married.
They would come to see people,
   just as our people would go to him, to their settlement,
      their settlement, their settlement, their settlement,
      oh, over and over they would do that.
         The Dyaguma were true friends.
They would go to exchange things at Dyaguma.
Shell collars, shell collars, at Dyaguma.
   "Here is your mother's payment."
   To Isanganga.
   To Isanganga, to her younger brother.
Pok, pok, oh, so much payment for his wives.
The same in the case of Tagupage, to Grandfather, to Agifu,
Father's father [here Tsangaku is talking about Kambe's father's
brother].
      To her younger brother.
Pok, she did have shell collars.
   Dyaguma shell collars, bah!
   Scattered, scattered, all over the place,
      the shell collars.
   That's what she said, Kanga, the wife who had been paid for.
   And um, unworked shells strung together,
   unworked shells on burity cord, their unworked shells on burity
   cord, unworked shells on cord.
      Something like this, they had those things,
      all around there.
They must have been making them all the time!
      [Kakangafu, holding up some blue Czechoslovakian seed
      beads, which I had brought from New York, said, "They
      didn't have any of these?"]
They certainly didn't, they didn't.
                                          ["Oh."]

Mm. Believe me, another time they approached the settlement,
Kanga approached.
    Um, that person, also the married man.
    That other person, she went also
        with him.

Now we were interrupted by a visitor who had come into the house to
ask Tsangaku for a certain kind of cooking pot, which took some time
to find. After she chatted with her neighbor for a few minutes, Tsangaku
came back to her hammock and continued.

So listen.
So they were there.
    They were friends,
    they would travel back and forth.

                              ["I see," I said.]

    We would go there.
        To the Dyaguma.
        For shell collars.
        They would go.
    We would go.
    I'm telling you they did that in order to see Kagia.
        To see their friends.
    Believe me they did because he was there.
        He was with his wife.
So she gave birth to a girl,
    so her older sister.
    The wife called Asoko, she had a daughter.
    But while that was happening the younger sister didn't seem to
want to become pregnant.
    [sadly] Fukangaigu didn't get pregnant.
                [Kakangafu: "But the other one did?"]
    Yes, this one, her older sister Kangai.
    Believe me she did have a child. That person was a female,
believe me.
    Asoko's wife.
                    [Kakangafu: "Tagupage?"]
    That was his daughter's name.
                     [Kakangafu: "What?"]
    That was her name.
    ["So the person I can't address (a senior female relative of her
    husband) carries the name of his wife's daughter's offspring?"
    Kakangafu asked.]
    The mother of the woman who is married to your younger
    brother.

[Kakangafu continued, "That was Asoko's daughter?"]
The daughter.
[Kakangafu asked, "Tagupage's granddaughter?"]
Yes. The Dyaguma's granddaughter.
[I asked, "The Dyaguma's granddaughter?"]
Yes. The Dyaguma's granddaughter. That's what I was told.
The granddaughter of the Dyaguma.
Yes, they were beginning to mix in with us.
The granddaughter of the Dyaguma.
Yes.
Then, it finally happened. Then, believe me, it finally happened.
Kagia was clubbed.
They went to club him.
And an old Dyaguma man, let me think, Tïgoko.
I remember being told, that, um, Kagia was clubbed.
The Lahatua came to club him, I remember.
"I don't know if they had practiced their evil things," I remember
that's what Father told me.
"I don't know if it was because they had practiced their evil
things," I remember that's what Father told me. "That they
clubbed some of us."
["They clubbed some of us," Kakangafu repeated.]
"They clubbed some of us."
["They clubbed some of you," I repeated.]
I don't know, we people here never want to club people from other
settlements, believe me. "I don't know why they had to go and
club him, believe me."
[Kuɾoño, Tsangaku's co-wife, who was listening intently, joins
in for the first time, "Never. Oh no."]
[tightly] Believe me there never was any reason at all for them to
behave that way.

This was a delicate subject, because a man had recently been executed
for witchcraft. Apparently consensus was not as complete as it should
have been for the execution to have taken place.

Mm.
He was clubbed, when he was clubbed, he himself, Kagia was
clubbed,
he died.
Then they were told about it
by the Suya.
They spoke to the Dyaguma about it.
"Your Kagia is no longer alive.
He is no more.

The Kalapalo were killed
    by the Kuikugu who clubbed them."
They came to them, crying out, "Waa,"
    they came to the Dyaguma.
They were really mourning in their own way when they did
that.
Then, they came right here.
    In order to mourn again.
    Let's see, then the bow master,
        the bow master.
Then they came in their usual way.
    Those other men, mourning.
    The turtle eggs were beginning to hatch. "Let's look for turtle
eggs, let's look for them."
    They came.
So, now look, this was all happening at Tanguro.
    That was where the Dyaguma left their canoes, at Tanguro.
        They beached at Tanguro.
            They had came down the Tanguro.
    There were fish pools of theirs there.
        At Tanguro.
        Dyaguma fish pools.
    Only the Dyaguma could fish there.
    Those were their springs there.
    "Kagia's springs," where he fished.
        His own springs.
                            ["What are they?" Kakangafu asked.]
    They poisoned the fish there, that's what I was told.
    He himself poisoned the fish there.
The Dyaguma approached in their canoe.
    They were on the Tanguro.
So then, at last they beached their canoe, they beached their
canoe.
    Tutututu they carried their canoe on the land, putting out their
    campfire tsïzïzïzïzï, DEEP in the forest.
        As they went some people were looking for turtle eggs.
So after the Dyaguma had been clubbed, these others came in their
own way, "Waa," looking for him.
    Wiii.
        ["Let's see. Was Kagia already clubbed?" Kakangafu asked.]
    Yes,
        Kagia had already been clubbed.
[Kakangafu continued, "Who were the ones who clubbed him?"]
    The Kufikugu, Kufikugu [that is, the Kuikuro].

At first they were living at the settlement called Kufikugu.
  They went from Kufikugu.
After they had done that, when for some reason they clubbed that
Dyaguma,
  they moved to Lahatua.
    They decided on Lahatua.
        ["That's why they left Kuikuro, then?" I asked.]
  Yes, that's why they moved, why they left.
Then, that was all.
Afterward, two people went to do what I was talking about, Ofe
and his companion.
  His wife, his wife.
"Let's go look for turtle eggs."
  Turtle eggs.
  His wife spoke, his wife spoke.
        ["It was the dry season?" Kakangafu asked.]
  It was the dry season.
"Let's go look for turtle eggs.
  At that place."
    They approached the place.
  Coming around the bend along the bank, the others saw them
  now,
    the Dyaguma.
  They had traveled in their canoe all the way from their
settlement.
  ["From their settlement the Kalapalo had been going all
  along?" I asked.]
    That's right. [Yet another interruption. Kakangafu's
    daughter was now in a tantrum.]
So then, where did they go to? *Popopopopo*, in the canoe,
  further over to that side where Togoiñe had lived,
    they came right toward that place (they came toward that
    place)
      the Dyaguma, in their canoe.
        Their canoe.
A young woman was with them.
  One woman.
    Only one woman paddling.
    A woman.
Tadyoki, Tadyoki.
  And Mbenatu.
  A Dyaguma woman.
    She was one of their women.
    A woman.

She only had one breast, like this.
   Well, she was with them.
      Yes. Father said that, I remember.
Then, those others came toward them very slowly.
   Now she was turned away from her husband.
      His wife was turned away from her husband.
      Afilutsu was.
         Yes. From Ofe.
      The husband, the husband.
         Afilitsu was the wife.
"Here are the Dyaguma!" with that he rubbed out his fire and
ran over to the side,
      The husband was preparing to roast the turtle eggs, the
      husband.
      He ran away, he was frightened of them.
"Oh, ho ho," they called out.
"Where is Kagia. Where?
   Is Kagia?
   Is it true the Kufikugu clubbed some Kalapalo?"
"No. He's still alive. He's here.
   He's still alive. He's still alive. He's here."
      "You're wrong. You're wrong.
         The Suya told us about him.
         The Suya did.
'We've heard Kagia's been clubbed.
Killed with a Kalapalo by the Kuikugu.' the Suya told us."
      "No. He's still here. Go there and see for yourself.
         See for yourself."
      Her husband was still trying to hide from them because he
      was afraid,
      and so the woman at last
      went to them, went to them.

Kakangafu angrily smacked her older son, who had been sneaking bits
of the baby's food: "Shame, his fish!" Now all the children began weeping, so Tsangaku gave up her story as a lost cause.

   That's all. Some other time.

PART
4

13

Conclusion:
History, Ideology, and
the Personal Version
of Reality

During my attempts to understand the narratives in this book and what the Kalapalo storytellers were trying to say to me, I found valuable two concepts which tend to be applied to modern and modernizing societies rather than the nonliterate, relatively detached communities in the Alto Xingu. These are "ideology" and "biography." Having used the terms in a somewhat implicit manner in the early sections of the book, I turn now to more explicit discussion of the relationships between them to explore some of the consequences of recognizing these relationships in oral genres, so as to better understand narrative representations of history and of persons.

Understanding Subjectivity in
Kalapalo Narratives

In a study of Western biography, James Clifford writes that the most difficult task of biography is of "rendering personality as an experiential world," in which the external realities of living are portrayed as inseparable ingredients of a self. The difficulty is connected to the fact that Western biography is concerned with "delivering a self," with finding the particular coherence or unity of an individual life, attempting "not to portray a life experience but to shape a life." There is an emphasis on "closure and progress towards individuality, rather than openness and discontinuity," Clifford writes (1978: 45). And, considering the other side of the temporal bracket, because a "complete" life must have a satisfying conclusion, the biographical convention of narrative closure requires that the story end in the subject's death, retirement, or conversion, in other words a significant identity transformation. In the same vein, Sven Birkerts writes that biography is intrinsically compelling because it presents, however fanciful, a view of an individual's experience as a contained whole, a final design. "We may be bored by the substance of x's life [Birkerts says], but the perspective itself is exalting" (1987: 315).

These views of biography are closely connected, I believe, with a tendency to think of the personal "self" as some kind of concretized, unified, and (as is often hoped) consistent and harmonious "thing," be it treated as a mental structure, a set of bodily images, or a semiotic relation. Such ideas of "self" pose serious problems of objectification and reification.

It is here that Kalapalo stories, which describe the cross-fertilization between personal programs and social realities sharing a common ground, seem to offer interesting possibilities. When talking about individuals, the Kalapalo seem to be most concerned with action-oriented narrative processes, oriented, that is, to the actual strategies people use with one another for enacting emotions and formulating motivations. What to us may seem troublesome contradictions, paradoxes, and inconsistencies in feelings are represented not as incoherences or even pathological states but, more interestingly, as arising from the problems people experience in giving strategic voice to inevitable incompatibilities and paradoxes in their understandings of who and what they are.

To understand the nature of biographical content in these stories requires an approach that uses specification of names, labels, and other categorical differences between identities and relations per se as merely a first and perhaps superficial step, because this content is precisely what is problematic, what is emerging through (rather than being represented by) narrative. Many of the events are of speech-centered and generally dialogical actions that result in distinctively individual (though not always fully unique) versions of reality developed within and through particular social configurations. In order to understand these, one needs to become more deeply involved in a search for the individual voices and the cohesion and coherence that are created between them: how the narrators' descriptions of actions are connected to each other to form an intersubjective, emergent narrative process and where and how these voices are repeatedly, yet variously, heard. Thus my discourse-focused approach that investigates temporal organization and developmental processes seemed particularly appropriate. Insofar as this approach reveals the special ways that individuals develop within (and thereby change) their social configurations, experiencing time through social change, it is especially suited to searches for implicit forms of historical consciousness in stories.

Kalapalo History and Biography

To the Kalapalo, history is first and foremost biographical, in that the events of the past are remembered as stories about specific, named people. Ideas about these people pertaining to their emotional agency, motivations, and special goals, together with changes in their subjectivity, are far more important to the Kalapalo sense of history than objectified and generalized descriptions of events or of groups of people. In fact, the poetic structuring of Kalapalo narratives, the logical relations that organize events and their narrative sequencing, depends upon the emotional quality of relationships people have with one another, the feelings they provoke within each other, and the motives arising from those feelings.

Above all, historical actors are conversationalists—speakers engaged in dialogue. The Kalapalo make considerable use of this convention to the extent that most of their depictions of events are "speech-centered." The result is that all their narratives consist of extensive conversations, chiefly "oratory," and other instances of people speaking to each other. In fact, in all Kalapalo stories (historical or otherwise) the emotions and motives of characters (and thus the uniqueness of specific characters themselves) are realized through their quoted speech, rather than through labels or a narrator's more direct description of feelings and motives.

I have used the phrase "quoted speech" rather than "reported speech" because the Kalapalo understand these conversations to have been ultimately learned from actual participants in the events in question, actual reproduction of things people once said. We might question whether such words were "really" spoken in the past, though evidentiality often provides good reason to accept some conversations as well remembered. But this is to miss the more important point about quoted speech, which is that Kalapalo narrators use it to realize ideas of the emotional quality of interpersonal contact, which has a deeper truth for them than whether they are literally replicating speech. This is another important way individuals are shown to be intimately participating in one another's understandings of experience, even when these are disputed. Storytellers prefer not to label people's emotions, tending to show them to be a function of conversations. Where narrators do use verbs that represent emotional action ("he was furious") and nominalized verbs that represent emotional actors ("the angry one"), they always do so by way of conclusion to a piece of conversation, in order to qualify the quality of an interaction, especially where there is a need to make something explicit to a listener who might not be clearly following the story. Not only speech but song, expletives, animal calls, and ideophonic representations of actions involving inanimate entities all contribute in important ways to describing activities in an emotional mode involving different kinds of entities.[1] To give a third example, strategic use of pronouns and other kinds of referencing of persons (as we have seen in considerable detail, for example, in the story about Tapoge) also qualify emotional actions.

The fact that a person's decisions to act are motivated through interaction instead of by personal introspection is a real difference between Western and Kalapalo biographies. A character's subjective version of reality emerges from an interactive, interpersonal field of interpretation, planning, and the formulation of goals, as well as the comprehension of consequences as they are spoken about with others. Such interpretations are constituted as speech-centered events (rather than, for example, "thoughts" or even "utterances") during which people comment upon, validate, or dispute one another. Understanding and experiencing anew, in other words, are far from solitary activities in these stories. So, while as biographies these narratives are focused upon individual persons, the focal narratives are always joined to those of others through the expressive convention of quoted conversations. The latter inform us about all the interactive and especially transactive conditions that led to personal decisions to act, thus providing not only descriptions of what happened but procedural explanations of why, always related to characterizations of encounters between persons. Thus the events that are described do not "just happen" but are made to appear part of an emergent, developmental process. In this regard, quoted speech, as the critical element in an event that is "speech-centered" but which may also involve bodily action, plays a critical role in how the Kalapalo understand personal as well as social development.[2]

Such explanations may vary both in scope and content according to who is listening. Since (with regard to Kalapalo) we are talking about an oral tradition in use among a nonliterate people, we are necessarily dealing with memories of individual persons that have been reworked through poetic and theatrical conventions into an *akiña*, or dialogically constructed narrative performance, the conditions of which must also be given some attention. Hence my emphasis upon the rhetorical and expressive devices used by Kalapalo narrators to structure their narratives.

Conventions in Western Biography

By characterizing certain Kalapalo stories as biographical, I am rejecting claims that the "biographical attitude" is lacking outside Western writing and that (as a literary form) autobiography in particular is not a traditional (or indigenous) Native American literary form but one that was adopted by literate people or those who collaborated with anthropologists and historians.[3] In this view, biographies and autobiographies are treated (too uncritically, in my opinion) as if they represented the same "attitudes" toward individuality and personal autonomy. Brumble, who has written thoughtfully about this problem, delineates six kinds of preliterate "autobiographical narratives" among Native Americans, but he takes care to distinguish these from "autobiographies," which he defines in terms of several negative criteria derived from Western writing: the absence of full life accounts; the lack of a connection between notions of an individual self and the narrative; the lack of chronological ordering; the absence of early childhood experiences; and the absence of "turning points" or "climactic moments" with no connections made between events. For Brumble, "preliterate autobiographical tales were likely to be discreet stories of episodes in a life, rather than the story of a life" (1988: 85). According to him, the numerous recorded dream accounts and stories of great deeds performed by named individuals, such as the coup tales of the Gros Ventres, Sioux, and Crow, are autobiographical tales but not autobiographies in that they are not concerned with the "complete lives" of individuals. I would consider some of these stories biographical rather than autobiographical to the extent that they were not told by the person who directly experienced the events in question but had become part of oral tradition.

The Western concern with whole lives in biography has much to do with the need to explain what is special about a person. Our own autobiographical consciousness is focused upon the distinctive nature of a private self. Western writers follow the characteristic sequential scheme of a more generally typical narrative structure. They set an individual's personal development within a linear frame, being concerned wherever possible with complete birth-to-death progressions of particular lives (though the earliest experiences are often inaccessible and thus subject to extreme conjecture). These writers tend to seek the causes of the very individuality they are shaping in motivations, whether conscious or unconscious. Psychological biographies, which deliberately interpret people's lives according to theories of personality, see these lives (and ideologies, insofar as they can be linked with specific persons) as realizations of certain implicit, original undertakings arising from early childhood experiences. While such writers have increasingly incorporated social contexts into their biographies, emphasizing the individual's attempts to adapt to social circumstances and especially the patterns of change in familial circumstances throughout a person's life, social context is treated less as emergent meaning than as a background environment so that the person's lived experience in the world becomes obscure, decontextualized.[4] As the distinctive settings in which a person is situated are separated from the described "person," the autonomy or "thingness" of personhood is granted at the expense of interactive relations.[5]

As Arnold Krupat has suggested, the place of the individual person in special social configurations is much more important in Native American societies than is the sense of autonomy or separateness from others. Krupat writes, "That egocentric individualism associated with the names of Byron or Rousseau, the cultivation of originality and difference, was never legitimated by native cultures, to which celebration of the hero-as-solitary would have been incomprehensible" (1985: 29). In Kalapalo, however, narratives are often focused on personal versions of reality, upon individual persons making unusual decisions for reasons unique to their life situations. The special ways that individuals develop within their social (and often cosmological) configurations are so meaningful, so understandable (because they constitute a kind of explanatory argument in which links are made between events), and (apparently) so memorable that they become the substance of stories that eventually join existing oral tradition.

Kalapalo stories about warriors are certainly not biographical in the ways I think we would most anticipate if we use as models the work of notable Western intellectual and literary biographers. Most Kalapalo stories differ from Western biography in making use of rather brief time frames. Kalapalo biography (much like the North American autobiographical oral narratives described by Brumble) are episodic, placing emphasis upon only certain critical times in a person's life, without tending toward the kind of closure mentioned by Clifford that we would expect. Kalapalo warrior biographies describe events occurring over very short periods of time: a single lunar period, or even during the course of a single horrible day. This same focus upon crisis, and the resolution of essentially personal difficulties, is typical of the community and family stories told by Kalapalo. Although the latter have a greater temporal perspective, they too concentrate upon critical situations involving relationships between persons and have a biographical character for this reason.

Contrary to the expectation that biographies must be "life-historical" progressions of particular lives that realize certain implicit, original projects, Kalapalo biographies are not necessarily stories of personal experiences in the classic Eriksonian life-crisis contexts: the events surrounding puberty, marriage, childbirth, and the death of a parent. Only in the case of narratives about those primordial beings who constitute what I have elsewhere called the "human pedigree" (Basso 1985) are there anything like "life histories" presented. This is because such myths are concerned with the character of entities whose actions resulted in the original humans; they are ontological in theme, explaining human nature through their representations of the logic of the character of these primordial protagonists. Life-crises contexts are the focus of Kalapalo attention only insofar as they lead to pivotal occasions of reformulation of meaning in people's lives, moments of profoundly significant decisions to act, when ideas about identity, personal agency, and responsibility for the consequences of action are suddenly thrown into relief by their questionable relevance to new and unexpected situations. In this regard, either a person's exit from puberty seclusion (signifying the end of sexual abstinence) or the failure of a marriage is a particularly important Kalapalo context for both men and women, as we have seen.[6] Such life-historical contexts as early childhood experiences, childbirth, and the death of a parent receive little attention [one exception is the story of Tapoge]; the death of a child or a friend, however, is treated as a turning point in several narrated lives. Generally, though, Kalapalo stories represent individuals in the here and now as socially contextualized, action-oriented, and discourse-centered selves, engaged with the practical immediacy of incompatibilities and paradoxes in their understandings of who and what they are.

Although the depth of narrated time is shallow by our own standards, the details of each story create a strong sense of individual character and, even more important, the shaping of moral understanding arising, not (just) from formative events in childhood but from those special moments of decision and choice during which a person's distinctive individuality is portrayed as achieved through actions that involve deliberate use of strategy and selected preferences. And it is often the case that the individuals involved clearly expressed a wish—at the very moment of those crucial decisions—that stories of their deeds be passed on to others. For this reason, at least some of the biographies are in an important way autobiographical as well. The manner in which this is achieved makes such stories distinctive among all the Kalapalo tell.

As narrative speech (akiñatunda), these stories are told in very similar ways regardless of their varying subject matter. There is always an active dialogic relation between the narrator and a listener-responder, who by responding (itiïtsa) contributes to the structuring of the story; second, narrators use a variety of conventional expressions to create hierarchically organized rhetorical units; third, quoted speech is used extensively to realize the specific character relations of the story. But it is in regard to the particular ingredients of quoted speech in the warrior biographies that (above all) they are shaped as distinctive among Kalapalo narratives. The self-conscious references warriors often make to their actions as substance for future storytelling—"Let my life be something to tell to those who come after"—suggest a joint-authorship of the story, an embedding of autobiography within biography. The warrior contributes as much to the story as a conscious actor aware of a future audience as do the people who tell about his life years later.

Finally, we have the autobiographical stories, narrated memories, and testimonials (the latter similar to Brumble's "self-vindications"). Here, the social configurations in which the individual tellers are embedded are clearly foregrounded: personal self-consciousness of the narrator is subdued. Yet the absence of the personal "I" does not mean there is no personal voice. I have argued that the developmental progression which emerges in Kalapalo narratives constitutes a kind of explanatory argument that connects events, which are, above all, speech-centered. In autobiographical stories, this progression is also important, and we need to look at the particular details of its configuration through quoted speech in order to see the autobiographical voices emerging among the voices of the other participants. So, although Brumble's characterization of Native American autobiographical stories as lacking "critical moments" and "turning points" may be true for some (but certainly not all) Kalapalo stories, this does not necessarily preclude arguments that connect events in an explanatory fashion. This occurs, to repeat, through the emergent narrative structure itself, and for Kalapalo, that structure cannot be separated from what participants in events are made to say.

Ideology and the Personal Version of Reality

In his well-known paper on ideology, Clifford Geertz writes, "It is a loss of orientation that most directly gives rise to ideological activity, an inability, for lack of usable models, to comprehend the universe of civic rights and responsibilities in which one finds oneself located" (1973: 219). And when this universe is perpetually changing, then we would have to expect that the motives ideology engenders would be also suspect. Under these circumstances, experimental, exploratory activity (what Ricoeur called a "confrontation with basic ideals" [1986]) would emerge and become highly valued.

Many Kalapalo biographies (and their trickster stories as well [Basso 1987b]) exhibit this kind of activity. Action in an experimental mode (is this "experimental subjectivity?") might become highly valued during times of such cultural sea changes—and the more general suspicion that things are not fixed and assured might arise as a key element of an inherently subversive ideology. At the same time, the individual actors who were most experimental might, like the Kalapalo tricksters, also become suspect and dangerous through their unpredictability.

Ricoeur and others have questioned the appropriateness of speaking of ideology in premodern contexts, assuming that people do not confront each other over basic ideals in such cases.[7] Anthropologists, on the other hand, are skeptical about whether such "universal agreements" ever existed, stimulated in large measure by an anthropology of language that has begun to show a deep appreciation, thanks to Mikhail Bakhtin, of "the heteroglossic, centrifugal forces in speech communities" (Hill 1986: 2). Our concern with the role of language in experiencing human connection—the interactive, transactive, interpretive phenomena of speech-centered events—often forces us to consider the reasons behind instances of confusion and misunderstanding, leading us to focus more sharply upon conflict, resistance, argument, debate, challenge, and deception. These are matters of intense concern to anthropologists who long ago discarded the idea that social life necessarily functions to create coherence and order.

Anthropological considerations of ideology often point to how changing notions of identity and shifting dimensions of ethical judgment emerge during ideological processes. Twenty years after Clifford Geertz wrote of the orienting function of ideological activity in times of pervasive disorientation, Eric Wolf, who views ideology mainly as a matter of codification of distinctions and of classification, discussed ideological alternatives as systems of ideas and their enactments used by groups and classes "to define their place in the field of force generated by a mode of production" (390). Talal Asad (in a review of Wolf's formulation) writes of ideology as a kind of political discourse that involves the construction of motivations, transformation of commitments, and reorganization of experiences (1987: 594–607). For these writers, then, there is an unexplored cognitive dimension to ideology that involves reasoning, particularly the attempts people make to clarify (and make effective) the actions and ethical dimensions that are constitutive of specific identities.

From the perspective of individuals, this process of clarification can only be effective insofar as a person is able to feel that desires and hopes are valid and capable of being realized—if only by others. Put simply, the choice of ideological material to believe in creates hope, even for those for whom the future is anything but auspicious. There is much need for a close examination of this dimension, using more fine-grained analyses than authors concerned mainly with ideological content and the behavior of entire classes of persons have chosen to develop.

Kalapalo narratives not only "justify" power or demonstrate how "expressions circulate in the social world" (Thompson 1984) but show how individuals try to reorient themselves with respect to relations of power and direct their activities in new and different ways. This process of "figuring out" comes to be much more interesting than "justification" in Kalapalo narratives. In stories people tell about their pasts, conversational dialogues are most apparent when emotional events and problems of motive are foregrounded, and it is in such contexts that the speaking personality appears in all its surprising idiosyncrasy.

The study of speech-centered events in narratives can therefore tell us much about how people understand and remember the place of subjectivity in the constitution of ideology, just as with history. A close analysis of historical narratives provides the opportunity to understand some of the ways people engage in this work of personal adjustment to new situations and contribute to the construction of ideological shifts. It is this psychological dimension of ideology that closely connects it to the biographical and autobiographical motives, the concern to ask "why" about a life, to question the foundations of particular, historically located conceptions of subjectivity, to probe the sources of motivation. When recurrent dramas and unique crises are preserved in memory through oral narrative, attempts at reformulation of personal identity and of standard interpersonal activities will be included in the story. It may be that this is so because the struggles to reorient identity, often in the face of terrible odds, are struggles that involve narrativization (or textualization) as a way of achieving coherence. The very fact of acting in the hope that someone will preserve one's story is thus at once a performance, an optimistic personal strategy, and an ideological process—a claim of authenticity and legitimacy.

Although ideological ferment is associated most often with the open, conflictual situation of modern society, with its rapid changes in older structures and challenges to traditional authority and precepts, anthropologists working with native people in South America have discovered considerable evidence of those changes (what Geertz called a "pervasive sense of disorientation"). In lowland South America centuries of brutal invasion, occupation, and enslavement by Europeans have resulted in new ethnic allegiances and identities, responses to the new conditions imposed upon them. Sometimes, people from very different kinds of communities, often speaking different kinds of languages, fled from the centers of European expansion to form new societies. As these refugees encountered one another while exploring new places where they hoped to settle, mutual fear and distrust sometimes resulted in violent confrontations. Yet once the sheer immediacy of survival was assured, some tried to peacefully establish contacts leading to mutually beneficial relationships. Although not always successful, such undertakings must have involved extended and patient efforts, during which notions of personal commitment and obligation with respect to membership in a moral community were subjected to particularly intense scrutiny.

Ideas regarding commitment to a newly forming community, the organization of labor, exchanges of goods for trade, relationships with parents and with in-laws, such crucial matters as what one ate, the weapons one used for killing people and animals, the labels one used to identify oneself (and one's enemies), and, above all, the typical demeanor required of men and women in their relations with one another all reflected upon what most needed reinterpretation: notions of personal identity with respect to membership in a moral community.

The Kalapalo stories tell us that events leading to the emergence of such communities must have included vivid—and unforgettable—moments during which local values were subject to particularly intense scrutiny and people found themselves in crises of reorientation. While stories from many parts of lowland South America are very clear about these matters as they involved an increasing awareness of the terrible contrasts between Europeans and Indians, we must recognize that it was not always Europeans who were present to be resisted and commented on but other Indians. Native people focused attention upon one another and also inwardly, upon their own communities. As with Native South American resistance and reorientation to European culture, the importance of reformulation of ideas about local relations became supreme.

Viewed as the rhetoric of conflict arising from the challenging of values, and especially notions of the public self and its duties, we find that ideology was indeed an active force in such societies. What Paul Friedrich called "political ideas in action" emerged among native people as part of the processes through which new societies were being formed as a consequence of European invasion and settlement of the Americas (1989: 301). While this observation would seem to support the idea that such peoples are "premodern" insofar as ideology emerges among them only when they are forced to come to terms with Europeans, I suggest that Europeans were not necessarily always present to resist and comment upon directly. Rather, some ideologies were the consequence of people trying to form new kinds of societies out of remnant, refugee groups who were forced to move away from their homelands, finding themselves struggling with other native peoples they encountered.

Evidence for ideological ferment has been preserved in narratives like the ones included in this book, and they have much to tell us about what happened to people during such times of disorientation and what it felt like to participate in events of those times. From the stories, we learn how people tried to reorient themselves, contributing thereby to a very gradual and subtle construction of ideological shifts. These changes are not represented in lengthy disquisitions, arguments about abstract principles, or rhetorical forms familiar to the readers of *The Federalist Papers* or viewers of the "MacNeil/Lehrer News Hour." We must be prepared to accept as ideological more discreet phenomena: the politically pragmatic efforts of individuals to reorient themselves with regard to personal ambiguities and to difficult relationships within their communities.

The special importance of these stories about the past for the Kalapalo rests, finally, not in the fact that they represent a new ideology, a set of collectively accepted images that animate social life. Rather, it is precisely because they describe people who clearly shaped their own fates. Their special biographical character rests in the fact that they describe experiences of individuals taking chances, exploring alternatives to their lives, making strategic choices when conditions forced them into new and untried situations. No longer able to return to the old ways, often forced into an unknown environment by enemies, these men and women made decisions to act that signified to those who followed after them special abilities in giving meaning to the conditions around them and thus to project forward, to clearly imagine and take responsibility for the course of their futures. The warriors in these stories stand out most vividly as men who tried to reconfigure certain basic values central to their particular designated roles. Their actions thus transcend the time of cannibalism and blood feuding, of desperate migrations in search of a place to live peacefully.

When we look at the more personal features of these historical narratives—their biographical character—we come face to face not with the monological functions of "distortion," "legitimation," "justification," "authenticity," "integration," and "identification" typically associated with ideology (and a narrator's voice) but emotionally charged dialogical processes of challenge, resistance, debate, and the negotiation of meaning, with the struggles that take place as people try to understand and experience anew. As V. N. Voloshinov wrote, this "behavioral ideology" (a name he gave to what he described as the "inner and outer speech that permeates our behavior") "is in certain respects more sensitive, more responsive, more excitable and livelier than an ideology that has undergone formulation and become official" (1987: 88). The rhetoric of conflict that is developed within Kalapalo stories about the past becomes merged with the rhetoric of conventional ideology in the practice of contemporary life, so that the usual authoritative resources for telling about "how people were" project a voice struggling for dominance—a voice radiating that "sideward glance" at the voices of others.

NOTES

1. Introduction

1. This area is a zone of floral transition between the scrublands of the central uplands (the Planalto Central) and the high Amazon rainforests.

2. For more detailed accounts, see Agostinho da Silva (1972) and Galvão and Simões (1964: 132).

3. The names Matipu (or Matipuhy) and Nafukwa are usually used in the anthropological literature for these defunct village groups. When speaking to outsiders in Portuguese, these terms are also sometimes used by local people. However, when speaking among themselves, the Carib speakers use the proper village names Wagifïtï and Dyagamï to identify individuals who originally belonged to those communities. Wagifïtï are descendants of the original Oti group and thus most closely related linguistically to the Kuikuro. Dyagamï, one of several related communities formerly located near the Rio Kuliseu, spoke a language that, according to contemporary people, was identical to Kalapalo. The Dyagamï people, survivors of measles and influenza epidemics as well as attacks by the Txição, upon moving north began to intermarry with the also seriously depopulated Wagifïtï. Today, the descendants of these two groups occupy two settlements: Mïgiyape, after the lake of that name, where the Trumai once had a settlement, and Angafunga, after a smaller lake to the south of Aifa, formerly the site of a Yawalipiti settlement. Because of considerable intermarriage as well as political difficulties, certain families have moved several times between the two settlements.

4. From ngi "wild thing (of the forest)"; "uncultivated plant" + ko (plural) + go (animate relator suffix), hence the gloss "fierce people." Although use of the word has been extended to mean any non-Xinguano person or people, "fierceness" (itsotu) is the first thing people ask about when they hear of a new group. As late as 1982, there was continued sensitivity to the possible presence of hostile outsiders living in remote areas which fed this fear of the strange Indian. Often mentioned were the so-called Agafïtïkuegï, the "other Agafïtï"; Agafïtï refers to the original Yawalipiti settlement. More recently, Kalapalo realize that if any of these marginal natives had survived into recent times, they were probably no longer alive because of the kagayfa who were beginning to move into the region. According to Seeger, Suya fought and later assimilated survivors of the iaguma while living at the settlement called Otoko (now Diauarum) near the Rio Suya-Missu, above its confluence with the Rio Xingu. This site was visited by Steinen in 1884 (Seeger 1981: 50).

5. Murphy and Quain (presumably using information given Quain by the Trumai) mention a revenge attack by Kamayura, Mehinaku, Waura, and Trumai that was once launched against the Suya (1955: 11).

6. I describe how the Kalapalo classify living beings (ago) and other entities in detail in Basso (1973: chap. 3). There, I discuss some of the ways this set of categories can be used for identification of particular kinds of relationships between humans and other entities. In that connection, I present the dietary practices Kalapalo follow in different situations.

7. See Whitehead (1984) for a discussion of the historical evidence for cannibalism among the Carib-speaking peoples (as well as other native peoples) of the northern regions of South America.

8. The Trumai language is treated as "isolated" but may be related to the language of the Javahe and Karaja people located along the Rio Araguaia to the east of the Xingu (see Monod-Becquelin 1975).

9. In the story about Saganafa (chapter 3) a man is said to "act like a Christian" through his adoption of non-Indian customs during his residence among those people. In another story, people who are apparently Indian (but not of the Alto Xingu) are included in a group of *kagayfa*. (See Dole 1983–1984 for an attempt to connect this story with Brazilian history. Dole suggests the "followers" were Bororo Indians.)

10. In Basso (1985) I discuss Kalapalo ceremonial gatherings and the importance of different kinds of songs performed in connection with those events.

2. The Language in Storytelling

1. Her story is tragic, for she was married at the time of her puberty seclusion against her will, despite her parents' agreement to give her to this outsider. Not long after, returned to her parents during pregnancy, she died in childbirth. Her husband built a memorial to her near the canoe landing for the old community along the Culuene. This place is now known to the Kalapalo as "Dyaqui."

2. Basso (1986) is an extended analysis of the significance of validation and verification in a Kalapalo story.

3. Analyses of evidential categories are usually built upon epistemological attributes indexed by grammatical and other linguistic features (as in, for example, the important work in Chafe and Nichols 1986; Givon 1982; Hoff 1986; Haviland n.d.). Basso (1988) includes a short critique of this approach, which is also criticized by Givon. In Kalapalo (and apparently many other languages), evidentials qualify actions to an extent that they take on modal properties, having some of the semantic effects of adverbials in English. In Kalapalo, though, rather than qualifying bodily happenings, evidentials give special emotional force to speech activities, which are thus performed "assertively," "doubtfully," "in wonderment," "defiantly," "politely," and so forth. There seems to be no Kalapalo equivalents for these English words, which may be connected with the fact that Kalapalo don't report speech but rather quote it (and, with the exception of formal oration, usually represent speech as conversational). Speakers' feelings are qualified (relatively infrequently) by narrators, but, more usually, the quality of a speech event is suggested by how speakers use various kinds of evidentials.

4. Kambe's Testimony

1. While shifters of listening were recognized by the structuralists as not exclusive to historical discourse (and, indeed, absent from many kinds of such discourse), in Kalapalo narrative they are most important for constituting an authoritative voice, necessary for historical understanding.

Regarding the idea of testimony, Young (1988) writes: "In its English past, 'testimony' derives from the Latin for 'witness' (*testi*), while 'witness' in turn derives from both the abstract concept of becoming conscious of (or to know) something and literally seeing a thing. To testify is literally 'to make witness'—an etymological reminder that as witness and testimony are made, so is knowledge. . . . The very figures of witness, testimony, and documentary thus point respectively to having seen events, having been part of events, finding significance in events, and then teaching about and finding meaning through the transmission of events" (15–16).

5. Warriors

1. Ancient Tafununu Lake settlements were called Tefukugu, Kugufi, Netunugu, and Faifua.

6. Ahpïü's Story about Wapagepundaka

1. Although Ahpïü uses much the same imagery to describe the clubbing of people (lines 268–274) and the killing of game animals (lines 729–735), he does distinguish between hunting equipment and the technology of fighting (as in lines 466 ff., when he refers to "bladed weapons"). In some of the other stories, clubs made at the battleground from tree limbs are used, much as Wapagepundaka cut something for his wife to use as a club at their campsite.

8. Kudyu's Story about Tamakafi

1. Tafugi, "Minnow," was the name of a settlement included in a list given by Carib-speakers to Hermann Meyer. Located along the Rio Suya-Missu, it might have been occupied by the Ge-speaking Suya, although the *angikogo* in this story are not identified as such (Krusche 1977).

2. In Basso (1985) I present a translation of the story of Yamurikumalu origins and an extensive discussion of the women's Yamurikumalu ritual.

3. See Basso (1985) for stories and discussion of the imagery of Ñafïgï.

9. Kudyu's Story of the Wanderers

1. For a detailed discussion of experiences created through Kalapalo musical ritual, see Basso (1985: Chap. 7).

2. This was the only occasion on which I heard such a remark used. When I asked about it, Kudyu told me that it was the correct thing for the *tïitsofo* to say to the *akiñoto* when the story ended. But no one else ever used it as far as I could tell.

10. Ausuki Tells of the Trumai People

1. Brazilian linguist Bruna Francetto identifies this site as located near the headwaters of the Rio Burití (a tributary of the Rio Xingu to the immediate west of the Rio Culuene). See also Francetto (1983, 1986: 75–77) on the original settlement cluster called Oti (*cerrado*), occupied by various Kuikuro groups.

2. Much of this is described in Murphy and Quain (1955) and will not be repeated here.

3. Although Murphy and Quain allude to this story, it is absent from a comprehensive collection of Trumai stories published by French linguist Aurore Monod-Becquelin (1975).

11. Ugaki Tells of Afuseti,
a Woman Stolen by *Angikogo*

1. The name is usually written (following Steinen and Meyer) as Naravute. This group was eventually completely decimated by disease by the 1940s, with the few survivors joining other Carib-speaking communities in the Alto Xingu. It was one of the communities visited by Dyott.

12. Tsangaku Tells of the Dyaguma

1. I was told many stories about such incidents, particularly in connection with my earliest attempts to collect genealogical information, when people helping me were always very careful to describe how specific individuals died. See Basso (1973) for schematic descriptions of some of these incidents.

13. Conclusion: History, Ideology, and
the Personal Version of Reality

1. In Basso (1985) I discuss in detail this poetic process in Kalapalo narratives.

2. Just about half of all the lines in "Tapoge the Bow Master," 143 of 263, are quoted speech. In "Wapagepundaka," of 846 lines, 424 are quotations of speech. In "Tamakafi," of 755 lines, 305 are quotations.

3. Brumble (1987, 1988); Clifford (1978); Krupat (1987); Misch (1951); Weintraub (1978).

4. Consider the following from a recent introduction: "We cannot even begin to encompass a human being without indicating for each of the stages of his life cycle the framework of social influences and of traditional institutions which determine his perspective on his more infantile past and his more mature future" (Cocks and Crosby 1987: 15–16). Brumble's discussion of "tales of acquisition of powers" (1988: 45–54) concludes that this type of story comes closest to modern autobiography because of the detailed connection that is made between events.

5. There are some important exceptions to this biographical convention of "backgrounding" social environment, as seen in the biographical writings of Existentialists Karl Jaspers, Jean-Paul Sartre, and Martin Buber. Of particular interest in the present context is Buber's biography (1969) of the Baal Shem Tov, the founder of Hasidism. This work draws on the storytelling conventions of the Hasidim by using their own stories to simultaneously tell about the achievement of a distinctive point of view, the development of ideological conflict arising from popular recognition of this point of view, and the new social movement that resulted.

6. I present other important stories that emphasize these themes in Basso (1985: esp. Chap. 6) and throughout Basso (1987b).

7. Writers who restrict the notion of ideology to modern thought seem to want to emphasize the idea that ideology manifests a critical function which emerges in

connection with the development of social classes, from which arise challenges to traditional authority. In this connection, ideology is equated with distortion, but also (as Ricoeur points out) with Weberian processes of legitimation. Attempting to integrate the more positive ideas about ideology proposed by Clifford Geertz, Ricoeur adds to distortion and legitimation the ideological function of integration (or "identification," as he sometimes calls it), suggesting the importance of ideology's constitutive character, at least for "developing" countries (1986: 262). See also Thompson (1984).

REFERENCES

Agostinho da Silva, Pedro
  1972   "Information Concerning the Territorial and Demographic Situation in
          the Alto Xingu." In *The Situation of the Indian in South America: Con-
          tributions to the Study of Inter-ethnic Conflict in the Non-Andean Re-
          gions of South America*, ed. W. Dostal, 252–283. Geneva: World Council
          of Churches.
Asad, Talal
  1987   "Are There Histories of Peoples without Europe?" *Comparative Studies
          in Society and History* 29, no. 3: 594–607.
Bakhtin, Mikail
  1981   "Discourse in the Novel." In *The Dialogic Imagination*, ed. Michael
          Holquist, trans. Caryl Emerson and Michael Holquist, 259–422. Austin:
          University of Texas Press.
  1984   *Problems of Dostoevsky's Poetics*, trans. Caryl Emerson. Minneapolis:
          University of Minnesota Press.
Barthes, Roland
  1987   "The Discourse of History." In *The Rustle of Language*, trans. Richard
          Howard, 127–140. Berkeley: University of California Press.
Basso, Ellen B.
  1973   *The Kalapalo Indians of Central Brazil*. New York: Holt, Rinehart and
          Winston.
  1985   *A Musical View of the Universe*. Philadelphia: University of Pennsylvania
          Press.
  1986   "Quoted Dialogues in Kalapalo Narrative Discourse." In *Native South
          American Discourse*, ed. Joel Sherzer and Greg Urban, 119–168. Berlin:
          Mouton–De Gruyter.
  1987a   "The Implications of a Progressive Theory of Dreaming." In *Dreaming:
          Anthropological and Psychological Interpretations*, ed. Barbara Tedlock.
          New York: Cambridge University Press.
  1987b   *In Favor of Deceit*. Tucson: University of Arizona Press.
  1988   Review of Wallace Chafe and Johanna Nichols, eds., *Evidentiality:
          The Linguistic Coding of Epistemology. American Anthropologist* 90:
          216–217.
Bastos, Rafael Jose de Menezes
  1984–   *O'Payemeramaraka' Kamayura: Uma contribuição a etnografia do Xa-*
  1985   *manismo do Alto Xingu*. Separata dos Vol. 27/28, Revista de Antropologia.
          São Paulo.
Bauman, Richard, and Charles Briggs
  1991   "Poetics and Performance as Critical Perspectives on Language and Social
          Life." *Annual Review of Anthropology* 19: 59–88.
Birkerts, Sven
  1987   "Some Notes Concerning the Impossibility of Literary Biography." *Pe-
          quod* 23/24: 305–316.

Brumble III, H. David
    1987   "Sam Blowsnake's Confession: Crashing Thunder and the History of American Indian Autobiography." In *Recovering the Word: Essays on Native American Literature*, ed. Brian Swann and Arnold Krupat, 537–551. Berkeley: University of California Press.
    1988   *American Indian Autobiography*. Berkeley: University of California Press.

Buber, Martin
    1969   *The Legend of the Baal Shem Tov*, trans. Maurice Friedman. New York: Schocken.

Chafe, Wallace, and Johanna Nichols, eds.
    1986   *Evidentiality: The Linguistic Coding of Epistemology*. Norwood, N.J.: Ablex.

Clifford, James
    1978   "'Hanging Up Looking Glasses at Odd Corners.'" In *Studies in Biography*, ed. Daniel Aaron, 41–56. Cambridge, Mass.: Harvard University Press.

Cocks, Geoffrey, and Travis L. Crosby
    1987   *Psycho/History*. New Haven: Yale University Press.

Dole, Gertrude E.
    1983–   "Some Aspects of Structure in Kuikuru Society." *Antropologica* 59–62:
    1984   309–329.

Dyott, George Miller
    1930   *Man Hunting in the Jungle*. Indianapolis: Thornton Butterworth.

Eggan, Fred
    1967   "From History to Myth: A Hopi Example." In *Studies in Southwestern Ethnolinguistics*, ed. Dell Hymes, 33–53. The Hague, Paris: Mouton.

Fernandes, Florestan
    1949   *A analise funcionalista da guerra: Possibilidades de aplicação a sociedade tupinamba. Ensaio de analise crítica da contribuição etnografica dos cronistas para o estudo sociologico da guerra entre populaçoes aborigenes do Brasil quinhentista e seiscentista*. Separata da Revista do Museu Paulista, n.s. vol. 3. São Paulo.
    1970   *A função social da guerra na sociedade tupinamba*. São Paulo: Livararia Pioneira Editora, Ed. da Universidade de São Paulo.

Foucault, Michel
    1973   *The Order of Things*. New York: Vintage Press.
    1976   *The Discourse on Language*. In *The Archaeology of Knowledge*, 215–237. New York: Harper and Row.
    1980   *Power/Knowledge: Selected Interviews and Other Writings, 1972–1977*, ed. and trans. C. Gordon. New York: Pantheon.

Francetto, Bruna
    1983   "A fala do chefe: Generos verbais entre os Kuikuru do Alto Xingu." *Cadernos de Estudos Linguisticos* 4: 4–72. Campinas, Brazil.
    1986   "Falar Kuikuro. Estudo Etnolinguistico de um grupo Karibe do Alto Xingu." Ph.D. thesis, Postgraduate Program in Social Anthropology, Museu Nacional, Universidade Federal do Rio de Janeiro.

Friedrich, Paul
    1989   "Language, Ideology and Political Economy." *American Anthropologist* 91: 295–312.

Galvão, Eduardo, and Mario Simões
    1964   "Kulturwandel und Stammesüberleben am oberen Xingu, Zentralbrasi-

lien." *Beitrage zur Volkerkunde Sudamerikas* (Volkerkundliche Abhandlungen), Band 1: 131–151. Hanover.

Geertz, Clifford
1973   "Ideology as a Cultural System." In *The Interpretation of Cultures*, 193–233. New York: Basic Books.

Givon, Talmy
1982   "Evidentiality and Epistemic Space." *Studies in Language* 6, no. 1: 23–49.

Gumperz, John
1984   *Discourse Strategies*. Cambridge: Cambridge University Press.

Haviland, John
n.d.   "Fighting Words: Evidential Particles, Affect and Argument."

Hemming, John
1978   *Red Gold: The Conquest of the Brazilian Indians, 1500–1760*. Cambridge, Mass.: Harvard University Press.

Hill, Jane
1986   "The Refiguration of the Anthropology of Language: A Review of Problems of Dostoevsky's Poetics, by Mikhail Bakhtin." *Cultural Anthropology* 1: 89–102.

Hill, Jonathan, ed.
1988   *Rethinking History and Myth: Indigenous South American Perspectives on the Past*. Urbana: University of Illinois Press.

Hoff, B. J.
1986   "Evidentiality in Carib." *Lingua* 69: 49–103.

Hymes, Dell
1987   "Tonakawa Poetics: John Rush Buffalo's 'Coyote and Eagle's Daughter.'" In *Native American Discourse: Poetics and Rhetoric*, ed. Joel Sherzer and Anthony Woodbury, 17–61. Cambridge: Cambridge University Press.

Jaspers, Karl
1985   *Socrates, Buddha, Confucius, Jesus*. Vol. 1 of *The Great Philosophers*. New York: Harcourt Brace Jovanovich.

Krupat, Arnold
1985   *For Those Who Come After: A Study of Native American Autobiography*. Berkeley: University of California Press.

Krusche, Rolf
1977   "Unpublished Material on the Ethnography of the Upper Xingu Region (Mato Grosso, Brazil)." *Jahrbuch des Museums für Volkerkunde*, Band 31: 177–184. Berlin: Akademie-Verlag.

Lévi-Strauss, Claude
1966   *The Savage Mind*. Chicago: University of Chicago Press.

Meyer, Hermann
1897   "Uber seine Expedition nach Central-Brazilien." *Verhandlungen der Gesellschaft für Erdkunde zu Berlin* 4: 172–198.

1898   "Im Quellgebiet des Schingu. Landschafts und Volkerbilder aus Central-brasilien." *Verhandlungen der Gesellschaft deutscher Naturforscher und Arzte* 69: 135–145.

1900   "Bericht über seine zweite Xingu-Expedition." *Verhandlungen der Gesellschaft für Erdkunde zu Berlin* nos. 2 and 3: 112–128.

Misch, Georg
1951   *A History of Autobiography in Antiquity*. Cambridge, Mass.: Harvard University Press.

Monod-Becquelin, Aurore
    1975   *La Pratique Linguistique des Indiens Trumai, 2. Mythes trumai (Haut-Xingu, Mato Grosso, Bresil)*. Paris: SELAF (Tradition Orale, 10).
Murphy, Robert
    1957   "Intergroup Hostility and Social Cohesion." *American Anthropologist* 59: 1018–1035.
    1958   *Munduruku Religion*. University of California Pubs. in American Archaeology and Ethnology, 49, no. 1.
Murphy, Robert F., and Buell Quain
    1955   *The Trumai Indians of Central Brazil*. Monographs of the American Ethnological Society, 24. Seattle: University of Washington Press.
Ricoeur, Paul
    1986   *Lectures on Ideology and Utopia*. New York: Columbia University Press.
Seeger, Anthony
    1981   *Nature and Society in Central Brazil: The Suya Indians of Mato Grosso*. Cambridge, Mass.: Harvard University Press.
    1987   *Why Suya Sing*. Cambridge: Cambridge University Press.
Sherzer, Joel
    1987   "A Discourse-Centered Approach to Language and Culture." *American Anthropologist* 89: 295–309.
Steinen, Karl von den
    1886   *Durch Central Brasilien*. Leipzig.
    1894   *Unter den Naturvolkern Zentral-Brasiliens*. Berlin.
Thompson, John B.
    1984   *Studies in the Theory of Ideology*. Cambridge: Polity Press.
Urban, Greg
    1991   *A Discourse-Centered Approach to Culture*. Austin: University of Texas Press.
Voloshinov, V. N.
    1987   *Freudianism: A Critical Sketch*, trans. I. R. Titunik, ed. in collaboration with Neal H. Bruss. Bloomington: University of Indiana Press.
Weintraub, Karl J.
    1978   *The Value of the Individual: Self and Circumstance in Autobiography*. Chicago: University of Chicago Press.
White, Hayden
    1978   *Tropics of Discourse*. Baltimore: Johns Hopkins University Press.
Whitehead, Neil
    1984   "Carib Cannibalism: The Historical Evidence." *Journal de la Société des Américanistes* 70: 69–88.
Young, James C.
    1988   *Writing and Rewriting the Holocaust: Narrative and the Consequences of Interpretation*. Bloomington: Indiana University Press.

INDEX OF STORIES

GENERAL INDEX

Boldface page numbers refer to photographs.